Living with the UN

The Hoover Institution gratefully acknowledges
the following individuals and foundations
for their significant support of the
Koret-Taube Task Force
on National Security and Law
and this publication:

KORET FOUNDATION

TAD AND DIANNE TAUBE
  TAUBE FAMILY FOUNDATION

JAMES J. CARROLL III
  JEAN PERKINS FOUNDATION

Living with the UN

American Responsibilities and International Order

Kenneth Anderson

HOOVER INSTITUTION PRESS
STANFORD UNIVERSITY   STANFORD, CALIFORNIA

The Hoover Institution on War, Revolution and Peace, founded at Stanford University in 1919 by Herbert Hoover, who went on to become the thirty-first president of the United States, is an interdisciplinary research center for advanced study on domestic and international affairs. The views expressed in its publications are entirely those of the authors and do not necessarily reflect the views of the staff, officers, or Board of Overseers of the Hoover Institution.

www.hoover.org

Hoover Institution Press Publication No. 609

Hoover Institution at Leland Stanford Junior University, Stanford, California 94305-6010

Hoover Institution Press assumes no responsibility for the persistence or accuracy of URLs for external or third-party Internet websites referred to in this publication, and does not guarantee that any content on such websites is, or will remain, accurate or appropriate.

First printing 2012
18 17 16 15 14 13 12   7 6 5 4 3 2 1

Manufactured in the United States of America

The paper used in this publication meets the minimum Requirements of the American National Standard for Information Sciences—Permanence of Paper for Printed Library Materials, ANSI/NISO Z39.48-1992. ⊗

Library of Congress Cataloging-in-Publication Data
Anderson, Kenneth, 1956– author.
    Living with the UN : American responsibilities and international
    order / Kenneth Anderson.
        pages cm. — (Hoover Institution Press publication ; no. 609)
    Includes bibliographical references and index.
    ISBN 978-0-8179-1344-1 (cloth : alk. paper) —
    ISBN 978-0-8179-1346-5 (e-book)
    1. United Nations—United States. 2. United States—Foreign
relations—2009– I. Title. II. Series: Hoover Institution Press
publication ; 609.
    JZ4997.5.U6A63 2011
    341.23'73—dc23   2011037056

For Jack Simon and Richard Anderson

*"Maintain power in as decent a
way as would be yet the most effective."*

Thomas Berger, *Arthur Rex*

*"Ne serait-ce point une
Amerique lasse de son métier?"*

Stendhal, *Le Rouge et le Noir*

CONTENTS

ACKNOWLEDGMENTS

This book began a long time ago, in the midst of the UN reform efforts of 2005. It was originally conceived as a short essay on the United Nations, legitimacy, and global governance—and went through successive drafts until it at last became clear (even to the author) that all of these topics together and "short" were not compatible. It was eventually narrowed to US-UN relations, the topic it currently addresses. Although the fundamental question of defining "multilateralism" and "engagement" was present from the beginning, the election in 2008 gave greater impetus to that topic, as those terms began to feature ever more often in the diplomacy, and particularly the United Nations diplomacy, of the United States.

This book is a short foreign policy essay. It deliberately eschews the scholarly apparatus that would turn it into a law review article or academic monograph; the notes are limited to a small handful of substantive comments and citations to direct quotations, and very little else. The bibliography is aimed at the general reader and inquiring student and so focuses on secondary sources that are readily available, rather than leading into the fascinating but sometimes hard to research archives of the United Nations or academic literature not available to readers lacking research-library access. The aims of the book are modest policy ideas, not original scholarship or an exhaustive academic argument. The intent, rather, is to gather into a single usable, readable handbook a set of tools, heuristics, rules of thumb, policy templates to guide United States relations with the United Nations. The emphasis is on the present Obama administration, but certainly the author believes that these heuristics are applicable for future administrations of either political party.

The book in its current form owes an enormous debt to Benjamin Wittes, senior fellow at the Brookings Institution, a member of the Hoover Institution Task Force on National Security and Law, and a good and generous friend. In this instance, he reached back to his skills as a former *Washington Post* journalist and took a still unwieldy and untidy manuscript and cut it (the "drive-by edit," he called it) into its current length and form. Without his skills, the term "short" would scarcely be applicable here and, likewise, such readability as the book possesses.

My thanks also go to the two editors of the Hoover Studies series, Tod Lindberg and Peter Berkowitz, whose patience waiting for this manuscript knows no bounds. But they have also contributed a great deal of sense and readability to the manuscript through their edits and probing questions, not all of which I am able to answer. I have received helpful feedback on various chapters of this book from members of the Hoover Institution Task Force on National Security and Law, and I thank them and particularly Stephen

Krasner, Matthew Waxman, Jack Goldsmith, Philip Bobbitt, and Ruth Wedgwood. I am grateful to all of them; I am, of course, solely responsible for errors that remain. I should also like to thank two people who have been mentors to me in these fields and dear friends over many years, although, alas, I have grave doubts they will find the arguments of this book persuasive: Aryeh Neier and Henry Steiner.

I am also grateful to the Hoover Institution, its staff and director, John Raisian, for support over several years working on this volume, and to the staff of the Hoover Institution Press. Thanks also go to the Gingrich-Mitchell Task Force on the United Nations, a Congressionally sponsored task force on UN reform organized through the US Institute for Peace, on which I was privileged to serve as an expert during the 2005 UN reform process. Also, thanks are due to my law school, Washington College of Law, American University, and its dean, Claudio Grossman. Finally, thanks and appreciation go to my wife, Jean-Marie Simon, and my daughter, Renee, who offered love and support throughout this process.

Kenneth Anderson
Washington, DC 2012

INTRODUCTION

As President Barack Obama enters his fourth year in office, his administration continues to seek a definition of the United States' relationship to the United Nations. This is not to say that the Obama administration has not announced one. From the first euphoric days of the new presidency, and particularly the new president's first, electric appearances at the General Assembly and the Security Council, the watchwords have been *engagement* and *multilateralism*. That language continues down to the present day. It is exemplified, for example, in the Obama administration's 2010 National Security Strategy, which emphasizes "engagement" and cooperation "with" and common global action "through" multilateral institutions. Speeches and pronouncements from US officials solemnly endorse engagement and multilateralism as the order of the day, at seemingly every opportunity. American policy is multilateral engagement; even if America pursues its counterterrorism war with hardheaded force and few niceties, at the United Nations and other international institutions, the American attitude and affect with the community of nations continues to be humility and humble good-fellowship, a continuing yearning for world approval and a belief that the Obama administration is uniquely positioned to get it. The attitude has grown slightly stale, coming on four years and an election relentlessly focused upon domestic issues. The United Nations and relations with it have been rendered mostly part of the background noise of foreign policy, an effect rather than a cause. Yet the watchwords remain the same: engagement and multilateralism.

Americans and non-Americans, allies and enemies, have wondered from the beginning what those terms mean as actual policy of the United States of America. They continue to wonder, three years on. What does it mean in practical terms to work through multilateral institutions? What does it mean to engage, with multilateral institutions, with friends, allies, and even enemies? Does multilateral engagement mean that the Obama administration has discovered a way to overcome the collective-action problems of a hopelessly divided United Nations that no American administration has ever managed to discover before? Is multilateral engagement instead just a rhetorical stalking horse for announcing American decline—the planned obsolescence, as it were, of the superpower and global hegemonic power? Or, is it just talk that does not actually mean anything at all? The hoopla that surrounded the new president's election is long since gone; likewise the hoopla that enveloped his first appearances at the United Nations. Even four years on, the relationship between the United States and the United Nations remains unsettled. Nor is this merely a matter of the Obama administration; any subsequent administration, of either party, will have to address these same questions, in a world of great domestic and global uncertainty on fundamental questions of economic power and stability, of shifting demographics, and of attendant shifts in the global security environment. These questions will not go away any time soon.

Clearly the US-UN relationship has gotten past the tumult of the Bush years—9/11 and then the Iraq war debates in the Security Council, particularly. Those years and their acrimony are rapidly receding in collective memory. But what replaces those muscular tussles, no one seems quite to know, apart from a discernible American absence, a space that is not quite filled by the Obama administration's words. Is the relationship being set by the terms of presumed American decline in power and stature, and the rise of the ballyhooed "multipolar world"? Alternatively, is the United States merely reverting to the long-term, stable mean of its relations with the United Nations, the traditionally pragmatic US view of international law and institutions as an occasionally interesting sideshow, but always a sideshow, the Goldilocks mean: neither too cold nor too hot?

The US ambassador to the United Nations since the beginning of the Obama administration, Susan Rice, came in for some criticism early on for supposedly spending little time at the Turtle Bay headquarters and the US mission in New York, preferring to stay in Washington and work the Obama administration rather than the international missions. The flurry of diplomacy around the Libya intervention and Arab Spring revolutions have allayed that charge, though diplomats still complain privately that the list of issues that truly matter to the administration is short. She and the Obama administration speak constantly of engagement yet during much of the last three years do not think it much worth the time personally to show up and engage. Ironically, perhaps, Rice's predecessor in the Bush administration, the endlessly excoriated John Bolton, on the other hand, engaged personally and relentlessly. He treated the institution itself, and not merely its agendas, as one long negotiation in which he was the United States' lawyer, paying attention to every minor contract clause for fear of the consequences of a single misplaced comma. Their diplomatic interlocutors at the United Nations are critical of each, publicly or privately, but for quite opposite reasons.

The more important question, however, is this. Which of these two, Rice or Bolton, more accurately gauged the fundamental relationship of the United States and the United Nations: the ambassador whose administration speaks endlessly of multilateralism and engagement with international institutions but then seems to find that the center of the universe is, for all that, Washington, or the ambassador whose administration seemed to speak only of unilateral, sovereign power and yet who was a constant, and for many constantly irritating, presence at UN headquarters on every jot and tittle? Which of them more accurately priced the United Nations' value to the United States? What model will their diplomatic successors in subsequent American administrations choose?

Consider the last great period of hoopla surrounding the United Nations in which the United States had to take account of its fundamental relationship to the institution: the grand international debate over "UN reform" back in 2005. This period may be lost in the mists of recent time a scant few years later—does anyone but Ambassador Bolton in his memoirs even recall it? But it was a big deal back then. It was former Secretary-General Kofi Annan's last hurrah.

Enthusiasms and passions ran high. Many UN watchers anticipated fundamental reforms in the UN system, starting with the composition of the Security Council. Annan was always the "rock star" of secretaries-general, and he threw all his considerable personal influence and charisma behind the idea of remaking the United Nations for the new century. Many people who now scarcely seem to remember the episode seemed then to believe that the moment was propitious for deep institutional reformulation. They catalogued what the institution of the United Nations was *not*, and they catalogued what it should be. And they catalogued the conditions in the world, from global security to environmental problems to climate change to malaria and AIDS to human rights, that ought to benefit from global coordination today and global governance tomorrow—to be proffered from the United Nations.

The believers in UN reform in 2005 included many decidedly practical people, people not given to global utopianism. They included people only too familiar with the United Nations' penchant for grandiosity and bathos, who understood perfectly that the natural state of the United Nations was, and is, perpetual stagnation. The result was peculiar. Very little reform came to pass; nothing unusual in that for the United Nations. But it produced surprisingly little reform even merely on paper—an odd result at the United Nations. Reforms at the United Nations usually produce a vast amount of reform on paper and very little reform in fact. But the "Final Outcome Document" of the 2005 General Assembly reform summit had surprisingly little of the grand proposals submitted by various expert groups and diplomatic confabulations.

The "Final Outcome Document" had plenty of the usual pomposity, utopianism, and windy exhortation, to be sure. But reform of the composition of the Security Council, for example—and the single most important issue for many aspiring great powers—proved entirely impossible. As did a treaty definition of terrorism—despite Annan's personal, genuinely heartfelt support. And the grand bargain between the global north and global south, "aid-for-security," proposed by some senior UN advisors, did not significantly figure in the final product. Some of the measures looked like one-step-forward-one-step-back. The final document mentioned the concept of responsibility to protect (R2P, in the jargon), for example, but cabined it with new requirements of Security Council approval that would have made diplomatically more difficult, if not have precluded altogether, NATO's 1999 Kosovo war and other such efforts in the future, such as a purely NATO intervention in Libya. Other measures, however, looked more like awkward steps sideways: the embarrassing, ugly Human Rights Commission morphed into a new institution functionally indistinguishable from—and no less embarrassing than—the old, giving the world today's embarrassing, ugly Human Rights Council.

The entire 2005 effort was accompanied by that signature feature of grand UN negotiations, the fervid assertions that, if the organization did not finally act now, then disaster will this time surely follow. But then the organization does *not* act, disaster does *not* follow, and the organization lurches on much as before. The overheated rhetoric is yet again quietly forgotten and buried. And so it goes until the next crisis of apparently galactic proportions. Today, a few years on, one can see the 2005 reform summit for what it was: simply another of the United Nations' rhetorical flourishes for maintaining the status quo.

Lethargy punctuated by crisis is an important sociological cycle embedded within the political economy of the United Nations. In 2009, the United Nations went through another such spasm, this time around climate change and the just-as-rapidly-being-forgotten Copenhagen summit. Irrespective of an issue's intrinsic merits, the cycle of crisis rhetoric and then collapse is the same—after UN reform came Copenhagen, and after climate change will come something else. The point is fundamental to understanding the United Nations. Periodic, episodic crises ironically serve to reinforce the United Nations' chronic stability. Punctuated equilibrium is a structural feature of the United Nations that has to figure deeply in how the United States deals long-term with the organization.

Looking at this peculiarly stable dynamic of eternal crisis-gridlock that envelops the United Nations, one has to ask why, given its manifest and permanent failures, the United Nations persists. It precedes even the question of US-UN relations—why this insistence upon "engagement" with an institution of such manifest gridlock? It might seem both a loaded and impertinent question, particularly if one is a UN grandee or one of its many apologists. But it is actually the right question. The long-term persistence of a large, seemingly influential, visible, engaged and engaging, institution on the world scene which, on its most basic fundamentals, persistently fails to accomplish very much even by its own standards has to raise questions. How and why does the United Nations survive, rather than failing in some crisis and disappearing, to be replaced by some other institutional configuration? Why has the United Nations not gone the way of the League of Nations? And, if it does persist under these conditions of long-term, repeat-play failure, might that be because the common understanding of the institution turns out to be inaccurate and it is serving some purpose or function other than that which we imagine?

Plainly, those possibilities have consequences for policies of multilateralism and engagement. But engagement can mean many things, or nothing much at all, and so can multilateralism. "Engage" is an easy slogan but not really very helpful as a matter of policy, as though it were an end in itself. It is not. Equally, embracing "multilateralism" leaves more questions unanswered than answered, starting with the question of whether multilateralism necessarily or particularly means "the United Nations."

The puzzle of what engagement really means is made more puzzling still by the fact that the Bush administration in fact "engaged" rather more with the United Nations and international institutions than one might have suspected, listening to the criticism or, for that matter, listening to the Bush administration itself. Neither the Bush administration nor its critics had, at least at crucial moments and for radically different reasons, much interest in acknowledging just how engaged diplomatically with other states was US foreign policy, certainly from 9/11 onwards. And the Security Council, in particular, was always a crucial multilateral focus of that engagement. Despite the charges of unilateralism, the Bush administration was multilateral at least in the sense of enlisting other, indeed many other, countries in its ambitious uses of force. The Obama administration, through its reliance upon targeted killing and drones as its preferred mode of counterterrorism, arguably worries about it less—while this is sound security policy, it certainly requires less "engagement." The Bush administration had the apparatus of Security Council backing in its Afghanistan invasion and in its antiterrorism measures covering terrorist financing, travel lists, and many other matters—behind-the-scenes international legal authorities on which the US depends today and will depend in the future. In its war making, even in Iraq, the Bush administration led coalitions of states, and the numbers were not small—coalitions of the willing or perhaps just of those who realized that one could not free ride on US security forever without at least a token appearance when the United States went to war.

Ironically, the area in which the Bush administration was perhaps most insistently unilateral, truly unilateral, was not in the use of force, making war, or any expression of US interest at all. Bush unilateralism was most on display, without apology or cavil, in its approach to AIDS in Africa. This might seem a remarkable assertion. But there, the Bush administration insisted that accountability to a single chain of authority, budget, and command, and, finally, measurable effectiveness, mattered more than internationalist sensibility. Unilateralism was at its bluntest in a program of pure global altruism. The gap between the perception of Bush unilateralism and its actual multilateral engagement with other states was so large that it suggests that the questions of multilateralism and engagement are as much issues of style and posture as of substance. Unilateralism was always something of a pose and an attitude, whether struck by the Bush administration or railed against by its critics.

The implication of the criticism made against the previous administration, however, is that the United States is not really being "multilateral" and does not really "engage" unless it actively does so through the United Nations. This is at bottom what the international-law academics, think-tank wonks, nongovernmental organization (NGO) activists, and the rest mean when they say "multilateral engagement." Multilateral engagement is, in this vision, not simply a coalition of states. It has to be *through* international institutions and international law, which is to say, through the framework of liberal internationalism. No matter how many states are involved, it is just congeries of states in the Westphalian anarchy of international power politics without the United Nations.

All of which puts rather a premium on the contemporary debate over this question of US engagement with the United Nations, a debate that has become sharply polarized and partisan—notwithstanding the notable lack of purity on both sides. One extreme is the conservative reflex simply to reject the United Nations as flawed, failed, and decidedly not in the United States' interests or, really, on its moral compass. It finds expression at this writing in legislation being proposed by some in Congress to use the power of the purse to force the administration to address certain "values" issues at the United Nations, particularly US participation in the Human Rights Council, on the one hand, and eternal issues of UN budget and management in an era of US austerity, on the other.[1] "Shut it down," one conservative intellectual tells me flatly. He speaks for many on the American right. And to be clear, I am not wholly unsympathetic to the sentiment.

1. Howard LaFranchi, "UN Chief Asks Congress to Protect Funding. Republicans Less Than Thrilled," *Christian Science Monitor*, April 7, 2011, *available at* http://www.csmonitor.com/USA/Foreign-Policy/2011/0407/UN-chief-asks-Congress-to-protect-funding.-Republicans-less-than-thrilled.

But it is not merely a point of realism to observe that the United Nations is not going anywhere. It is not shutting down, and indeed it has a huge role in shaping "soft-law" attitudes and norms that have a mischievous way of binding American policy. To fail to engage at all means to cede this ground to people who do not have American interests, or, very often, American ideals, at heart. The United States has to deal with this reality and so do American conservatives. Conservatives also need to understand that the issue of the United Nations is not always simply a matter of seeking to contain a hostile and ineffective organization, nor is it simply a matter of seeking to block the perennial move by the international soft-law community to use international law and organizations as an end run around the US constitutional rule of law, the sovereign and self-governing America of Lincoln's impeccable definition of sovereignty: a "political community, without a political superior." Much, much more importantly, American conservatives need to be clear that, despite all that, there *are* tasks that the United Nations, however badly, does carry out—tasks that the United States properly *wants* to see carried out but which the United States cannot or will not do itself.

The other extreme, however, is the liberal reflex to believe that the United States *must always* engage with the United Nations—because of the glorious future promise of "global governance"; or because there is no other United Nations; or because of the presumed inherent moral superiority of universal institutions over merely sovereign national ones; or because one is a cosmopolitan for whom only the international legal order is truly legitimate; or for whatever complicated reasons. Whatever those reasons, this was the opening position of the Obama administration, particularly in the president's two maiden appearances, at the General Assembly and the Security Council. And it continues up to the end of the president's term, though today as the mostly rhetorical flourishes that other nations have figured out define large parts of US foreign policy. Unfortunately, the rhetoric often takes place through US reengagement with the worst enterprises of the United Nations, such as the Human Rights Council, and through other such initiatives in what, mistakenly, the Obama administration imagines are merely cost-free exercises in symbolism and values.

Such exercises are rarely cost-free. On many matters, the United States ought *not* to engage the United Nations, its staff, mechanisms, people, committees, commissions; it ought not to engage the United Nations with statements, meetings, attendance, membership, and, in particular circumstances, with particular bodies and issues, it should decline to pony up any money. On some issues, that is, its position ought to be oppose, obstruct, reject, disengage, and make engagement costly for others. One of the points of this book is that, perhaps counterintuitively to some, the issues on which rejection is the most important are the supposedly cost-free, merely symbolic, issues of values. The answer to the question of "engagement" cannot be "never"—but likewise it cannot be "always."

My purpose in these pages is to argue that the answer to the question of when the United States should engage with the United Nations is a resounding "sometimes." It depends. It's complicated. Whether in a unipolar world or in a multipolar world of competitive powers, the United Nations has genuinely useful functions to perform. In no sense does this book deny that; on the contrary, it tries to take the United Nations sufficiently seriously as to offer a hard-nosed assessment of what it should be and what it should do and what the United States should materially and morally support it in doing. Despite the extensive and severe criticism I offer of the United Nations throughout this book, the useful functions of the institution are many and varied, and the United States should support and promote them. But those useful functions are typically specific and discrete. Notably, they do not include political governance or global governance. Indeed, clinging to the aspiration of global governance—the chimera of governance at some glorious, but somehow always receding, moment in the presumed future—does the institution no favors in the present. Really, such fantasies of the United Nations' friends do the institution far more damage than its enemies ever could.

In any case, at this historical moment, the conclusion that friends, allies, and enemies alike have drawn about the Obama administration is that in point of fact it is not about either of these alternatives, the conservative democratic sovereigntist or the liberal internationalist. The Obama administration uses these and many much more fancy terms, but it does not actually mean anything at all by them. Not concretely, in the sense that they mean *this* but not *that*. Future American administrations will have to take account of this—accurate—perception on the part of the rest of the world. Sometimes, after all, engagement will not serve American interests. Sometimes the proper mode of engagement will be explicitly or implicitly hostile efforts to obstruct UN activity. If the Obama administration or its successors finally adopt that position, however, even just as a *possible* policy, the

result might be surprising, at least to the current architects of
mostly content-free engagement.

Confidence and certainty might go up, to start with,
at least once believed. However irritated or even angry
America's friends and allies might be at any particular
American assertion that it means this and not that, on any
particular question, just knowing that the United States has
taken a position and *actually means it* is a structural comfort in a radically uncertain world that the Obama administration to date has rendered yet more uncertain. Even on
the Libya intervention—the Obama administration's most
muscular use of the United Nations to date—friends, allies,
and unfriends alike are left with a troubling sense of high-
minded policy ends with far less defined means—what one
expects, in the end, of a powerful but indecisive player inside
a multilateral institution, not a hegemon that has the ability
and even legitimacy to speak from outside it. Syria poses a
far more severe test. On many matters other than Libya, on
the other hand, the administration comes to the end of the
term with a distinct sense of having lost its religious zeal
for international institutions, of going through the motions
mostly—yet trapped by intellectual and ideological stance
within those motions.

In any case, I argue in these pages that the goal of the
United States over the short or long run cannot be simply to
make the United Nations more efficient and effective, however much one might wish it so. The Obama administration
might today be bored with its own internationalism; its experience, together with the Bush administration's, offer important lessons for the future and for other administrations. For
the United Nations is an institution that is, in myriad ways,

simultaneously inefficient and *also* profoundly and structurally anti-American. It would be very easy to sign onto a vapid program of wanting to see a more responsive, better-run, and generally more effective United Nations. That is not, however, always in America's interest, nor does it reflect a strategy to sustain America's ideals for a better world. A genuinely effective United Nations would almost certainly be, in very important matters, more *effectively* anti-American—"anti" to both its policies and its ideals. In many matters, the US interest toward the United Nations is simply containment in some form. The stasis that afflicts the United Nations is very often not a bad thing.

The world, after all, does not have a genuinely shared vision of what the United Nations, or global governance, or the role of the United States, or universal values relating to human rights and many other matters, actually should be. If things really were shared in that way, then the problem would be one of execution and delivery—questions of efficiency. But we lack a shared vision. Indeed, if anything, the world is moving farther apart regarding universal values, not closer together, as authoritarian states rise in the world periodically flush with cash, as still-communist China reaches for global great-power status, and as communalist religion comes to play a more strongly competing role with liberalism in the global arena.

A not inconsiderable part of the deep moral and political vision of the rest of the world is hostile to the United States, to its values and not merely its policies. That is so in ways that are not cured by replacing George W. Bush with Barack Obama, or John Bolton with Susan Rice, or with any subsequent US administration. While some modest parts of the United Nations are like a commonweal of shared values, other (and often the most important) parts are not and so cannot be treated as merely questions of efficacious execution of shared policy. And other parts are simply deeply and irremediably anti-American. These parts all require separate and nuanced mechanisms of engagement. But, strange as it might sound to the Obama administration, it is not "nuanced" unless it concretely includes the very real possibility of non-engagement and outright opposition.

Another reason to reject the "always engage" approach is its supposed endpoint. Francis Fukuyama usefully defines liberal internationalism as the proposition that international power politics will finally be replaced by and subordinated to international law and institutions. At stake in the debate over engagement and multilateralism for the United States, therefore, is the question of whether the United States sees itself engaging with other states and institutions *as* a sovereign and always *for* a sovereign and *among* sovereigns or, instead, whether it sees multilateral engagement—*always engaging* and always engaging *at the United Nations*—as a means of reaching toward global governance. "Always engage" with the United Nations means reaching past sovereignty, reaching toward liberal internationalism's promise of the subordination of anarchic international power politics of sovereigns to a system of international law and institutions.

This is the deepest issue raised by the nature of US engagement with the United Nations: What is the implied view of global governance *tomorrow*, through the behavior of the United States as a sovereign actor with other sovereign actors *today*? Liberal internationalism is not truly on offer today but exists only as an aspiration for tomorrow.

So the divide between the former Bush administration and the enthusiasts of always engaging the United Nations is not really a debate about today but one of attitude and affect with respect to global governance in the future. Do we embrace it as a faith in the future or instead recoil from it as a profound violation of the sovereignty of a self-governing polity? On this fundamental issue of ideas, ideology, and belief, there is a sea change from the early days of the Obama administration to its end: from rapture to ennui. If the reaction to the argument of this book at the beginning of the Obama era would have been a defense of liberal internationalism and its intellectual engagement, today the reaction may be distinct boredom—the debate itself is passé. *Nil admirari*—don't get all worked up; these are debates today not of excitable utopian vision but of straitened material circumstance. The debates that matter are not about the ideals of global governance for their own glorious sake but instead the *necessity* of global governance as the only orderly response to American decline.

The intellectual move from four years ago to today, from global governance as an ideal to global governance as a necessity, seems to me not really to change the debate over multilateralism and engagement very much at all. This is particularly so if one is attempting, as this book does, to speak to future American administrations. I attempt in the succeeding chapters to set out the meanings of multilateralism and engagement with the United Nations in a fashion that can actually guide policy. I recognize at the outset that, extracted from the general issues of foreign policy and given the fact that the United Nations is, for the United States, more of an effect than a cause in foreign affairs, any discussion that focuses directly upon US-UN relations will automatically be somewhat exaggerated; it can always be said, with cool skepticism, that the issue does not merit such attention. By taking the United Nations out of context, I elevate it to the level of a strawman in the foreign affairs of the Obama administration.

This form of skepticism could be said of nearly any policy issue, however; and, in any case, many of those who are part of these policy debates have long seen the United Nations as more important than that, as more important, in fact, than I do. Imagine a sophisticated shrug of the foreign policy shoulders—no one ever took the United Nations so seriously as that, you debate a shadow—until, of course, the moment the cool skeptic wants to have a reason to tell the United States government that it must do this or must not do that on account of the UN Charter, or what the General Assembly said, or because the Security Council has not given permission, or because a UN special human rights rapporteur said so.

So I am skeptical of the skeptics who say that they do not have the belief in liberal internationalism, the special form of foreign policy idealism, that attaches to the United Nations. I think they do. That said, the first move in understanding US-UN relations is to understand that there are many UNs, for the United Nations is a collection of institutions, organs, actors, functions, motives, and motivations. Once the multiplicity of the "United Nations" is on the table, then it becomes possible to see that there are multiple ways of engaging (or not) with it—or with them. I attempt to provide approximate rules of thumb that can guide US policy as the presumptive starting point for how, or how not, to engage with the United Nations in its particular parts and functions.

The book proceeds in two parts. Part 1 lays out certain general features of the United Nations relevant to understanding it and its relationship to the United States—the conditions that define the United Nations (including the current fact of a loose US hegemony, even if one that is under pressure both internal and external). I argue that the effect of the many contradictions and ambiguities that characterize the United Nations is that its general condition is one of stasis punctuated by episodic but inconclusive crises, resulting in what I term an ironically "happy equilibrium." It does so, however, looking to the future of US-UN relations in an international environment shaped by a rising multipolarity that risks weakening the hegemon and, as a consequence, raising global uncertainties and threatening the provision of global public goods by the United States. Part 2 turns the focus away from the nature of the United Nations in order to lay out the optimal behavioral characteristics of the United States toward it. This part offers "heuristics" for US engagement through consideration of particular parts, themes, and functions of the United Nations. The book concludes by offering a vision of a better, but also more modest, United Nations. That vision is unlikely to be realized or even attempted. But at least it should be on offer.

This book goes to press as US-UN relations undergo one of their periodic flurries of activity. This flurry of activity is largely the consequence of events in the world that do not go to the primary concern of this book, multilateral engagement as a leading foreign policy agenda of the United States. The results of these events, and their UN cognates, will not be known until well after this book appears, so it is worth noting where the discussion leaves off. The Libya military intervention is still underway at this writing; Tripoli and the Gaddafi regime have fallen, although at this date the town of Sirte is under siege and under NATO air attacks, and Gaddafi himself has not been located. Libya is discussed briefly in the text, primarily to note that the intervention fits a certain model of Security Council action.

Meanwhile, the situation in Syria is characterized by increasing use of violence by the Assad regime, unclear moves by the opposition to adopt arms, but seemingly no prospect of intervention by the NATO powers, with or without the assent of the Security Council. Assent for intervention in the Security Council seems highly unlikely, given Russia, China, and many other states' statements that they believe that NATO has acted beyond its Security Council mandate in Libya. The lesson for US-UN relations and humanitarian intervention is that efforts to institutionalize the practice of "responsibility to protect" at the UN tend strongly to result in less ability of the United States or NATO to act, because institutionalization of "responsibility to protect" authority in the Security Council conveys a veto—one that is likely to be exercised if the Syria situation were put squarely to a vote. There is agitation for the Human Rights Council to report on Syria; if this occurs it might or might not be salutary. But the Arab League always has its own agenda. At this moment that agenda appears to be sharing responsiveness to Arab mass revolutions. But the future of Syria in UN discussions is very unclear.

As the General Assembly opens its session in early September 2011, the prospect of Palestine seeking UN membership has loomed larger. It is unclear at this writing whether the United States will be able to head off a vote or other General Assembly action. This matters for Israel in a number of ways, including an increased ability to use public international institutions to go after Israel and its officials. The US ability to influence the General Assembly is, however, limited, and it is an important lesson of this book that although the Security Council will always be an important venue for the United States, the General Assembly is at best an institution to be contained—in terms of budget, legitimacy, and every other metric. This extends to many other dependencies of the General Assembly.

None of this is new, except that the possibility of a very serious attack on Israel through UN institutions raises the question of a US diplomatic response, primarily through withholding dues and other budgetary contributions. The general approach of this book is to be very careful in deciding to pull triggers on general UN dues—the Charter-mandated regular UN dues—for reasons stated in the text. It is very cautious on refusals to pay the regular assessed dues of the United Nations. On the other hand, this book urges that, while using budgetary threats as calibrated pressure, to be resorted to at the end of a process of other pressures, individual UN agencies should be evaluated carefully for whether the United States should make voluntary contributions on various metrics—effectiveness of the mission, corruption, promotion of anti-American initiatives, singling out of Israel or the United States, etc. There is some talk at this stage, for example, that UNESCO might choose to "recognize" Palestine even if the General Assembly or the Secretary-General does not; in that case, the reasons for withholding contributions or (once again) quitting the organization seem to be of far more benefit than harm to the United States. Current US law already makes certain requirements in this area, and the approach of treating the United Nations as a collection of entities for this purpose rather than a single entity is correct.

Finally, the reader will see in the pages ahead that Israel features relatively little in the discussion of US-UN relations. Of course, the treatment of Israel is a central part of US deal-ings with the UN, as well it should be. Nonetheless, this aspect of US-UN relations is well covered by other authors and venues, and treating it on its own would require a book-length discussion. Instead, this discussion is quite deliber-ately about everything else. Given that lacuna, however, it bears stating at the outset that Israel is the exception that proves the rule. Much of this book is devoted to pointing out ways in which the United Nations is incapable of overcom-ing basic collective-action problems. Yes, many of the United Nations' troubling aspects are that it, and its members, want to pursue wicked ends, illiberal and authoritarian ends. But another part of the United Nations' many problems lies in its inability to overcome the willingness of member states to promise things and then default on their promises later. The problem of the UN collective, however, is that the individual defections are individually rational.

In the case of Israel, and Israel alone, apparently, the insti-tution and its member states manage to rouse themselves from their general torpor and rent-seeking sloth finally to come together on attacking Israel. The peculiarity and the irony is that only by reaching to fanaticism, zealotry, bigotry, demonization, and hatred—and on this issue alone—is the institutional UN able to overcome the otherwise daunting rationality of the failure of its members to act collectively. The United Nations acts collectively most of all, it seems, when its members act irrationally.

Part One
CONDITIONS

1 SICKLY SAPLING, GLORIOUS TREE?

What exactly is the United Nations and, for that matter, why is there still a United Nations at all? How has it managed to survive over time, from 1945 down to the present—given its long record of underperformance, frequent outright failure, and even more frequent irrelevance? On the United Nations' core issues—collective peace and security, development, and universal human values and rights—its record is mediocre, unless one counts sheer institutional persistence as enough. And that record is particularly poor concerning the issue from which the collective sprang in 1945: international peace and security through the collective itself. Why, then, has not the ruthless evolutionary logic of history pruned it as a failed institutional sapling in a relentlessly competitive forest, as the League was pruned?

The textbooks in international law and organizations provide one set of answers to account for the persistence of the United Nations. They tell us the heroic story of the United Nations' founding in 1945 and the first meetings in San Francisco; Eleanor Roosevelt et al. They tell us about the

efforts of the Second World War Allies to create an organization that would be able to establish true collective security
and avoid the fatal—and predictable—errors of international organizations that yielded, among other things, the
failed League of Nations and the naïve Kellogg-Briand Pact.
They describe the present-day organization as an attempt
to provide global governance in a recalcitrant world. They
tend, above all, to tell a progressive moral history—"Whig
history"—of advances toward greater and better international
order through international law and organizations.

Accounts from the field of international relations tend to
be more skeptical, but their skepticism comes typically from
a realist perspective. The skepticism is descriptive rather than
normative. These international-relations accounts do not necessarily challenge the *normative* goals of the United Nations
and international order but instead note just how difficult the
task is and the limited success the institution has had.

But descriptive and normative accounts of the United
Nations, successes and failures, seen from the outside are not
the only accounts that matter. One would get a rather different perspective on the United Nations than either of these
big-picture, external accounts, by contrast, perusing the
institution's finances. For those (few) willing to delve into
its internal budget, management, fiscal control, accounting,
managerial structures, and labor relations, a striking organizational beast emerges. The organization's priorities are
mirrored in its budgets and fiscal structures that allocate its
resources. This is a picture of the United Nations characterized by rent-seeking and sometimes outright corruption, lack
of fiscal discipline or control, and a chief executive officer, the
secretary-general, who has no exact idea how many people

work for his organization. These are not facts that many experts on UN diplomacy choose to pay much attention to. Rather, the diplomats often find them tiresome when forced on their attention, for they distract from the grand issues of diplomacy and international law that make the United Nations exciting. The international-relations specialists find that they distract from accounts of power relations among states at the United Nations. But they are surely relevant, too, in establishing the terms of US-UN relations.

Yet none of these accounts of the United Nations, useful and interesting though each may be, provides much of a basis for guiding the United States in its dealings with the United Nations. That requires an account not merely of the United Nations' heroic self-conception, its less-than-stellar record, or its tawdry organizational reality—but also of its intellectual and ideological trajectory, in relation to those of the United States, from the past into the future, and those in relation to the ideals and interests of the United States. We need ways of explaining the United Nations so as to explain and predict how it will evolve and whether and when that evolution will support US ideals and interests or conflict with them.

So let us shift to another, quite different means of explaining the United Nations. The master issue, in this explanation, is the institution's source of legitimacy. The key to relations between the United States and the United Nations is fundamentally to address their contrasting—sometimes supporting and sometimes competing—legitimacies. Doing that begins with a close look at the source and nature of the United Nations' legitimacy and how the peculiar limits of that legitimacy contribute to the institution's most persistent large-scale feature—paralysis, a very particular kind of paralysis, to be sure, because it consists of marching, constant marching, but marching *in place*. Call it *immobilité perpétuelle*.

The United Nations consists of deep contradictions. More exactly, the United Nations consists of *antinomies*—profound, connected opposites that are "baked into" the institution's structure, history, incentives, and motivations. So. The United Nations is an independent institution with independent global claims to govern; the United Nations is a mere instrumentality of the member states. The United Nations is an institution based around the sovereign equality of states participating in a universal institution; the United Nations is committed to certain values and yet, at least in principle, there are standards to be met by states as a condition of joining and participating. The United Nations is the talking shop of the nations; the United Nations is a genuinely shared society of the world and not just the meeting ground of states' politics. The United Nations is merely the humble servant of its states-party; the United Nations is an independent governmental actor directly representing the "peoples" of the world. The secretary-general is merely the ministerial servant of the member states of the United Nations; the secretary-general is something approaching, albeit weakly, the "president" of the world. The United Nations is about global governance; yet it is said to be governance without a global government.

But the most powerful of the United Nations' many and varied antinomies is the one that ironically turns the institution's very failures into its most potent source of legitimacy. The distinctive salience of the United Nations is that it is a failure today—and a hope for tomorrow. And this is so even though it is *always* a failure today, each and every day—and yet *always* a hope for tomorrow. Imagine the United Nations as a sickly sapling. Sickly as it is today, however, it still holds out the promise of growing to become a glorious overarching tree—the glorious sheltering tree of global governance—but tomorrow, and always tomorrow. The tree never seems to grow or overcome its pathologies; it always remains the same sickly sapling. But likewise the promise of tomorrow, too, always remains as glorious.

This paradox points to one of the fundamental reasons for the persistence of the United Nations over time. The chronic promise of tomorrow provides a reason to put up with the chronic failures of today. Everything the organization does today, no matter how ineffective, ineffectual, corrupt, rent-seeking, or just plain wrong, has to be excused on the basis of what the organization will someday be.

It does not finally matter what the scandal, the appallingly bad behavior, the failure of management or of execution or of fiscal control happens to be. It can be wholesale mismanagement and corruption through the Oil-for-Food program (does anyone still recall that multi-billion-dollar scandal?) and the flight of a senior UN executive to his extradition-free home state. It might be rape and sexual predation against the young, not only by UN peacekeeping troops trading sex for food but also by UN civilian staff in African conflicts—followed by stern pronouncements of zero tolerance but no actual criminal prosecutions. Or it might be the unveiling of a $23 million mural on the ceiling of the UN Human Rights Council chambers—the main sponsor, Spain, having raided its international development aid

budget to help pay for it. It might be the relentless orches-
tration of reports, statements, declarations, resolutions, and
investigations by that same Human Rights Council, beneath
its magnificent mural, and its members and various "independent" experts and NGO enablers against a single state:
Israel. Or it could be the utter and disastrous inability of the
United Nations to actually get aid in a timely fashion to vic-
tims of the 2004 tsunami, as its aid czar held press conferences and sent observers to reconnoiter and finally fell into
the usual default activity of blaming the United States. Or—
at the largest political levels, looking backward across UN
history—it might be UN inaction in genocide in Rwanda
and Bosnia.

This leaves aside the question of whether the United
Nations' general inability to create positive outcomes, even
when not acting badly but merely inefficaciously, is a reason
to wonder about whether it is an organization worth having
around in the long run. It leaves aside the dangling question of whether the United Nations might be better replaced
with some other structure of global political coordination.
After all, such institutions of global coordination as do exist
with some effectiveness—the World Trade Organization,
for example—are formally reckoned part of the UN system
through, as it were, branding but in fact are governed under
their own mandates. Those successful global coordination
exercises share a couple of defining features. First, they tend
to be about economic matters in which a reasonably large
group of states have reasonably overlapping interests, whatever
their other conflicts. Second, they see their activities as fundamentally self-limiting to that particular activity, function,
and justification—not leading beyond it into grand political

projects, regardless of how much theorists of governance would like to see themselves gradually building into some grander political structure. The successful and reasonably effective institutions of global coordination have a deeply Burkean sense of limits: the length of time it takes to elaborate limited institutions of coordination and how quickly that coordination can be eroded or even toppled.

These are not the qualities of the United Nations as such; its mandate is by its nature political and invites expansion on every metric save effectiveness. Indeed, rather than inviting grander political projects in global governance, the United Nations' manifest failures ought rationally to invite the question of whether the United Nations' existence has the unfortunate effect of impeding the very possibility of the emergence of an alternative structure—some evolution towards something else, something with fewer contradictions, antinomies, and ambiguities. But the deepest of these is the way in which future promises lock in failure today. The rhetoric that surrounds the United Nations, the rhetoric that gives us the persistent ideal of "The Parliament of Man," has this constant and peculiar trope. It is always looking *beyond* the dismal present day of the United Nations to the glorious transcendental future of global governance, always on offer, but always on offer *tomorrow*. Call it "UN platonism."[1] Or maybe call it—the *nonfalsifiable* idea of the United Nations. It amounts to an infatuation with "global governance" as an ideal platonic form.

1. I borrow a phrase from Michael Glennon. Michael J. Glennon, "Platonism, Adaptivism, and Illusion in UN Reform," *Chicago Journal of International Law* 6 (Winter 2006): 613.

There are apparently *no* circumstances in the real world in which the ideal of the platonic United Nations could be found definitively wanting. The persistence of global hunger? Inevitably it means we must commit ever more deeply to the United Nations and give more to its development program. An outbreak of epidemic disease sweeps the planet? Clearly, we need to invest more in UN agencies and should have done so earlier. Nuclear war breaks out between regional powers? The problem must surely have been that insufficient emphasis was placed on engagement through the United Nations' multilateral disarmament and nuclear nonproliferation negotiations. The United Nations always remains the default answer, no matter what the question and no matter how badly its own failures contributed to the problem.

If it is somehow not the answer for today, then certainly it is the answer for tomorrow. And even if it is not the answer right now, we should act as though it *were* in order that it may *become* the answer for tomorrow. For some people, this is a general proposition, directly an article of faith about global governance and the United Nations as its historical vessel. Others maintain that they have an open mind, and so the United Nations might not necessarily (as a matter of historical necessity) be the answer to global coordination. But somehow, there turns out to be nothing in fact that could alter their commitment to the institution, because of what it represents for the future or, at least minimally, because it always turns out to be the hypothesized least-bad alternative. The first is straight-up UN platonism; the second a functional, constructive UN platonism. However one gets there, the final result is the same. Future possibilities hold the present hostage, and so every failure must finally be excused.

No matter what the question, the answer is somehow always a greater and deeper commitment to the United Nations. It has to be reckoned a nonfalsifiable faith, not a reasoned judgment.

Although Americans are not likely to do so, one might object to all of this on grounds that it applies with almost equal force to any of the leading sovereign states and their claims to legitimacy because they, too, have their manifest real-life failings. The United States, in particular, might be thought vulnerable to the charge, given how much it wears its constitutional idealism on its sleeve. America, after all, has not always lived up to its promises, and its reality has sometimes brutally betrayed its lofty ideals. If the United Nations might be judged a mistake, are there circumstances under which the Americans making this judgment ought, on the same standard, also to judge the United States a "mistake" or a "failure"? And if not, is the United States not *equally* nonfalsifiable as an ideal? Why, the skeptic might ask, should we set the standards for the United Nations' performance so high by comparison to that of sovereign states? Every institution has corruption, every institution has greater and lesser amounts of rent-seeking behavior by officials, and every institution has the problem of "capture" by particular constituencies. So what? One would never conclude that the general failure of the Congress is a reason for giving up on the United States. Such a judgment makes no more sense when speaking of the United Nations.

But this objection assumes an important prior conclusion about the United Nations as compared with sovereign democracies: that the United Nations is a necessary, non-contingent element of governance in the same way that the sovereign and ordered state is necessary and noncontingent with respect to governing society. It is hard to imagine governance in a world without the state. But of the United Nations one might easily say, we have no need of that hypothesis.[2] Moreover, the relative magnitude of the successes and failures in states differs enormously from that of the United Nations; the successes of leading states in the present require no recourse to fables about the future. The history of material improvement that has come about within societies over the last several centuries has required the condition of the state. It is, to be sure, not the sole political condition, but it certainly has been a mandatory element. One of the mysteries of contemporary Western elites is their sometime eagerness to dismantle and toss away the institutional engine of governance that has been necessary to produce such progress as humankind has experienced. States cannot be considered as possibilities for irrelevance to their societies' material and social progress by any stretch of the imagination.

By contrast, the United Nations has never been shown to be actually necessary to any of its declared ends, save perhaps the self-fulfilling aim of "universal harmonization" through the United Nations. The possibility that the United Nations really is a fifth wheel on the engine of history is a live hypothesis and indeed likely. It is hard to say that anything

2. As Laplace said of God. In any case, on at least one momentous occasion, the proposition of the United States as an ideal *was* tested, in the crucible of the Civil War; after 700,000 lives, the attempt to falsify it failed. The same has been true of other leading democratic sovereigns. The form of the nation-state persists, it would appear, for more reasons than merely its ability to persist. Certainly the form of the nation-state and its persistence is owed to more than its glorious promise for the future. One cannot say the same of the United Nations.

of crucial importance has required or necessarily depended upon the United Nations in the way that matters always have with states. To look into the future and say that, down the road, something hugely important historically or morally or politically both *will* and *must* take place with respect to the United Nations is a description of nonfalsifiable faith, especially as the event-horizon recedes, by a day as each new day passes.

Nor is it necessary that the United Nations be *this* United Nations—that is, one with a grand vision of its future role. Let us accept for argument's sake that the United Nations is not going away and it will not be replaced wholesale with some new institution. Neither will some "caucus of democracies" or other combination of global coordination emerge and render the United Nations irrelevant on any current political trajectory. Even so, why not aim toward a United Nations of few pretensions to glorious global governance— a United Nations aiming not at cultivating an overarching tree but instead at creating a series of low, sturdy, limited hedgerows that perform competently their precise and limited functions? Even accepting the general idea of a "United Nations," would this not be a better vision of the institution than a vision that cannot possibly come to pass and which, in loudly announcing itself but failing to bring itself to pass, will cause much greater damage in its wake?

Yet when liberal internationalism dreams, it dreams of overcoming anarchic and violent power relations through universal global governance. That is so even when liberal internationalists themselves, in the Obama administration and everywhere else in the world, are tired and a little bored with their own idealism. The dream presupposes two key things.

First, it requires a profound diminution, at a minimum, of the effective sovereignty of states, at least where sovereignty is understood in its traditional way, as a "political community without a political superior." Second, "global governance" sufficient to take over where the anarchy of sovereigns leaves off requires a form of global constitutionalism in an ultimately federal world, at least weakly, a world of states subject to universal global law and enforced by global institutions of law.

Some academic and policy literature devotes itself to denying the second proposition as fulminations of "right-wing bloggers and some politicians," so as to turn it into a mere strawman claim.[3] The international community, confronted

3. Thus, John Ruggie, writing in the foreword to Thomas G. Weiss and Ramesh Thakur, *Global Governance and the UN: An Unfinished Journey* (Bloomington, IN: Indiana University Press/United Nations Intellectual History Project, 2010). I refer in part to the burgeoning "global constitutionalism" literature in international law and politics, particularly among European academics believing that the rise of the EU is a model for the rise of a new global order. For a sharply skeptical, realist critique of this whole line of thinking as formulated within the orthodoxy of international law, see Eric Posner, *The Perils of Global Legalism* (Chicago: University of Chicago Press, 2009); for a quite different kind of critique based around a more traditional and politically pragmatic view of international law, rather than Posner's radically realist skepticism, see Michael J. Glennon, *The Fog of Law: Pragmatism, Security, and International Law* (Chicago: University of Chicago Press, 2010).

But Ruggie need look no further in this regard than the series preface (written by editors Louis Emmerij, Richard Jolly, and Thomas G. Weiss) in the book for which he writes the foreword for a small example. The editors of this series of works by the UN tracing its history—to be less generous, the UN congratulating itself fulsomely on the UN's contributions to "economic and social thinking and action"—say of global governance and global government: "The global financial and economic crisis of 2008–2009—as well as many less serious previous crises—underline the risks, problems, and enormous costs of a global economy without global government. . . . Although countries, especially the major powers, may not yet be ready to accept the need for some elements of global government. . . . [e]lements of global government will emerge."

with objections to its utopian appetite, suddenly puts on a modest countenance and downcast eyes as if to say, "But that's not us, we have no grand desires to govern anything." That is easy to say since the United Nations does not govern very much now. Nor is this a prediction that it could or would do so in the future. What it is, rather, is a statement that this is what it dreams of doing, and, whether there is any possibility of it coming to pass or not, thinking in those terms for the future alters its behavior today.

That is all this argument requires. But it grants too much in any case. For there is a very large literature devoted either to ways in which this governance *can* turn into government or else ways in which governance *must* turn into government, in order to persist over time. So to argue, indeed, is the intellectually plainest way to proceed; the idea of global governance without government was always a counsel of despair, invented in the 1990s because it was evident that government was not on offer. The syllogism that governance requires effective government is clear and compelling realism in service to a certain liberal internationalist idealism. By contrast, the syllogism that one can have global governance without global government is the reaching hypothesis and at the least invites the suspicion that it is an answer invented post hoc to make the best of the inability actually to achieve the highest goal of global government. It is a more honest argument, certainly, than the current one that global governance is all economically constrained states can afford; it is not so much a positive dream but the consequence of straitened necessity.

Not everyone, even among the world's elites, shares that global dream—quite irrespective of whether the daunting collective-action problems of global governance could ever be resolved. The dissenters are not only, and not even most importantly, American irredentists atavistically attached to American sovereignty. Elites of the rising great powers— China, Russia, Brazil, and India, for example—are frank in their nationalism, even when willing to use the language of internationalism to particular ends, usually as a means of cajoling the United States. The rulers of China, in particular, clearly believe that their country's global rise is not just on account of having so many people but on account of that state's national and linguistic coherence, as a society. Global Islam has its own allegiances and understanding of universalism. Still, there is a culturally significant number of preceptors among the global elites whose personal and professional lives remove them from the petty, parochial nation-state loyalties that are such an impediment to the great dream. They live as though in the jet stream, and their political dreams are borderless because they reside as though in the air.

According to liberal internationalism, then, governance ideally ought to be global. We are not there yet, but that is what ought to be pursued as a political end, whether as its own ideal or as today's economic necessity. Governance should be global, and for many of the visionaries, global governance should emanate from and center upon the United Nations, which the terms of the United Nations Charter itself imagine as a "centre for harmonizing the actions of nations." No effective global coordination or cooperation will last over the long term except if managed by a single global governor, able to enforce law and regulation in the classic definition of law as command backed by the effective threat of coercion, the argument goes. That argument appeals to realists, for whom the test of law really is a command backed by an effective threat.

Equally important, however, is the idealistic argument—the argument that has often appealed to the global bourgeoisie and elites alike as a form of cultural affinity—that the world and, indeed, history are gradually progressing toward a unified world in which individually sovereign states will gradually give way to a global government for the cooperative good of all. Particularly given that nation-states are established precisely on the principle of the ability to exercise ultimate control over activities within their territory, why should a global political system not require precisely such reach? It is an argument from idealism that takes the successful nation-state as the model for what a global order ought to look like, even though that means supplanting the nation-state itself. It is a form of constitutionalism—global federal constitutionalism—and is often represented as such.

On the other side of this debate is the defender of national sovereignty. The defender of sovereignty usually comes off in this debate as a retrograde, a defender of crude sovereignty and the privileges of states simply because they are states. This is how Americans, or anyway American sovereigntists, are often painted—vulgar defenders of nationalism and an American exceptionalism, which in turn gives rise to a claimed American sovereignty privileged over that of other sovereigns. As with the arguments for global governance, however, both a realist and an idealist argument lie beneath the "sovereigntist" position. The realist argument is obvious: multilateral state actions will often take place more effectively through the simple combined energies of self-interested states while still acting as individual states, coalitions of the willing, than through structured international-governance institutions into which their sovereignty is subsumed.

Less obvious, however, to those who assume that the sovereigntist position merely reflects a love affair with American power is sovereignty's powerful appeal to idealism. Indeed, it is perhaps the more compelling argument, because the idealist argument explains why the realist case is worth making. It asserts the intrinsic value of a self-governing political community, a democratic political community, one that obtains its legitimacy from the consent of its members. Such political communities can recognize not just their self-interest but their *comity*—their parallel and homologous interests—with other similar political communities. This yields them interests in coordination and cooperation within the limits of the interests and ideals of the democratic political community that gives legitimacy to government. There is, to be sure, a big problem in a community of states in which many are not democratic, and many only marginally so, but that fact, while conditioning relations among states, does not obviate the link between democratic self-governance and sovereignty within the states that are democratic.

The democratic sovereigntist argument views suspiciously the form of political cosmopolitanism that seeks a shift in ties gradually from the nation-state to the organs of planetary governance. We *will* become citizens of the planet and not just its inhabitants, says the liberal internationalist. In order to do so, we will necessarily become citizens less of our merely partial and selfish and nonuniversal once-sovereign communities—and all that according to a certain material logic of economic globalization and the integration of markets requiring global integration of governance, too—a sort of historical materialism revived for the purpose of dignifying what is otherwise a remarkably utopian cosmopolitanism. In turn, the democratic sovereigntist skeptic worries that being a citizen of the planet has as its primary characteristic not solidarity but instead something closer to . . . *undefinedness.* "American citizen" may be a parochial, partial, vulgar, and unworthy public identity, but at least it has the virtue of standing for something in a way that "citizen of the planet," however strategically mellifluous, does not.

But this is an old argument, this argument from democratic sovereignty as an ideal. When China and others of the rising world act as self-interested sovereigns, they are also acting according to an idealist argument. The legitimacy of those regimes is in several cases genuinely the legitimacy of democracy—India and Brazil, for example. But it is also, notably in the case of China, the legitimacy of rising living standards, wealth, and economic growth. Even the rising nondemocratic great powers today act in the larger world not from atavistic attachment to sovereignty, or from game-theory dictates of realism in the anarchy of states, but because—even if not necessarily by democratic consent—the *internal* legitimacy of the regime is at stake. And that internal legitimacy is profoundly bound up with economic growth.

The point is sometimes overlooked, this crucial relationship between internal legitimacy and sovereign action in the world. China is not democratic, but it has great internal legitimacy premised on the ability of the Communist Party to deliver economic growth. It has all the privileges that attach in international relations to a state apparatus able to act coherently with respect to the rest of the world. But even though not democratic, the regime does have to fulfill certain internal expectations to remain legitimate. Indeed, the lack of democracy itself puts greater pressure on economic growth as a source of internal legitimacy in China. All of these rising great powers, not just China, and whether or not democratic, are attached to internal, nation-state legitimacy as the ground for acting in the larger world of nation-states; they do not act from dictates of interstate realism alone.

This was on display in the 2009 Copenhagen summit on climate change. Europe—and to some extent the United States or at least the Obama administration—presumed that the only "idealism" was that of acting "globally" to combat a presumed "global" evil. Anything else was merely selfish self-interest. It was always assumed that the irredentist Americans, even in the Age of Obama, would have to take into account internal democratic legitimacy in the United States and the possibility—likelihood—that even a Democratic Congress would reject a Copenhagen climate change deal imposing great costs on the US public. It was assumed at Copenhagen, however, that the rising powers would function solely according to some realist premise of pure interstate self-interest. Hence China, India, Brazil, et al. could always be bought off by the first world, if the rich countries wanted to pony up. Or at least they could be sufficiently bought off so that they would sign a final-deal document, whether or not they intended to keep to it.

In the event, therefore, interstate realism at Copenhagen dictated that the rising great powers should take the money. Yet they did not. Though the internal diplomacy is only slowly emerging for scholarly scrutiny, it appears that irrespective of interstate realism, the internal legitimacy of regimes deeply bound up with rising living standards and rates of growth dictated no acceptance, not even on paper, of any deal that would compromise their long-term economic growth. The conditions of internal regime legitimacy, on one reading of the Copenhagen climate summit, trumped strict realist rationality.

In one sense this is quite peculiar, on a realist calculus. Why not sign and then defect from the promise down the road? Well, one reason is that not signing deliberately sends an important signal to one's own population. It tells them that the source of regime legitimacy, internal economic growth and rising living standards, will not be imperiled even as an abstraction. It will not be put up for negotiation, even for a piece of paper that the regime could abandon— insincere promising and defection. The lesson is that it is a mistake to assume that idealism is always on the side of liberal internationalism, or even that the counteridealism is always a democratic ideal of a self-governing community. In today's world, the sovereigntist counteridealism might well be, not a democratic ideal, but an authoritarian ideal of permanent economic growth. Authoritarian state-directed economic growth is a two-edged sword for an authoritarian regime— something other than democracy that the regime can use as a basis for internal regime legitimacy, but concomitantly something that, in an importantly idealist way, the regime *owes* to its own population when dealing with others in the world. There are few things on which such regimes are held to account internally; but this might well be one of them, particularly if the regime has put this on the table as its metric of legitimacy.

Such issues as democracy and economic growth—neither of which is a question for the United Nations—are what arguments over "real" legitimacy are about when serious nation-states have them, however. The limited—and, by UN enthusiasts, persistently overestimated—legitimacy such as the United Nations does possess, for particular functions, is premised on something that is frankly not sufficient to guarantee the long-run survival of nation-states: the promise of the future. It only suffices for the persistence of the United Nations because the expectations in the present are so low. The contradictions between the unprepossessing present of the United Nations and its always-and-ever presumed better future contributes mightily to the single most striking feature of the United Nations today: general and unyielding stasis. The United Nations is frozen on many issues between contradictory visions and missions, frozen between the inglorious present and the apparently glorious future that grants it contemporary legitimacy. It is at once caught within and paralyzed by these gaps, and it is consequently unable to make choices and then move forward. The United Nations lives in the interstices between the present and the future. The most salient and remarkable sociological feature of this posture is that it is so *stable*.

To say that the United Nations is perpetually caught in stasis is likely to elicit a weary shrug and the response, from many long-time observers of the United Nations, tell me something I didn't know. After all, the organization was practically frozen in amber from the beginning of the Cold War to the end. With 1990 came a resurgence of idealism around the organization's possibilities, but it mostly fizzled over that decade. The United Nations' disastrous performance in the Rwandan genocide and its failures in the Yugoslav wars were just two of an accumulation of episodes in the 1990s that convinced even many UN supporters that the institutional United Nations was something to laud as an ideal but not something to take seriously in fact, at least in the sense of ever *relying* on it in the present.

The growth of "global civil society," and its successes with such campaigns as the landmines ban and the Ottawa landmines convention, injected brief new energy into the idea of a self-reinforcing, mutual legitimation between the United Nations and global NGOs. Global civil society would provide the United Nations with a natural global constituency, and the United Nations would then empower global civil society as the "representatives" of the world's peoples. Together, they would enable the United Nations to do a kind of end run around the member states, as well as around the United Nations' notable "democracy deficit." But by the end of the 1990s, and certainly with 9/11, the idea that global civil society would be able to supply the United Nations with legitimacy sufficient to act in serious matters, beyond the will of the member states, likewise fizzled. September 11 and the Iraq war caused Annan to realize that the Secretary-General's fundamental constituency was, and always would be, the Security Council. As historian Paul Kennedy noted in his book on the history of the United Nations, by the mid-1990s, the post–Cold War vision of the United Nations had been ideologically and idealistically exhausted—a scant few years after the fall of the Soviet Union.[4]

Since then, there have always been surface movements of one kind or another—the United Nations' Millennium

4. Paul Kennedy, *The Parliament of Man: The Past, Present, and Future of the United Nations* (New York: Random House, 2006).

Development Goals, for example—seeking to offer a new ideological and motivating vision that treats the United Nations not merely as a locale for conducting global *politics* but as a shared *social* project. There are also conflicts over structural issues, such as the composition and role of the Security Council in a world in which, to say the least, power relations have shifted away from Europe. Tensions over the relationship between the United Nations as the ideal vehicle for "collective security" and the United States as the world's actual (for the moment) security hegemon always simmer. But beneath those surface movements, there are not so many changes.

The considerable and real anger expressed years ago during the Security Council's Iraq war debates exemplified the antinomy. The United States would go to the council to seek its blessing for the Iraq invasion, for example—but it would not, in the final analysis, obey a contrary vote. The Iraq crisis raised questions as to whether the United Nations would remain relevant as an organization even in fundamental questions of international security; as James Traub observes, the fear of the United Nations, even the Security Council and, more pointedly, the Secretary-General, being rendered irrelevant in an era of dominant American power haunted Annan and his senior advisors.[5] Events did not resolve those questions, of course, or even alter their terms materially. The United Nations and the Security Council did not become irrelevant in international security—but they did not become more relevant, either. Contrary to what the

5. James Traub, *The Best Intentions: Kofi Annan and the UN in the Era of American World Power* (New York: Farrar, Straus & Giroux, 2006).

theorists of the post–Cold War United Nations hoped, the Security Council had not finally become a vehicle for collective decision making in matters of great-power politics; it remained at most a talking shop for those great powers. As in all such debates at the United Nations, they produced words and not deeds.

The stasis created by a mutual expectation that each country participates but is not bound, promises but then need not deliver, goes to things big and small. Countries promise money for Millennium Development Goals but then do not pony up (and without cavil, apology, or embarrassment in these straitened times, even among the Europeans); countries promise on the Kyoto Protocol but then do not reduce carbon emissions; global civil society, according to UN officials' own speeches, will rejuvenate global political society but then it does not. All this insincere promising might be customary and predictable—but it is finally corrosive to institutions, whether sovereign states or organs of the United Nations itself. It turns the United Nations into a kind of weird machine in which the disconnect between word and deed is practically automatic. The result is a UN Energizer Bunny that marches and marches—but has managed to march itself into a cul-de-sac. Unable to find a way forward or a way out, it simply continues to march, but forever marching in place. Movement takes place. The mechanism hums and throbs. Something is always going on, there is always some activity. But movement does not proceed discernibly in any direction (save only for the consolidation of the anti-Israel consensus, the organization's one discernible collective action, successful, one might conclude, precisely because it is religious and ideological in its zeal, not rational).

And so one looks forward, to the United Nations' elusive promise of tomorrow, without ever actually getting there.

The last serious attempt to break the stasis from within was Kofi Annan's 2005 UN reform effort. Backed by his considerable charisma, it was a serious attempt to build as his legacy a United Nations for a new century. But Annan's last gasp push for reform did not take. There was the big conference in September 2005. There were bits and pieces of change, some worthwhile and some grotesque. But then again, there is always a big conference with the United Nations. There are always many words. And there are always small, ultimately insignificant changes. And then internally things go on much as before.

The truth of the matter is that big changes—and even small but significant shifts in tone and emphasis—at the United Nations almost invariably take place on account of upheavals from the outside. It is by nature a derivative institution. The fall of the Berlin Wall and the collapse of the Soviet Union, for example, gave rise to unequivocal US hegemony for several years and the stability of great-power relations. This allowed the language of human rights and related universal values to consolidate themselves within the institution during the 1990s—the consolidation of "universalism" through American hegemony. It is a far from insignificant contradiction, this human rights universalism through hegemony, one that the Obama administration and American friends might mark as the American administration contemplates, under soothing cover of "multilateral engagement," the downsizing of that hegemony.

One can thus imagine two contemporary extra–UN movements over the coming years that might shift important aspects of the United Nations' static internal arrangements. One is the rise of multipolarity (discussed in greater detail in chapter 3). This might occur as part of signaling an American decline that, in its turn, could only too easily trigger a multipower scramble amidst new security, economic, and posthegemonic instabilities, particularly in Asia. A multipower scramble could have significant impact if accompanied by continued rise in the influence of authoritarian states such as China, Russia, Venezuela, Iran, and their satellites and sympathizers; because many of these states are essentially resource-export authoritarians, much depends upon the price of oil and whether the US decides to develop supplies inside the US and increase supplies from Canada. Inside the United Nations, multipolarity could mean a shift away from what has been, for several decades, human rights as the apex value and toward other kinds of values-talk that does not require the same sort of finger-pointing at serial human rights abusers: climate change, for example, or development goals would be more comfortable. Or it could mean simply the redefinition of human rights to ever more powerful forms of illiberalism; same words, same sanctimony, but radically different meanings.

American decline and the rise of multipolar power politics could also easily produce international security crises—more North Korean military adventurism or an Iranian nuke and attendant military response, for example. The threats arise, especially in Asia, from a multipolar world and what might properly be called the Obama administration's *withdrawal into multilateralism*. Withdrawal into multilateralism is the best way to understand America's current strategic fusing of multilateralism and American decline. Obvious to everyone, these are not the threats that defined the decade after 9/11. The past decade's threats and attacks by transnational non-state-actor terrorism will of course continue. But they are far from the only kind of threat. Some of the most serious of the other threats have been long held at bay by the belief of all parties in American hegemony, its power and resolve to use it, most of all in preserving the peace of the Pacific.

So looking to the future, multipolarity thrusts the United Nations, and those that look to it as collective security or as any other kind of collective-action entity, back into the conflicts of nation-states in classically Westphalian anarchy. The easy days of the 1990s are over. Half of the Obama administration's foreign policy team seems still to live in those glory days of liberal internationalism; a not insignificant chunk seemed to believe, during the first heady days of the administration, that a decline in US power equals the rise of the liberal internationalist order, the decline of one begetting the rise of the other: a zero sum equation for the welfare of the world and a bit of comeuppance for the hegemonic bully, not simply a regrettable condition of the world but, well, hooray for American decline! Now that that decline appears to be a real, rather than merely academic, possibility, there is less mea culpa than a slightly desperate search for ways to spin dross into gold. Meanwhile, the other half of the Obama administration—the "New Liberal Realists"— never harbored illusions about decline begetting a new world order of global understanding. Not Carter, but Kissinger, they nonetheless deploy the same language of their idealist cohabitors as the tool for softening the terms of American strategic withdrawal from hegemony and think themselves one step cleverer than Kissinger to do so.

The second extra–UN movement (taken up in chapter 7) is the increasingly confident rise of Islamic states that see the United Nations as a tool for promoting a new content for the old language of human rights: group identities and the primacy of religion, meaning without cavil Islam and global Muslim religious sensibilities. The decision on the part of the world's democracies not to stick to a "deep but narrow" conception of inalienable human rights has left the content of rights-talk open to change, which includes becoming a language for quite illiberal enterprises such as the "rights" of religions or religious followers against, for example, blasphemous Danish cartoonists. The pressure to rewrite the content of the language of rights comes even as the Western democracies shift to a very different language of values, one more focused on the environment and climate and development, whether framed in rights language or something else. Just as "human rights" replaced "world peace" as the apex language of values at the United Nations in the 1990s, one could imagine the content of those rights changing over time, even as rights themselves recede in prominence.

As this book goes to press, we have seen the Arab Spring, and the Gaddafi regime has just fallen, but not Syria's Bashar al-Assad at this writing. This book makes no special predictions about where those Arab Spring revolutions will go over time—perhaps liberal democracy breaks out, perhaps using Twitter means one is for the rights of women, perhaps the use of social media betokens a specially progressive mind. Or perhaps not. The point is that unless these good things actually and sustainably come to pass, a core point of this book is to say that it is a mistake to appeal to things that are supposed to happen because of the presumably inevitable flow of history to the good. This assumption is a big part of why it is impossible to do much to improve the United Nations in the first place.

The key point, however, is that these changes, if they happen, will take place not because of any quality of the United Nations itself but because of external forces. In between the United Nations' externally imposed moments of disruption are long periods of stasis, often accompanied by intellectual and moral exhaustion. The stasis is largely defined by the United Nations' own internal interest groups, and, to the extent that the United Nations evolves at all as an institution in these periods, it does so in a very slow drift. The forces that bring about change at the United Nations are combinations of real-world power relations in the external world and ideological shifts.

Historian Paul Kennedy is not alone in diagnosing the intellectual and political exhaustion at the United Nations, in the 1990s or now. Many observers have expressed it as a matter of frustration and have penned many books, theses, and articles to explain the problem and how to fix it. The customary explanation for the United Nations' deep stasis is that the United Nations is mostly a consensus institution or set of institutions. It has many stakeholders, and many hold what amounts to a veto, a "hold-up" over actions that might conflict with their desires: member states, groups of member states, UN officialdom itself, individual diplomats, NGO advocates, philanthropists, and outside donors. It is a long list of claimants. It is mostly a wonder that any changes take place internally at all, the argument goes. We should understand UN stasis as a collective-action problem in a structure that encourages consensus, as well as "bloc" voting along such axes as geography and ideology. Everything is blocked, because everyone holds a veto, and only events from out-side the United Nations can break the hold-up, and that only occasionally.

This explanation does not go far enough, however. In any case, we should be skeptical of an explanation that so conveniently takes everyone individually off the hook, so to speak, for a general failure—while leaving the institution in place in a dynamic world. It is not just the endless deadlocks created by multiple stakeholders that make it so hard for the United Nations to pursue a vision and a mission. Nor is it only the corrosive nature of insincere promising, defection, and free riding. To these, one has to add the deadlock produced by the antinomies and ambiguities surrounding the very categories that the institution is supposed to exemplify. Once again: Is it an "association of member states" or is it an institution with genuinely independent power, authority, and legitimacy beyond, and even above that, of its members? What is the role of the secretary-general? Under the Charter, he is the humble servant of the member states. Kofi Annan, on the other hand, successfully sought to expand the role and prestige of the office to the point that, for many in the world, it was a kind of weak president of the world. Part of the dissatisfaction that many have expressed with Ban Ki-moon is precisely that, at least by comparison to Annan, he eschews the world president role and remains far more diplomatically circumspect. Is this a step forward or backward?[6]

6. James Traub, in a sort of update to his 2006 book on Kofi Annan and UN reform, exemplifies this line of criticism of Ban Ki-moon as being too much the diplomat. See James Traub, "Good Night, Ban Ki-Moon: The U.N. Secretary-General Must Go," *Foreign Policy*, July 22, 2010, *available at* http://www.foreignpolicy.com/articles/2010/07/22/give_ban_the_boot.

These questions, in turn, implicate all of the earlier questions concerning the relation between the United Nations and national sovereignty. John Ruggie, as both a leading political scientist and former senior UN official and continuing outside senior advisor, has described a struggle between UN "traditionalists," on the one hand, and "modernizers," on the other.[7] The traditionalists look to the authority of member states for the United Nations' legitimacy and authority. The modernizers, by contrast, look for legitimacy and authority elsewhere, directly among the "peoples of the world" in order to imbue the United Nations with authority that does not depend upon the will of states. On all of these questions, one has to ask both: which is it now and, more importantly, which is it to be?

The United Nations and its public intellectuals and theorists are almost always able to elide these difficult questions. They do so with the very simple response of pushing them off into the World of Tomorrow. Time becomes a universal solvent, so to speak, of anything that appears intractable today. Given that anyone important in the UN system has a veto over action in the present, if only by a refusal to act or cooperate, the fundamental ambiguities cannot be resolved, and the baseline choices announced by these antinomies cannot be forced. All the hard questions are permanently kicked down the road into that beautiful tomorrow that forever justifies the inadequate today.

It is perfectly acceptable within the sensibility of the United Nations, by the way, to make note of this, perfectly acceptable, that is, provided one goes through a certain ritual bewailing

---

7. For a discussion of Ruggie's views, see Traub, *Best Intentions*, p. 383.

and expression of public frustration that shows, so to speak, that one's heart is in the right place. At one point or another, everyone with a stake at the United Nations is permitted to be the designated mourner for the inability of the United Nations to do what it is supposed to do. One bewails the inability to answer the questions that, at bottom, the collective does not want to have to answer. The conceptual antinomies and strategic ambiguities *both* make the organization's continued daily existence possible *and* ensure that it remains most of the time in a frozen state—save for those rare moments when events from the outside punctuate the equilibrium. It keeps the organization always marching, but marching in place and justifying its lack of progress with reference to the glorious future toward which it is conspicuously not progressing.

This quality of forever marching in place has implications for US-UN relations over the long term, however, and across presidential administrations. They are implications that broad American political movements, conservative and liberal, and both political parties need to assimilate. Conservatives need to get their minds around the United Nations' *permanence*: the United Nations exists, and it is not going away. But liberals, for their part, need to get their minds around its *stagnation*: it is not likely to become something radically different from what it is now, either, and suddenly wake up and start doing jolly good things.

And despite the periodic fits of wailing about the institution's state, the truth is that the United Nations' "culture" is not really unhappy about that fact. After so little internal change over so many years, perhaps it is time to conclude that the United Nations is *not* an institution in which everyone desires change of some kind but just cannot agree on what kind of change or how to get there. Perhaps the more honest conclusion is that the United Nations is an institution and a petit-society reasonably content with itself, pretty satisfied with its condition and its actions. Maybe, just below the surface wailing, it is an institution that is fundamentally *happy*.

Subpar equilibrium? Sure. Permanent and stagnant? Plainly. Unhappy about it? Not really. Ritual complaints and bewailing of the problems are a fundamental part of the institutional culture—in part as a means of rent-seeking from those who pay its bills. But that is merely the surface of a society that is materially and spiritually pretty happy with itself. Even its complaints and demands for change are themselves part of the marching in place.

The United Nations is not just in equilibrium, in other words; it is in *happy equilibrium*. The challenge for American policy makers is not to figure out how to disrupt that happy equilibrium, either in order to push towards the elusive tomorrow or in order to shut it down. Neither will happen. The challenge, instead, is to figure out how to engage that happy equilibrium with eyes wide open about its nature— where to use it to do things the US could not do itself, where to press it to more efficient activity, and where just to work to disengage and contain its damage.

2 MULTILATERALISM AND ENGAGEMENT

The United Nations' pattern of long periods of stasis punctuated by cycles of apparent crises is a profoundly subpar state of affairs, even if, within the culture of the United Nations itself, it is a happy equilibrium. The crises never quite force resolution of the institution's internal contradictions and instead peculiarly contribute to the stability of the institution, but at an equilibrium that is worse than it might otherwise be. Moreover, it is a subpar state of affairs characterized not merely by pervasive equilibrium inefficiency but by deep and ineradicable anti-Americanism as well. Indeed, the anti-Americanism and conjoined anti-Israelism are the genuinely dynamic and moving parts of the institution—really, the only ones. Under such conditions, when and how should the United States engage with the United Nations? What are multilateralism and engagement supposed to mean under these circumstances?

The response sometimes given by conservatives—*never*—cannot be correct. Its attraction is obvious, but the

United Nations is here to stay. Even as hostile a skeptic as
John Bolton acknowledges flatly that the United Nations is
not going away. But if that is right, then the United States
must have a defined relationship to it. At the same time, the
response sometimes given by liberals and the near-mantra
of the Obama administration now year on year—*always*—
likewise cannot be correct. Liberals and liberal internationalists in particular need to understand the disadvantages not
just to the United States but even to the United Nations
and the international community of an "always engage"
response—particularly the ways in which it undercuts more
nuanced strategies of engagement with particular UN organs
and activities but not others.

The correct answer and the best policy response is the
most obvious one: "Well, *sometimes*." But is "sometimes"
just policy mush? Not entirely. It can actually offer useful
and relatively specific guidance for whether, when, and how
to engage—or not. It can offer policy heuristics, general
rules of thumb, for how to engage with parts, activities, and
organs of the United Nations. These rules have exceptions,
but they are good reflexive starting places for policy.

Engagement is not a policy. At most, it is a process and,
most of the time, merely a slogan. It only means something
if it can be applied to different parts of the United Nations
in different ways that suit the characteristics of those parts
and functions. The Security Council is not the same as the
General Assembly; issues of global security are not the same
as issues of UN symbolic values and human rights. The
Millennium Development Goals are not the same as the
Human Rights Council. The World Food Program is not
the same as the Durban conferences on racism. The body's

different functions and components require different forms
of engagement, and some of them require no engagement
at all.

The basic rules of engagement for the United States with
respect to the United Nations run roughly as follows:

◆ *Security Council*: "always engage." Engagement with the
Security Council includes, however, a willingness to use
the veto as required in particular circumstances; "always
engage" does not mean "always go along." It also means
a particular understanding of the Security Council as having a primary role as talking shop of the great powers—a
role that will increase in importance as multipolarity rises
but which will also grow more strained as the permanent,
veto-bearing members (P5) are ever less representative of
the multiplying, true powers.

◆ *The General Secretariat*: "always engage." Engage, however, by continuing to play the unpopular managerial
reformer, insisting on accountability, managerial effectiveness, and fiscal rectitude. It also means, insofar as possible,
supporting the secretary-general in his largely thankless
task of trying to be the executive officer of an organization that, by design and history, has no real space for a
CEO—supporting the secretary-general but also insisting
that he *manage*.

◆ *UN specialized agencies, particularly in international
development, the environment, and global health and
disease*: "sometimes engage" and sometimes "parallel
engage." Effectiveness in grappling with the underlying
global problem is the issue; engage *through* those that are
effective and incentivize them with funding, even to what

amounts to a budgetary buyout of the agency, but be willing to engage in *parallel* activities on the same problem, outside of the United Nations' agencies and agendas, particularly in international development.

♦ *The General Assembly*: "contain," which is to say, "engage sometimes" but always be prepared to "disengage" or "actively oppose." The General Assembly is an organ of the United Nations fundamentally to be contained in a material and ideological sense because it is unreformable and will always be fundamentally anti-American. Any resources allotted to it will either be misspent or spent on anti-Americanism; budgetary resources to the General Assembly should be as limited as possible and, as much as possible, dispersed to rent-seeking and other mechanisms for keeping people pointlessly occupied.

♦ *The Human Rights Council and other UN "values" institutions and processes*: "disengage and actively oppose." The Human Rights Council (HRC), like the commission it supposedly replaced, exists largely to protect the world's human rights abusers, and engaging with them in the HRC can only water down American critiques of these countries' human rights records. The rest consists almost entirely of attacks upon Israel, partly from pure ideological motivation and partly as a mechanism of distraction. The Arab League's current, urgent desire to align itself with anti-autocratic-regime sentiment and protest among Arab populations does not alter that long-run trend, nor does it turn it into a vehicle of human rights within the UN or elsewhere; its stance is a function of the Arab street at this moment, not any discernible embrace of human rights as such. Moreover, the trajectory of the United Nations on symbolic issues of "universal values" and "human rights" is fundamentally illiberal, and the essential role of the United States is to stand as the immoveable outsider on core issues of free expression and secular liberalism, opposing without apology or compromise what is otherwise the long march of illiberal states. The same is true of other UN values forums, such as the Durban conferences.

Subsequent chapters return at greater length to this basic policy guidance on particular topics. For present purposes, this is merely a window on the range of proper US engagement with different UN functions. The proper approach to engagement is neither *never* nor *always*; it is always complicated. "Nuance"—or "smart" diplomacy or whatever the buzzword of the moment is—is not nuance if it means "always." Nuance instead means responding to particular organs, functions, and circumstances within the United Nations—and not others.

Yet engagement as an ideological proposition for the Obama administration operates simultaneously as an ambition for it, on the one hand, without having a clear sense of what it means apart from the irony of "multilateral engagement" simply meaning "disengagement of specifically American power." It is also a key part of its seemingly never-to-end indictment of the foreign policy of the Bush administration. That indictment is not altogether fair: as with many foreign policy agendas of the Obama administration (and not just counterterrorism and national security) the differences are often less in actual policy than in tone. The Bush administration "engaged" quite a lot with UN processes, indeed sometimes too much. After all, the negotiations for the first infamous "anti-racism" (read, anti-Israel, sometimes anti-Jew) conference in Durban (Durban I), took place with the participation of the Bush administration in its first days (before 9/11). Until political circumstances finally forced Secretary of State Powell's famous walkout, the Bush administration was as eager then as the Obama administration was in its first year to bet on its ability to alter the outcome of ideologically driven UN exercises. Given that they predictably end in tears, the proper policy response is instead rejection and obstruction.

Yet the character of the Bush administration's form of engagement differed from the Obama administration's in that it often consisted of *disagreeing* with whatever the main body of the United Nations had already concluded was the correct policy. The Bush administration dared reasonably often to "engage" by saying that it would not necessarily go along with the "consensus." For the consensus-builders of the United Nations, to be sure, this was not real engagement after all. Engagement under conditions of consensus negotiations was supposed to mean, if not precisely agreeing straight-out, at least a certain pro forma negotiation over minor terms followed by a graceful agreement to go along with the consensus as a whole. Engagement apparently by definition did not include (at least in the eyes of the Bush administration's internationalist critics) engagement in order ultimately to disagree.

Alongside engagement, the Obama administration has also embraced multilateralism, which it similarly wielded as a charge against its predecessor. Multilateralism matters because it addresses a crucial, but otherwise unanswered, question about engagement—engagement *with whom*? Like engagement, however, it is a fraught term and subject to strategic ambiguity. First, for an action to be multilateral, is it enough to engage with a group, any group, of states? Or, alternatively, need the word mean something considerably stronger: engagement with some international-governance structure like the United Nations or perhaps engagement with sovereign states mediated through the processes of the United Nations?

The difference between these various visions of multilateralism lies beneath the argument over whether the United States had to garner permission from the United Nations to undertake the Iraq war or could instead lead a rather sizable "coalition of the willing." Critics called the United States–led coalition "US unilateralism." But it was unilateral only if multilateralism requires the authorization of the UN Security Council. Ditto NATO's 1999 Kosovo war. For Russia, it was American, or NATO, unilateralism, because multilateralism could come only through the United Nations; for European NATO countries, by contrast, the involvement of NATO as an institution meant that the war was more than unilateral.

The Obama administration began by embracing a strong form of multilateralism: engagement at and through the United Nations. The practical effect of this move was to give various actors and groups of states at the United Nations—often America's ideological, and often actual, enemies—great negotiating leverage over the United States. The administration initially seemed to think that in exchange for this leverage, the United States would gain goodwill, legitimacy, and political space for diplomacy to play to US benefit. Within a year or two, it was clear that although the United States

continued to hold out for the United Nations or, at least, multilateralism, as the space for addressing proliferation issues,
such as those posed by North Korea or Iran, and other essentially forward-looking issues, the (renamed) war on terror and
America's wars were quite off the table for discussion—the
United States might offer a detailed account of many matters
of human rights, but its drone attacks are still not even admit-
ted, let alone discussed. It has grown noticeably more impa-
tient with being tasked to explain its national security policies
in international forums, and this represents the ascendency of
the New Liberal Realist wing, not pandering to conservatives.

The administration also placed, and indeed continues
to put, peculiar faith in global public opinion and following
it, as though the globe were a single polity measurable by
Gallup, and countries like politicians following electorates.
This vision of how to measure global power and influence
is frankly absurd, and one need not hold to any strict realist
power theory to think so. The world is not an electorate, and
countries are not politicians. The world consists of societies
and countries and political systems and, whatever it is that
the global opinion polls and international media believe they
measure and whatever they think it means for politics, global
relations are mediated through institutions of power, nation-
states above all.

The United States' striking concessions at the General
Assembly and the Security Council in the administration's
first outings, followed by its other obeisances in such forums
as the Human Rights Council, have not borne much fruit;
again, the Arab Spring is too early to assess, and calls for
Human Rights Council-sponsored investigations in Libya or
Syria betokens merely transitory Arab League concern for the

shifting opinions of the Arab Street. But they are not forgotten everywhere; at the time, they spurned and frightened our
friends, emboldened our enemies, and pushed our allies—
those attached to us mostly for interests rather than shared
values—to reconsider the persistence of American power.
Even if today the administration has a much more workman-
like attitude toward the United Nations and what it offers as
a forum, this is because those appearances did their damage,
on the one hand, and because the rest of the world took its
measure of the administration and drew its own conclusions
about cant and content. Because this is so much a game of
perception—that is, signals being given today on apparently
symbolic issues that, for lack of better proxies, stand as the
best-available guides to future US behavior—the United
Nations and its organs, including its apparently hard-powerless
"values" organs, matter rather more than one might have
thought. Symbolism at the United Nations is leverage—but
not in the way that the Obama administration, to judge by
its maneuvers there, appears to have imagined in its first days.

The administration appears, even now, to think that
symbolic gestures at the United Nations are easy ways to
gain influence at little cost—it is all just words, after all.
Especially in the "values" arena of human rights, the administration seems to think get along–go along is all gravy; easy
benefits and no costs. But it would do better to think of its
words today, particularly in the "easy" forums, instead as
price signals. The world, in its various postures toward the
United States, anxiously seeks forward indicators of what
the United States will be—not so much *do* but what it will
be. Will it revert to the mean of a pragmatic, loose American
hegemony that allows much latitude to friends and enemies

and allies alike, while offering broad global public goods? Or is it genuinely signaling a new era of decline in which, for the first time, America itself believes? Not even global popularity polls suggest that the United States has gained much, if anything, for what it has yielded, and it turns out that in large areas of the world, America is less popular than ever.

Blame it on real-world American policies, blame it on disappointed expectations beyond the policies themselves, blame it on the peculiarly American habit of inviting everyone (enemies included) to judge it by the standard of perfection, blame it on Predator drones, blame it on the tendency to desert perceived losers and hegemons in decline: the United States is bearing, as the economists might say, the transaction costs of being a dominant actor that has signaled lack of staying power: everything *except* further decline becomes so much more difficult. The administration ironically today comforts itself with what its critics told it in the first place when it proposed global public opinion as a metric. The task of the United States is not to win elections in the world. True, but it is also to lead its friends and allies and to contain, hedge up, restrict, obstruct, if not always smite, its enemies. To which one might add what the administration has not yet: the "world" is not stupid, and it is perfectly capable of seeing through "multilateral engagement" to "American disengagement."

It requires no geopolitical wizardry to understand that the United States will hold to this current vision of multilateralism—the multilateralism that says the United Nations is a necessary party in big things—only up until the moment when it no longer wishes to. When the perception

of costs and benefits shifts sufficiently, the Obama administration will decide that "multilateralism" need merely mean
assembling the allies in the world that the United States can
conjure up for the particular issue at hand. Its partisans now
see its engagement as a win, because engagement is good
on general internationalist principles. But when the Obama
administration finally comes to the moment when it opts not
to engage with the United Nations and instead falls back on
its friends and allies—those that remain—that will also be
spun as a win. After all, it will show that the administration
has a tough, no-nonsense side, too.

In the world in which the rest of us live, however, policies
involve tradeoffs, not win-wins consisting of bait-and-switch
with oneself. As a real matter of tradeoffs, not foreign policy
narcissism, switching midstream in America's definition of
"multilateralism" involves an important loss of credibility.
Strategic ambiguity is occasionally an effective signal; most
of the time, as a political price signal, it is costly. It invites
others to make potentially disastrous miscalculations. While
Obama's partisans celebrate the ambiguity and say they can
have their cake and eat it, too, others in the world will note
that the administration said one thing when it was convenient and later did another.

The advocate of UN multilateralism today, of a multilateralism that may give way to weaker forms when convenient
down the road, may respond that hypocrisy is the norm in
international relations. No one seriously plans on anything
different. But that is not quite true. The United States has
actually shown striking long-term consistency, long-run
reversion to the mean of loose hegemony, in the basics of
its global security strategy and what its multilateralism

means—a subject we consider in the next chapter. The United States might be thought a vulgar gun-toting, often-times swaggering, hegemon, but it has also built up a considerable reservoir of credibility as to what the vulgar, gun-toting, swaggering hegemon will do when it says it will do something. Credibility of that kind takes a long time to amass, and relatively little time to squander. Switching from one form of multilateralism to another is one way to dissipate that credibility and trust.

And in the meantime, strategic ambiguity concerning the meaning of multilateralism will not net the US gains on such difficult topics as Iran or the South China Sea or other long-term trouble spots. Because the United Nations is controlled, particularly in the vocal General Assembly and its appendages, by actors and states that range from actively hostile to the United States to increasingly indifferent, the effect of invoking a multilateralism of the United Nations is mostly to raise questions about future American behavior among friends and enemies alike. That is true, ironically, even when the friends themselves are rather slavishly devoted to fetishizing the multilateralism of the United Nations.

Another ambiguity embedded in the term "multilateralism" is subtler but arguably more serious over the long run. Does the term implicate, on the one hand, relations among sovereign states today—without any view that even highly cooperative, structured, and closely coordinated relations among sovereigns are intended to lead to global governance of a liberal internationalist bent over time, so that the burdens and benefits are those of today and realistic expectations of tomorrow? Or, on the other hand, is today's multilateralism conducted in the utopian hope and expectation that these actions lay the foundation for genuine global governance tomorrow?

It is conceivable that the best diplomatic activity by the United States today and for the sake of today alone will turn out to coincide with that action which produces the United Nations of liberal internationalist global governance tomorrow—conceivable but not very likely. Far more likely is that conditioning the multilateralism among sovereign states today on the hopes and dreams for the United Nations of tomorrow will deform US multilateralism today and constrain and warp the nature of US diplomacy with respect to both friends and foes. Nonetheless, it is a seductive stance. It enables one to demand of the American democratic sovereigntist that he should support multilateralism because American policy of engagement is merely about robust engagement with other states through the vehicle of the United Nations. But it also enables one to turn about and demand of the liberal internationalist that he support multilateralism because it lays the foundation of global governance through the United Nations tomorrow. But telling one faction one thing and another faction another, using the same word, is a dangerous exercise in wanting it both ways.

Unfortunately, the concern that the United States, by embracing an "always engage" approach to the United Nations and its processes, has undertaken a policy at once mistaken if followed and in any case unsustainable is not a strawman. "Always engage" has been the US policy in the Obama administration, stated repeatedly during the Obama campaign and since the president's inauguration many times by the State Department and the US mission to the United Nations. This is unsurprising, as engagement is an article of faith for many of the administration's globalist supporters. They do not consider that a policy of engagement with the United Nations would be far more meaningful—because more credible and more believable—if it followed some kind of policy heuristic more refined and nuanced than the chipper, chirpy, touchingly all-American but unfortunately unsustainable, all-engage all-in. So: Is "multilateral engagement" anything more than "American disengagement"?

Engagement means diplomacy. It means negotiating, offering things, demanding things, talking, meeting, issuing statements, drafting agreements, and other such activity. When one looks back across the Bush years, or really any Republican administration, the complaint made about relations with the United Nations frequently comes down to a failure to engage with its processes—engagement with the process being the stuff of successful diplomatic outcomes. Of course, this is equally the stuff of *unsuccessful* diplomatic outcomes as well. The problem, then, is to identify when to engage and when not and to specify what engagement means for different parts and activities of the United Nations when these processes have a reasonable chance of yielding desirable outcomes.

The view that the United States must always engage with UN processes is really an argument that it must undertake activities in ways that other parties, other countries, and the United Nations itself, regard as within the accepted mechanisms for negotiating and arguing and lobbying. Although the United States is still the superpower and must act like a superpower to provide the world with needed order and resources, the argument goes, it must do so *within* the structure of the United Nations. It must do so as the biggest player in the system, but always still respecting that system as such, from the inside. It should not act from the outside, as a player that can, if it wants, do something different. It can dissent, and bring its national power to bear in its dissents, but it is not to do so in ways that call into the question the structure of UN governance itself and its role cabined within it.

The trouble is that the global security system, to cite one example, does not work this way, and it is not just the United States that does not want it to work this way. And in any case, why should the United States not want to bring into question important aspects of UN governance? There are aspects of it that are deeply anti-American and indeed illiberal and that the United States should actively seek to undermine, even dismantle. One may say that the United States can work to reform these things better from the inside, but little if any evidence supports this claim. All that happens when it tries is that it gets held hostage by claims about the necessity of the system as a whole as a reason to acquiesce in bad ideas and bad ideologies.

In arguments and debates on the question of engagement, proponents proffer a certain bait-and-switch. On the one hand, they contend, those who would disengage are questioning the legitimacy of the whole UN enterprise. Yet on the other hand, they also argue that the specific negotiation is really not that important and wonder why opponents are treating it so seriously. Well, which is it? Are UN negotiations so vitally important that one must not attack them—or so utterly unimportant that one need not bother attacking them? The answer, of course, is that one should preserve the options of delegitimizing, taking seriously, or participating farcically in a UN negotiation depending on the circumstances—and that is precisely what a policy of "always engage" precludes.

If engagement is always "on," one deprives oneself of the ability to apply pressure by threatening to walk away or not come to the table to talk in the first place. No preconditions for talking? Hitting the reset button?—only an American could believe that the world so easily begins anew. Possibly only the Obama administration ever believed that all discussions, with any dictator or despot in the world, could begin without preconditions, as though it were like clearing the computer cache. Only Americans, perhaps, could believe that all these complicated situations in the world have no history to them, or anyway no relevant history—because somehow the Americans do not think other peoples' histories are relevant to them. It is a touchingly American sentiment, in some ways—the world anew—because the Americans proposed that it be so. The good part about this is that it expresses a deeply American optimism and hope, but other peoples' histories do not disappear because we wish it so. So the bad part is, engagement on these apparently generous, humble, other-regarding terms amounts to—what is the proper word?—unilateralism, imperialism even: a world made new, empty, clean, a tabula rasa, on American command.

Moreover, as suggested above, a policy of "always engage" never truly means always engage. It means always engage—until some event causes you not to always engage. The Obama administration discovered this early on; it announced its engagement with the Durban II racism conference negotiations despite the sordid history of Durban I, in which the United States had also sought to engage, until anti-Semitism and anti-Israeli outrages finally caused then-Secretary of State

Colin Powell to walk out. With the United Nations being the same eight years later, by Durban II—only significantly more anti-American and anti-Israel—the same predictable scenario unfolded. The Obama administration announced its earnest desire to "engage"—with a hefty dollop of belief that America had the diplomatic ability to make things go its way at least on the most crucial issues and that its problem all along had been the incompetence and willful refusal of the Bush administration to engage in multilateral diplomacy through the United Nations. Once at Durban II, however, it eventually became clear that the United States was going to have to back out once again. Can anyone really believe that such walk-backs are cost free, whether in Durban I or Durban II?

The belief that engagement can now be different is compounded by the collective feeling of this administration's senior technocrats and intellectuals that this president has the ability to change whole global conversations at his option, not because of the power of the American presidency but because of the specialness of this president—at least during the first year or two. Though this early self-perception has largely faded, it set the tone for the administration's multilateralist and UN dealings. The United Nations is a place for talking, after all, and the Obama administration—president and advisers alike—place special faith in their ability to talk. "Always engage" is partly an expression of the administration's faith that it can alter the real world through talk—*and* that the United Nations is an efficient forum for using talk to shift the world. It is a little bit as though the administration's intellectuals, at least at first, regarded the United Nations metaphorically as a financial market, a sort of international politics clearinghouse. Talk and the written-down products thereof were a little bit like financial contracts, bonds and options and futures. With this administration's especially marvelous abilities at valuation, they were uniquely able to "price" relations in the real world with great efficiency and then alter the real world by mediating these pieces of paper at the United Nations, regarded as multilateral diplomacy's market-making center.

Not all of America's friends among world leaders were convinced—Nicolas Sarkozy, for one, as he indicated early on. That skepticism has spread; world leaders now face a difficult uncertainty as to whether the new American unreliability is a one-off of this administration that will revert to the long-term mean or whether the damage to American hegemony is sufficiently large that the United States lacks sufficient power to mean what it says, reflecting a "new normal." One difficulty among others for viewing the United Nations as a multilateral central clearinghouse in political talk-to-action is that without a contract-enforcement mechanism, the apparently efficient mechanisms for translating talk into real-world change break down. Indeed, the United Nations is a largely *irrelevant* market in *irrelevant* talk. Everyone knows this and has always known this, of course. But herein is the bait-and-switch that the Obama administration seems to find irresistibly clever: irrelevant multilateral market and irrelevant engagement talk?—fine. In that case, we can say anything we like at the United Nations because none of it really matters. If engagement at the United Nations translates to actual action, great; if it does not, great too, because we say it but it binds us to nothing. Either way, however, the result is a policy endorsing "always engage"—either because one thinks the United Nations is an efficient market for translating talk into change or else because one thinks it is so *inefficient* that it is irrelevant.

But there is something intellectually suspect about finding an instant way of reaching the same conclusion on the basis of radically inconsistent rationales: superidealism followed just as swiftly by superrealism. Can we really have it both ways? Is this bait-and-switch not a ruse played not on others, who have long since figured it out, but on ourselves? The truth and the correct practical policy lie somewhere in between. The United Nations is not an efficient market in talk for dealing on the world stage; it is its own world and what is said there stays mostly, though by no means completely, locked within its walls. At the same time, words do matter and they tend to bind the United States far more than they do most parties at the United Nations. Talk at the United Nations is cheap, but it is not free.

This is particularly true because talk at the United Nations so much of the time is expressed through the negotiating mechanism of *consensus*.[1] Insufficient attention has been paid in both the theoretical and practical international-law literature to the game theory of consensus in international relations. How does it work in practical terms at the United Nations? All parties sit together and work on a "rolling" draft, usually set out in advance by a chair or drafting committee that begins the process from a presumed point of general agreement. Negotiations proceed, article by article,

1. This discussion of consensus negotiations draws from Robert Mnookin, *Bargaining with the Devil: When to Negotiate, When to Fight* (New York: Simon & Schuster, 2010), although I do not suggest that Mnookin would agree with the arguments I make here.

line by line. In principle, any party can object to any line or article and either force discussion or amendment or, alternatively, put the clause in brackets as "under discussion" and return to it later.

One might expect that consensus would produce lowest-common-denominator outcomes in negotiations, since any single party has hold-up power. Curiously, however, for reasons noted below, it does not always do so. In any case, those who argue that the United States should "always engage" typically offer two reasons why consensus should affirmatively incentivize its participation. First, the United States has nothing to *lose*. Because the United States is always free to register an objection, the process will not go forward or will have to result in some adjustment of language to meet its requirements. The United States cannot be made to agree to anything it does not want. Second, the United States always has something to *gain* by engaging in a consensus negotiation. As many people have said, urging the United States to participate in processes as diverse as the Durban II negotiations and the formation of the Human Rights Council in the 2005 negotiations, one has to play in order to have any effect on the final outcome. The final document will not reflect American interests if the United States does not show up at the table to participate. The effect of these two considerations is, supposedly, to show that engagement is always a positive-sum game for the United States in consensus processes—and that consensus processes shield participants with particular strong interests to protect.

All of this might be true in abstract theory—but, well, not likely. Lawyers, diplomats, and others who undertake complex negotiations know that a policy of consensus in negotiations often produces surprisingly counterintuitive results. At the United Nations, consensus mechanisms often result in highly heterogeneous outcomes, as parties to the negotiation trade back and forth. It is true that consensus processes at the United Nations make sense for the United States in some situations, and those circumstances are important to acknowledge. For example, the United States overall does better with consensus approaches when it comes to things like the UN dues budget. Broadly speaking, in circumstances in which moral hazard plays a role, consensus might be a desirable negotiating mechanism, particularly if there are multiple players with the same concern. In the case of UN budgets, without some form of consensus here, the majority would simply impose greater and greater costs on the minority that actually pays UN dues; this is what happened over several decades of UN budgets until not only the United States but other rich countries also rebelled, resulting in a loose consensus budgetary mechanism.

But consensus serves the United States badly indeed in such matters as the rolling text of the Durban II racism conference or similar treaty, resolution, or statement negotiations. The reason is important. Pressures on the most powerful player not to break consensus in "shared value" negotiations are vastly stronger than in situations like those involving mere monetary dues. If the strongest player breaks consensus, it is accused of undermining legitimacy in a way that the smaller, less powerful players are not because the weaker players *cannot*. And mere haggling over dues does not raise the same institutional legitimacy issues that questions of values do. In large legitimacy and values debates at the United Nations, the largest player, the United States, inevitably faces the accusation that, if it does not go along, the legitimacy not just of this treaty phrase, or this treaty, will suffer. The legitimacy of the whole institution is at issue—and, in the case of the United States, as the strongest participant, every dissent from consensus raises the legitimacy of the whole institution, in a way that small or marginal participants could never do.

This consideration came powerfully into play in the UN reform negotiations of 2005. John Bolton, as then-US ambassador, insisted on offering a late-arriving, detailed, line-by-line series of edits to the reform draft document. Bolton was roundly attacked for challenging the whole basis for UN reform and, by extension, the legitimacy of the United Nations itself. He was accused of wanting to tear down the structure and of obstruction for no purpose other than that end. And given Bolton's famous skepticism about the institution, the suspicion was hardly without basis.

Yet I do not think that to be the most accurate understanding of Bolton's behavior in 2005. So far as I can tell, Bolton was under instructions to take the process seriously—which he did, and indeed entirely too seriously for what it was. Rather than seeking to tear down the building, he seemed to have set aside his own skepticism in order to treat it as a serious lawyer would treat serious negotiations in business or something in which the words on paper would actually matter. It is as though the US government had retained Sullivan and Cromwell to negotiate on its behalf. In such a situation, every line would (and did) raise a dozen questions and rewrites, and there would be (and were) standoffs and stubborn refusals to give way because the working assumption would be that the details of the language fundamentally mattered (whereas, in fact, they did not). What you agreed to, or not, would be enforceable in court.

In negotiations at the United Nations, however, the details of language only half matter. They do not matter in the sense that the vast majority of countries will sign anything the United Nations puts in front of them because they will follow it or not only as later suits them. No one especially cares, because as countries, they are not consequential enough for anyone to accuse them of hypocrisy or for it to matter even if someone does. The details also do not matter because no one is likely to raise or recall them, in most cases, in any important forum down the road. Everyone tacitly understands—or anyway is *supposed* to tacitly understand—that, unlike an enforceable contract, these are *just* words. There is no court to enforce them, and they were not drafted with the understanding that they would actually bind anyone or particularly—and herein the irony—that they would bind anyone of *little or no* consequence. On the other hand, the details of language do matter for the United States, because although its power means that it does not have to follow what it signs, its compliance will be remembered and harped upon relentlessly. Unlike most countries, the United States *is* consequential enough to have its hypocrisy noticed, and it thus must take care with what it signs.

And it was this asymmetry between US interests and behavior and those of other countries that made Bolton's behavior at the UN reform negotiations so striking. People expected Bolton to work toward strategic ambiguity where possible, but basically to go along where everyone else was going along. It was disconcerting, to say the least, to have him negotiate the terms as though the final document actually mattered.

But Bolton's method of negotiation does not work in circumstances of consensus negotiations. It does not even allow negotiations to open. While he intended the negotiations to be meaningful in the way that binding contracts are meaningful, consensus does not result in memorable or meaningful documents. In anything in which the text genuinely matters, in which it matters because it is enforceable, consensus does not serve, because everyone has a hold-up and will do what Bolton did. Consensus, rather, can only work where the outcome is either supremely important, but still within a shared framework of interests, or, alternatively, where the outcome is ultimately unimportant, and even there it creates distorted outcomes because of asymmetries—not precisely of power, but of legitimacy—among the participants.

In addition, consensus negotiation does not, as one might expect, necessarily result in merely the least-common-denominator language. On the contrary, it often leads to enormous pressures to trade off strong language on one matter (say, a provision about not offending religion) for something equally strong on another but *completely unrelated matter* (say, a provision allowing inspection of nuclear facilities). These are not necessarily pressures toward weak, least-common-denominator provisions, at least not when there is great strategic ambiguity and insincere promising in the text. The results, rather, might easily be diverse and heterogeneous *strong* positions, each of concern to only a few players and each likely to face routine violation by others.

Once again, however, the pressures to trade off strong provisions for *unrelated* strong provisions are especially great with respect to the hegemonic player. The hegemon is thus damned in any of three ways: by disengaging; by engaging farcically; or by engaging seriously. Indeed, ironically enough, the hegemon's *engagement*, if it means serious negotiations

including genuine objections, can be characterized as delegitimation of the international system just as readily as its overt
disengagement might be. Delegitimating obstruction, after
all, was precisely the accusation against Bolton for his pencil-
ing in of changes big and small as though it were an *actual*
negotiation solely over the substance of *this* document. It is a
no-win situation for the hegemon, at least if it does not want
simply to propose merely superficial flourishes to a consensus
document to which the world will then demand its (and no
one else's) rigorous compliance. And here, finally, the role of
the NGOs and nonstate players in the international community is likewise important. They do not have power as such,
but they are (self-appointed, to be sure) anointers of legitimacy in the international community. For them, the point
is not merely compliance as such but the ability to obtain
statements of symbolic value which can be used to impose
future reputational and legitimation costs on various players,
starting with the United States as hegemon.

The position of a very powerful, hegemonic player is thus
asymmetrical to that of others. If consensus were a binding
process, in which final outcomes mattered in the real world,
then smaller parties would feel compelled to use their hold-up
power to force a least-common-denominator result to avoid
risks to themselves. Given that there is no enforcement in the
real world, however, parties are willing to go with language
with which they will simply not comply and abandon their
promises without serious consequences later on. The United
States, as a dominant player, however, cannot so freely and
costlessly engage in insincere promising. Unlike the smaller
players, its assent to consensus language will be noticed
and commented upon, not merely as a matter of the content

of the particular negotiation in question but as a question of the system as a whole, and not just by states-party at the United Nations but by the whole network of global-civil-society kibitzers seeking to leverage themselves into players. No one scrutinizes smaller players in this way because, individually, they do not much matter to the system as a whole. While no one can force the United States to act against its will, the United States potentially pays a reputational cost that is different in kind from, and potentially, typically even, much larger than, that of other, smaller actors, if the United States engages in insincere promising and defection as the smaller players do.

What is more, while we may say that everyone has a hold-up, and that consensus is therefore win-win, in fact we know it *cannot* work that way. There are informal pressures not to disagree too much. Diplomats unctuously call it "good faith." Bolton broke those informal rules by taking the negotiation, as well as the supposed advantages of consensus, seriously. But, of course, no one *really* wanted it to be taken seriously, at least not in that way. Everyone understood that you are allowed a politely limited ("good faith") number of objections in the draft and then (if you are not the hegemon) quiet, never overtly disagreeable abandonment of your promises later on. The hegemon, on the other hand, is simply supposed to suck it up and not make delegitimating trouble.

What then can we say of the claim that the United States has to play the game in order to influence the process—that it has to be at the bargaining table to affect the outcome, that it has to be on the "inside" to have an impact? The claim is simply false. Whatever *else* is true of UN bargaining

processes, whatever else is true of smaller players, the United
States is *always* capable of having an impact, whether it is in
the negotiation or not. It might be more efficient, in some
matters, for the United States to use its influence from the
inside, but that is not always and automatically the case. It
is always capable of throwing its weight around, if it feels
like it, and whether or not it wins the day. The problem the
United States faces is that it is mostly not willing to force a
link between the effect of its pressures in capitals around the
world with its behavior at the United Nations; the United
States, too, assumes that multilateral engagement at the
United Nations is neither so beneficial nor so costly—that is,
it is sufficiently irrelevant to the real world—that it has any
reason to expend real-world diplomatic and political capital
on UN processes.

The result of all these considerations is that the United
States best preserves its power—given the asymmetries both
in its power and in the pressures on it—by being willing in
each case to make a decision at the *front* end about whether
to engage or not engage in any given consensus process. It
best preserves its ability to disagree by refusing to participate
automatically, by making an active decision about whether
or not to participate in the first place and by being willing to
break off participation, even midstream. The many insistent
demands that the United States always participate amount
to an attempt to impose a front-end reputational cost on the
United States as a means to pressure it to legitimate processes
that disfavor it, as well as a back-end cost for later failing to
keep its promises.

It is therefore easy but wrong to say that consensus
ensures that the United States should *always* participate

because it *always* has a hold-up and therefore *always* has something to gain. The pressures inherent in joining a consensus process—the implicit buy-in, the investment in the process, what the game theorists call "path dependency" in which, having taken certain decisions to engage, it is very difficult to back out without larger costs—all urge *greater* caution in joining consensus activities, rather than less. And for the United States, most of all, its decisions to play or not play actually matter. Saying yes to engagement and putting it on the "always engage" autopilot is a profound mistake, as well as an obvious one.

3 THE US GLOBAL SECURITY GUARANTEE AND UN COLLECTIVE SECURITY

The preceding section spoke of ways in which the United States' status as global hegemon peculiarly affected it as a negotiator and actor at the United Nations. The United States has held hegemonic geopolitical security power since at least 1990, if only in the sense that it is the sole security power capable of projecting military force globally. That is not precisely the meaning of *hegemony*, however, or at least not its full meaning. Hegemony is not solely about power, though power is a precondition for hegemony. US hegemony is a function of the fact that since 1990, however contested and buffeted by the others in the world, it has acted with the rough authority—rough legitimacy—to provide fundamental public goods to the world at large in matters of security. The same is true of fundamental public goods in economic relations, but, for purposes here, the security guarantee is crucial.

For decades, the United States has provided the security anchor to the world—a broad umbrella that has secured the conditions of trade, travel, intercourse, and commerce among nations. This was true in important ways during the

Cold War and provided the preexisting framework once the Soviet empire fell. The public goods the US security umbrella provides include not just such obvious and much-discussed matters as the peace of Europe and, up until now, the stability of the Korean peninsula and the South China Sea. It has included as well, for example, the freedom and relative security of the high seas—a result in large measure of the US Navy's having asserted rights of international navigation in straits and contested waters. These public goods are anchored in a broad concept of security, but they rapidly extend to commerce and intercourse globally. The breadth of these goods, and the acquiescence of nearly everyone in them—including, for that matter, many of America's enemies who nonetheless benefit from important parts of them—convey an important source of legitimacy that turns mere power alone into hegemony.

Madeline Albright, while secretary of state in the Clinton administration, famously called the United States the "indispensable nation" and encompassed in that formulation both power and rough legitimacy. Her statement was true—perhaps never truer—but it still displayed an important ambiguity: Did Albright's 1990s formulation mean that the United States was the indispensable party because it was the biggest player *within* the global system of the United Nations, made legitimate by and through and within the United Nations, just so happening to be the most powerful? Or, alternatively, was the United States the "indispensable nation" because it offered a *parallel* security and public goods system *outside* of the UN system—the one that states in the world actually trusted precisely because it was outside the United Nations' security order? The answer to this question plainly matters to understanding the relationship of the United States to the United Nations at its most fundamental level. Multilateralism and engagement, legitimacy and authority, mean different things depending upon whether the United States exercises the role of global hegemon fundamentally inside or outside of the United Nations' global order.

For a long time—so long, to be precise, as American hegemony was not an issue—it was impolite to speak, or speak very loudly, of American hegemony. It was a fact, like assumption about the tectonic plates, and frankly unnecessary to mention—either because it would be a breach of manners with friends or because it would be more powerful unstated as a threat to enemies. Indeed, there were no enemies in those days—merely those entities that had not yet been absorbed into The Post-History. That we have to speak of it now, to say what hegemony means, what American hegemony has meant and why its loss is such a collective one, speaks volumes, none of them happy.

The thesis that the United States is a power in decline is thus much in vogue today. Of course, variants of it have been favorites of writers, politicians, and statesmen over generations—almost a parlor game for intellectuals. It is a parlor game that tends, however, to turn historians into futurists. Proceeding from the unimpeachable, but also uninformative, observation that no empire in the course of history has lasted forever, it claims that the American empire is teetering. These analyses have a predictive track record as poor as they are undeniably popular.

The phenomenon owes something to the schadenfreude of intellectuals for whom the persistence of American power is something of an embarrassment, a bit of vulgarity upon the propriety and decorum of history. The financial crisis, US recession, and general inability of the United States to get its fiscal house in order are likely to spur more such talk, largely on the indisputable basis of American indebtedness to China and other global creditors.

For all I know, this might turn out finally to be the moment when the prophecies come true, for two reasons. First, current events disincline one to optimism; indeed, I find the arguments from financial and economic weakness broadly persuasive. Nonetheless, the path from financial crisis to economic decline to military decline and great-power overstretch, viewed within a frame of a few years rather than across multiple decades if not centuries, may ask unwarranted specificity for economic determinism as a predictor of history. And from a purely academic standpoint, one counsels historians to hold their fire until the future has become the past. Still, few doubt that the United States faces tests internal and external such as it has not faced in a very long time—and many doubt the strength of its institutions, not to weather the storm precisely but to come out on top and *not* in decline. If there were a moment for a declinist thesis any time since the end of the Second World War, this is it; the leadership quality of America's whole elite class has perhaps never been lower.

It is equally true that leaders of men and women and states and nations, their advisors and policy makers, cannot wait to act upon history: they, and we, must be futurists. And so the second reason: the leadership of the United States has today practically announced American decline and the withdrawal of American hegemony as national policy. Multilateral engagement need not necessarily be a stalking horse for the American disengagement from hegemony. But that does seem the best understanding of the Obama administration's repeated declarations (threats?) that the United States will "share" (externalize? de-internalize?) the burdens of global public order as it has never done in the whole postwar period.

A second in-vogue thesis, by contrast, postulates not American decline as such but the rise of new powers: the rise of new great powers, new regional powers, new local powers, and, as a result, the emergence of a "multipolar world." The charter members of the club of rising new powers include, naturally, China and India. They are supplemented by a group of rising new "resource-extraction democratic authoritarians" to accompany the traditional oil autocrats of the Middle East and elsewhere. The most important members of this club are Russia and, in a much less important way, Venezuela; and their rise, or not, depends at any moment on oil prices. All of these new powers are tightly bound to the existing Western powers, and to the superpower, through globalization and markets. China in particular depends upon American consumer demand and will for a long time even as it seeks to "re-balance" and even as America depends upon others' savings. The resource-extraction powers are tied to today's volatile global commodities markets. This second thesis posits not *absolute* American decline but less American power *relative* to the constellation of new rising powers. As a thesis about rise and agnostic on decline, it is likely more defensible than the thesis of American decline on the evidence actually available today.

Rather than exhaustively review the evidence for either of these theses, let us assume that the second (the rise of new powers) is strongly true and that the first (absolute American decline) may either be true now or may be becoming true or, at any rate, is intended by the Obama administration to come true. The question is what follows from those assumptions with respect to the interactions of three institutions: the United States, the United Nations in general, and specifically the Security Council. Let us consider this by returning to something asked at the outset. Why, given the nearly unwavering propensity of the UN toward collective-action failures on security matters, does the UN collective security system not simply break down and go the way of the League of Nations and other such efforts?

The simple answer is that a constituency of key players does *not* rely on UN collective security and need not worry for themselves about the promise, or lack thereof, of UN collective security or, to be perfectly accurate, *any* kind of collective security. These players, starting with the NATO members, rely upon the United States' postwar security guarantee, which protects the security of a wide array of countries in a cascade of stronger-to-weaker ways, starting with NATO at the top. Even countries that do not directly benefit from the NATO-style US security guarantee, however, nonetheless benefit from the global public goods flowing from the security provided by the United States. To see this point clearly, spend a moment contemplating what happens to the peoples who do not benefit strongly from the US security guarantee— Darfur, for example. The fate of countries and people who must actually rely on UN collective security as their only option is not a happy one.

Yet what happens to these security arrangements in a world in which rising new powers alter the equilibrium, particularly concerning the role of the Security Council? There are three ways to think about the role of the Security Council in relation to security arrangements in the broader world:

♦ the Security Council (in Kofi Annan's phrase) as the "management committee of our fledgling collective security system," in a genuinely collective and corporatist way

♦ the Security Council as concert of the great powers, who at least sometimes come together to establish and maintain order in the world but still as sovereign players acting in concert

♦ the Security Council as talking shop of the great powers, the place for diplomacy and debate in a multipolar world of increasingly competitive powers not typically in any concert; less still as manager of a collective for security[1]

In a world in which new rising powers increasingly compete with the United States, the Security Council will most often play the talking shop role. And the fundamental policy for the United States with this talking shop should always be engagement—engagement through active diplomacy in robust multilateralism expressing shared values when possible and through multilateral great-power politics or through a veto when not. This forum is different from the consensus forums discussed in the last chapter—largely because it is much smaller and operates by majority vote with a veto by the most important members. Holding such a veto, it is never in US interest to disengage from the politics and diplomacy

---

1. Kofi Annan, Address at the Truman Presidential Museum and Library" (December 11, 2006), *available at* http://www.un.org/News/Press /docs/2006/sgsm10793.doc.htm.

of the Security Council. This might seem obvious, but since there are significant areas of UN activity in which disengagement and active opposition are highly appropriate policy, it bears stating.

UN collective security was borne out of two contradictory impulses. On the one hand, it began with the realist recognition that collective security must be enforced by the great powers and, as a consequence, must be consonant with their interests or at least not too directly contrary to any one of their interests. On the other hand, it internalized an idealistic expectation that the Security Council would gradually evolve as an institution not just of great-power confabulation but of genuine global governance—into Annan's (wishful, but exceedingly telling) description of the Security Council as "our fledgling global collective security system."

The contradictions were present from the founding of the United Nations itself. The experiences of the 1930s, the rise of fascism, the collapse of the League of Nations, and the Second World War collectively left, as historian Paul Kennedy has written, the "American, British, and Soviet policy makers who were intent upon fashioning the world order in 1945 . . . in little mood for any of the flaccid well-meaning declarations that, they suspected, had given the League of Nations such weak legs."[2] But that instinct can, of course, lead in either of two directions: toward a harder, more realist vision of security or, alternatively, towards a stronger set of

2. Paul Kennedy, *The Parliament of Man: The Past, Present, and Future of the United Nations* (New York: Random House, 2006), quotations following from pp. 27–28.

declarations and assertions of international law and institutions. The framers of the Charter went in both directions, albeit with a far stronger nod to the great powers of the day both in the composition and rules of the Security Council and, indeed, in the Security Council's very existence.

In the realists' view, the League of Nations system had been simply "too democratic and too liberal." The creation of the Security Council explicitly as a gathering of great powers was a response to the weakness of the League of Nations and its paralysis, rooted in the fiction of equality between small states and great powers. In the Security Council, the great powers have mechanisms designed to ensure that their individual interests cannot be contravened to the point of leaving them with no desire to support the system. The existence of the veto—the structural feature of the UN system that perhaps most sticks in the craw of every state that does not have one—was, as Kennedy points out, deliberately designed to "weaken certain universalistic principles and compromise the effective response to possible transgressions of international law where a large nation was involved, but that was a lot better than no security system at all."

The realists of 1945 were highly aware of the "different capacities . . . of large versus small states" to provide security. The 1930s taught these realists that militarily weak countries like Czechoslovakia, Belgium, Ethiopia, and Manchuria were inherent "consumers" of security. They could not provide for themselves, not because of some lapse of national character but because they lacked the demographic, territorial, and economic resources. . . . By contrast, the big powers were . . . the "providers" of international security—again, not because of any special virtues of character but because only they had the capacity to withstand and then defeat Germany, Italy, and Japan.

The new system aimed to harness the military capacities of the great powers, provided that the matter at hand did not fundamentally contradict any great power's interests and was neither too remote nor too expensive. But it also tacitly acknowledged that if a powerful state should "decide to defy the world body and go it alone, there was little that could be done to prevent that happening." One function of the veto, from the standpoint of international law, therefore, has been to allow the permanent five Security Council members to ensure that resolutions of the council do not go against them in their vital interests *as a matter of making international law*. Without this safety valve, over time, the formal international law of the Security Council and the United Nations would lose any connection to the actual behavior of the very states supposedly establishing it. Unprincipled from a legal liberal internationalist view? Quite. But realistic, and a realist fudge that has the capacity to keep international law in the game, as it were, of international politics as they unfold.

Yet the idealist vision of a federation of the world, with the military capacities of the large nations in the service of collective security, was also deeply present in the founding of the United Nations. Despite the apprehensions of important diplomats who feared that the new UN Charter had set too high a bar for "this wicked world," the world's leaders and politicians, in the opening sessions of the General Assembly and Security Council in 1946, were far closer to the peroration of Truman's speech at the opening of the Charter for signatures: "This new structure of peace is rising upon strong foundations. Let us not fail to grasp the supreme chance to establish a world-wide rule of reason."[3]

The Cold War derailed both the carefully calibrated realist calculations and the global governance idealism. The bipolar struggle between the two superpowers in effect put the Security Council in cold storage for decades as an instrument of action. The peace that held during those years among the great powers and the superpowers owed much more to nuclear standoff and a fear of general conflagration than to the realist structures of the Security Council.

With the end of the Cold War, hopes for the United Nations surged and particularly for the ideal of collective security. With Bush père's call for a New World Order apparently to be based around reinvigorated international institutions, with collective security finally enshrined in the Security Council, with even a certain amount of global governance finally on the horizon—it is hard to overstate the excitement that many liberal internationalists felt in those heady days of the fall of the Berlin Wall. Even Saddam Hussein's 1990 invasion and annexation of Kuwait proved a perverse fortuity, at least from the abstract standpoint of evolving global governance. Because it was so nakedly a violation of everything the UN Charter stood for, everyone had a reason to object. Aggression, territorial conquest, the crudest violations of international peace and security, internal genocide and crimes against humanity, even the first large-scale use of chemical weapons since the First World War—everything bad

---

3. Kennedy, *Parliament of Man*, quotations following from pp. 46–47, including Truman quotation.

in a single package, as it were: a peg for every interventionist to hang his hat on and a rationale for every ideal and interest.

Yet the wars of the Yugoslav succession and Rwandan genocide in the 1990s forcefully brought everyone back to the realization that the Great Powers had *interests*, and that they also had *uninterests*, and moreover that collective security in the Security Council had not magically, with the end of the Cold War, solved the problem of collective action and free riding. This turned out to be true not just of the United Nations but even within the presumably much more unified NATO system. After all, NATO could not persuade itself for many years to intervene in the Yugoslav war and only did so when President Clinton decided the political costs of leaving it to the "hour of Europe" required the United States to reach past European dithering and use military force as an assertion of *American* interests in which Europe was invited to join.[4]

Adam Roberts and Dominick Zaum define collective security as a system in which each state "accepts that the security of one is the concern of all, and agrees to join in a collective response to threats, and breaches of, the peace."[5] Provided that the system's members share a reasonably common view of what represents a threat and breach to the peace, this ideal is desirable, of course. But even on its own assumptions, collective security faces daunting and well-understood problems of execution, in theory as well as practice.[6]

    4. Jacques Poos [foreign minister of Luxemburg], Yugoslavia Peace Negotiations (1991).

    5. Adam Roberts and Dominick Zaum, *Selective Security: War and the United Nations Security Council since 1945* (London: Routledge, 2008), 11.

    6. See David L. Bosco, *Five to Rule Them All: The UN Security Council and the Making of the Modern World* (New York: Oxford University Press, 2009).

Collective action is subject to promising when members join and commit to the common enterprise. If these promises are believed, then other members rely upon them. When the moment for action comes, however, a member may defect and abandon its promises. The enterprise might collapse on that basis—or it might succeed still, with the defecting member proving able to free ride upon the efforts of others. In a collective security game of several "rounds," potential participants will have to evaluate the promises made by others and decide whether the possibility of defection renders the common enterprise fruitless or whether the possibility of future rounds might persuade possible free riders to fulfill their promises. However the many versions of collective-action games are worked out, the fundamental problems for the game theorist to solve are those of easy insincere promising, easy or fundamentally cost-free defection, the strong potential for free riding, ensuing moral hazard, and copycat behavior. No one doubts that UN collective security through the Security Council is subject to an enormous, crippling disability in the form of collective-action-failure problems.

The system persists not because it actually provides security but because its formalities provide benefits to various parties, starting with the permanent members of the Security Council. Specifically, it provides a reasonably international public forum in which to argue security issues, a forum that provides certain procedural structures that help shape the underlying terms of debate. This is useful to those directly engaged in the debate; it is just as or more important to other states that are able to participate in the debate, even if their diplomatic interventions are not necessarily decisive—on balance, such debates are better being public, in a multilateral forum, than out of public view and out of the view of other leading players.

Yet arguments *about* security, and having a place for "the collective" to hold such arguments, are different from actually *providing* collective security. And it is hard not to ask why states cling so strongly, at least in their formal statements and representations, to a system that does not do what it proposes to do. So why is there no deep movement to get beyond the stasis of UN collective security and make it mean something more than it does? Save around the edges that constitute peacekeeping missions and associated activities, the system is in deep paralysis regarding collective security for the world as a whole, for what Kennedy describes as the "consumers" and "producers" of security. Coming on twenty years since the end of the Cold War, why has the system not evolved by now into something different, or withered away, or *something*?

The answer is the United States. Before, there was no need to say this, but today it must be put on the table for discussion.

Everyone admits, of course, that the United States is the superpower, more precisely the hegemon, even if it is a superpower and hegemon discovering its own limits and even if it is in decline. But there is an erroneous (if wholly understandable) tendency among proponents of the UN system to treat the United States as simply a large player, an overwhelmingly large player, even a hegemonically large player—but always a large player *within the UN collective security system*. Ramesh Thakur, a long-time United Nations assistant secretary-general, described the (imagined) relationship thus: if the "United Nations is the font of legitimate international

authority, the USA has unparalleled capacity for the maintenance of international peace and security."[7] This capacity is
unparalleled *within* the UN collective security system which
is, Thakur says, echoing many others, *the* source of legitimacy. The task of international diplomacy, then, is to capture
the United States and its capacities within that system. Even
when the superpower elephant breaks the rules and treats the
rules as inapplicable to it, the United States is still regarded
crucially as a player within the collective-action system. This
approach, however, obscures the reality that the system is not
in fact a unitary one and that, in its most important role, the
United States does *not* act within the UN collective security
system.

The persistence of the UN system lies fundamentally in
something not captured by treating the United States as
merely a dominant actor within a *unitary* security system.
The truest description of the international security situation since 1990 is, in fact, quite different. It is actually *two*
systems—parallel UN and US security systems, operating con-
currently though conjoined at several points. There is a weak
one, the UN collective security apparatus, and there is a
strong one, the US security guarantee. Understood this way,
the United States is not merely *a*, or even *the*, dominant and
most powerful actor within a system of security. Rather, the
United States offers a genuinely alternative system of international peace and security, a system for the provision of global
public goods, that is separate from the role it *also* plays as a
dominant actor within the UN collective security apparatus

7. Ramesh Thakur, *The United Nations, Peace and Security* (Cambridge:
Cambridge University Press, 2006), 49.

of the Security Council and such global public goods as the
UN system provides.

The parallel (and not merely "dominant within") actor's
willingness to extend a security guarantee to a sizable portion of the planet, explicitly and implicitly, alters the meaning, necessity, and quality of collective security at the United
Nations itself. In a diplomatic system characterized by insincere public promises, easy defection, moral hazard, and free
riding, the fig leaf is assiduously maintained that the United
Nations constitutes, or anyway offers, a collective security
system. But in fact, most leading players in Europe, Asia, and
Latin America, and even the Middle East, are unwilling to
test the strength of that system. Instead, they pay insincere
lip service to the UN system while actually relying on the
United States.

This is not, of course, any radical revelation; it has been
the basis for US global security policy and the fundamental
foreign policy assumption of much of the world—friend and
foe alike—for a long time now. It is a revelation only in the
current circumstance in which it is tossed aside remarkably
cavalierly, in the name of some new and untested formulation of US global security policy that, at a minimum, raises
radical uncertainties as to what the United States actually
intends and indeed stands for. For all the extant elite complaining and populist anti-Americanism, in other words, a
remarkable number of countries have counted the costs of
adherence to the US security promise and found it rather
better than their own, and better than the United Nations',
and better than anything else on offer, as to both benefits and
costs. After all, the United States does not even particularly
care when those under its security hegemony heap abuse on

it because, in the grand scheme of things, it understands that the system *incorporates* public rejection and protest by its own beneficiaries.

Part of the acceptance of US security hegemony by its beneficiaries includes their rational desire to displace their security costs onto another party, even if the providing party thereby has equally rational reasons to look to its own interests first, since it so overwhelmingly pays the costs. The US security guarantee, in other words, is not a collective security arrangement. It is not a collective security scheme, to be perfectly impolitic, even with respect to NATO. It works because it is not and so does not suffer from the risks of collective-action failures. This is why people in the world trust it. So long as their interests run sufficiently in train with US interests, they can trust the United States to do what is loosely within its interests—and loosely within theirs.

There are people in the world who must rely on the UN collective security apparatus. It is not necessarily their choice, and it is often not to their benefit. Although the American security guarantee is wide, even it does not extend everywhere. Darfur and many other places in Africa, for example, lie beyond it. One can construct a strategic rationale for why the US security umbrella ought to extend directly to any particular place. In Sudan one can talk about oil, and in other places one could construct hypothetical American interests based on the flows of refugees, destabilization of neighboring regimes, and so on. But however clever—or even accurate—these intellectual constructions of American interests may be, not even American power at its zenith could project universally; much less can it do so in an emerging multipolar world of increasingly competitive great powers.

To be sure, the American security guarantee is not an on-off switch. Even without creating a NATO or having any willingness to put military assets in harm's way, American power often can be projected to support one cause, regime, policy or another so as to increase regional or local security through bilateral aid, economic policies, trade incentives, and other such means—though soft power advocates are much too quick to see soft power where it does not exist or as a substitute for hard power rather than a leveraged effect of it.

But limits remain, and they are partly limits of American power and partly limits on American interests and just how far they can sustain the projection of American power. Partly, however, the limits arise from what can actually be done in the demimonde of failed and failing states, the world of disorder and endemic low-level but brutal civil wars, places in which, even if America were to identify a clear and overriding body of interests, it might not be able to bring meaningful order out of the chaos. Certainly the experience of Afghanistan is not currently persuading Americans or anyone else that these expectations should be very high. The lesson learned is simple, from a strategic security standpoint: stay away. You will not likely be able ever to leave; you will not likely create real or lasting order while you stay; and you damage your ability strategically to respond elsewhere. And if you need to act from a national security imperative—bring down the Taliban, pursue Al Qaeda, or whatever the future might bring—better to act in those zones, where possible, using not the full weight of the US military overtly and directly but instead proxy forces and force projected from unentangling remote, standoff platforms: these places are best dealt with, if at all, by locals, with backing and payments from the CIA to act as proxies, or by Predator drone.

As a strategy for the United States, the aim is not the creation of order out of chaos. That would be nice, but the United States is not able to do that and, in many cases, its very presence, no matter how good its political will, could well make things worse. In any event, there are a lot of places in which the United States need not even concern itself with the situation, because, however bad that situation may be, it does not offer any direct security threat, not even in the vague concern about failed states becoming terrorist havens. Moreover, some of the worst places in which the United States cannot find a strategic necessity to extend itself in any substantial way are not failed states in the sense of pure disorder but instead wicked but quite tightly run dictatorships and autocracies—Robert Mugabe's Zimbabwe, for example, or North Korea or (more loosely) Iran.

So the world can be divided into a series of "clubs" with respect to the parallel provider of security. The gold-plated, first-class club is the one that operates under the full benefit of the US security guarantee: not just NATO, but also Japan, Australia, South Korea, and a range of other industrialized, democratic allies. The next tier—business class, so to speak—includes many states that are not so fully guaranteed in the sense that America would go to war for them but still have an enormous security benefit in more passive ways. These include Latin American and those Asian states in which the US presence reduces considerably the pressure to arm against one's neighbors and the mini-states of the Gulf. The third tier—coach—benefits from a lesser but still important range of passive public goods, such as the freedom and security of the seas and the sealanes that supply China'a imports, for example.

The fundamental point is that all three of these clubs benefit from the US security guarantee in ways that are independent of whatever role the United States plays within the system of UN collective security. They benefit, rather, from a system that exists as a function of the postwar US role that began with NATO and extended outward from there. This hegemonic system has neither been nor wanted to be integrated into the system of UN collective security. Certainly one can appeal to Article 52 of the Charter (which refers to regional alliances) for the face-saving claim that NATO is somehow "part of" UN collective security, but suffice it to say that Russia and China do not see it that way, and other actors in the world are likely to feel as they do in a competitive, multipolar world.

Indeed, from the beginning, whatever hopeful and idealistic things various American politicians such as Truman said about UN collective security, US internationalism in security matters has always been multilateral and indeed internationalist—NATO—but only secondarily invested in the United Nations as a security system. The US security guarantee operates parallel to UN collective security, and, although in some situations the United States genuinely acts as a dominant actor within UN collective security mechanisms, its security guarantee—the one the first and second tiers rely upon for their safety—and the many direct and indirect global public goods that flow from it lie outside the UN system altogether. And that is precisely why those first and second tier countries trust in it.

The effect of this fact, however, is that neither the first tier nor the second has any significant incentive to invest in UN collective security for its own security—and neither tier does. They did not when they could afford to do so and will not as their welfare state models slowly decay from the inside out. They prefer to trust that their bottom-line security interest is close enough to the United States' that they can free ride on the hegemon and that the United States will not very much care. And the United States will not care very much, so long as it is able to assert *its* interests first and foremost, rather than endlessly negotiate them in the way a genuine mutual-assistance club would. NATO, at day's end, is only secondarily (at very most) a mutual-assistance club, because it has not truly solved the collective-action problems of mutual assistance. It is first and foremost a US security guarantee, trusted by NATO nations because they trust their interests to be sufficiently close to those of the United States that they can rely upon it, at least in the things that finally matter to their security.

This is also to say that the most successful collective security arrangement always owes its success in overwhelming part not to collective security but to the hegemonic guarantee of its principal member. Collective security is a rhetorical fifth wheel on the vehicle, at least since the fall of the Soviet Union. Moreover, the first and second tiers thus also have reasons *not* to take actions that might undermine the proven value of the US guarantee in favor of a UN collective security system that proposes no coherent answers to the collective-action-failure problems let alone to the dangerous insincerity of sovereigns with deeply opposed interests.

The third tier is far less invested in the US guarantee, despite its many passive benefits in the form of global public goods. But that does not lead it to greater trust in UN collective security mechanisms—particularly given that those mechanisms, invested in the Security Council, would frequently involve reliance upon Security Council members who in fact looked elsewhere for their own security. Countries facing particular circumstances sometimes do look to UN collective security—not failed states or countries with truly endemic disorder but reasonably intact states dealing with the end of a civil war or other such situations. In Central America following the 1980s civil wars, for example, UN collective security, through peacekeeping operations, had some very important successes in Guatemala and El Salvador.

These successes are one of the most important arguments for UN collective security as an activity for the United States to support. But it is equally important to understand that such success typically requires a reasonably intact state structure; a defined civil war with a defined opposition that is being brought to a defined end; no great-power opposition on account of its strategic interests; and the interest of the United States and other great powers, formally through the Security Council but also informally as a matter of politics and resources, to support the transition. In places like Guatemala and El Salvador, the United States acted along both of the parallel security system tracks, as it were—partly exercising US hegemonic security capabilities and relationships that have long existed quite apart from the United Nations, but partly acting as a dominant power through the United Nations and the Security Council. There are, of course, no strict lines; the division is partly arbitrary, and one role bleeds into the other. But if activities with respect to this "third tier" of states and security situations run them together, the core functions, legitimation devices, and justifications are separate and identifiable, by reference back to how the first and second security tiers of states view their own security.

Yet there is a fourth tier. It consists of the people, regimes, and places that fundamentally lie outside the US parallel security guarantee. To the extent that the United States extends something to them, it *is* as a powerful, sometimes dominant, actor within the UN collective security system—to which the United States contributes money through peacekeeping operations and other contributions both material and moral. American conservatives otherwise unenamored of the United Nations should understand that this is a valuable and important role, and worth paying for, partly because the legitimacy of the United States' global role does indeed depend, in part, upon its willingness to seek to extend something, including basic security, to those that it cannot possibly address directly. To the extent that anyone else extends security to these places and zones, it is likewise through the UN collective security system, at least in the loose sense of typically seeking UN approval, acting with UN mandates, and so on. Ironically, the legal letter of UN collective security receives its greatest expression in precisely the places in which the world's leading members have the least at stake and in ways that would not occur to them if it mattered to their *own* security. These people—trapped in many of the world's worst civil wars, wars of disorder, and failed states or, alternatively, the worst dictatorships, such as North Korea—have no choice but to accept UN collective security if even offered.

They would be "consumers" of security, in Kennedy's terms, at the mercy of possible "providers" of security who, however, act at their option. At least in those unfortunate circumstances, the general failure to come up with a convincing solution to collective-action problems in UN collective security is overwhelmingly evident.

The collective security problem is still more complicated than that, however. On the one hand, a collective-action game can consist of parties who each bring to the table resources of value to all, a game of "mutual benefit"; there are problems of defection and free riding even in these cases, which is why the success of NATO does not rest on collective action. On the other hand, the situation of this fourth tier is that they do not bring any resources to the table—to the contrary—so that any collective action undertaken is not collective in the sense of mutual benefit but merely *altruism*. In this case, the fundamental problem is not defection and free riding in an arrangement of otherwise mutual benefit but instead the fundamental question Why act at all if, for the providers of security, there is no mutual benefit?

Various answers have been proposed to try and get beyond simply the true, but not necessarily very motivating, answer of global altruism. They fall into one of two approaches: try to find a way to reframe the argument so as to turn altruism *into* mutual benefit or, alternatively, simply accept that it *is* altruism. The most noteworthy "reframing" has come from the United Nations itself: the secretary-general's High-Level Panel, addressing the issues of UN reform prior to the 2005 General Assembly reform summit, sought to recast the global security issue as one of mutual benefit rather than altruism. It argued—in much the way of those seeking to convince the United States to address this or that global situation by constructing an argument from interests—that the global north and global south were bound by the exchange of benefits: security for the global north and security and economic development for the global south, in a sort of grand bargain between the two. It was not very convincing; the global north, particularly, simply saw it for what it was, an argument for optional altruism, and paid it no serious attention.

What this acknowledges, however, is that the UN collective security system is typically not a system of mutual benefit but is in its most important features a system of altruism, at least as the system's security providers see it. It is always optional, however much parties say otherwise in the time-honored fashion of insincere promising, obfuscation, and obscurantism at the United Nations. And, in contrast to Kennedy's proposal that we see UN collective security as an understanding that big, powerful "providers" of security and small, weak "consumers" of security band together in an implicit contract, the one-sided nature of the "bargain" means that it is not an "exchange." Instead, UN collective security, when applied to the worst-off, pure consumers of security, is better understood as merely an option exercisable when and if the providers of security want to provide it as an act of global generosity. It entirely lacks mutuality and thus, unsurprisingly, predictability or stability.

Part Two
HEURISTICS

4 ALWAYS ENGAGE:
The United States and the Security Council

UN collective security faces a daunting series of obstacles in the way of ever becoming the system for international security—so daunting that it will likely never overcome them. In addition to those of the preceding chapter, we must add the juridical one of the literal language of Article 51 of the UN Charter. If taken seriously it would seem to require recourse to the Security Council for any use of force other than immediate territorial self-defense against an actual armed attack. Of course this is not how states actually behave and never has been—states' inherent right of self-defense means far more than that—so if collective security is supposed to be based on Article 51, it is a fiction long since overtaken by state practice and a different understanding of inherent self-defense. In reality, Article 51 serves as a rhetorical tool for those wanting to criticize how a state, in any particular circumstance, acts when that state does not seek collective security through the Security Council or at least Security Council authority.

As a practical matter, since the United States largely handles global security matters within its security umbrella, at least for anything important to it, and only in limited ways through the United Nations, UN collective security is about two things for the United States but also for most everyone else: one, civil wars and, two, circumstances in which states do not want their conflicts to go beyond certain bounds and for which Security Council action can offer a means of egress from conflict escalation. Neither of these functions is unimportant by any stretch. But UN collective security is not about great-power conflict. It is not even about many non-great-power conflicts. It is precisely because there are conflicts that do not impinge deeply on the great powers that, for example, peacekeeping operations under UN authority are even possible. As multipolarity spreads, however, and as that multipolarity increases competition among powers for resources and grubby commercial advantage in out-of-the-way places, great powers—China—might well discover that they have interests where previously they were indifferent.

Even if we take the idea of UN collective security at face value, in other words, it is not a mutual aid arrangement. To extend an observation of the last chapter, it is not even simple altruism; it is, rather, a form of *collective* altruism. And it is not merely collective altruism in a passive sense of "pass-the-hat" financing, but—for some party, somewhere in the UN system—collective altruism in the larger sense of providing active, in-kind resources such as peacekeeping troops or "lift" transport for peacekeeping troops and supplies. But altruism by itself is hard to motivate. Collective altruism is far more difficult to motivate than that of a single individual or small group of states when each looks to some abstract collective to act. Collective altruism requiring real action rather than merely passive monetary resources is more difficult than any of these. Moreover, even in those rare situations in which UN collective security might conceivably function as a genuine mutual-assistance pact, rather than as altruism, it has no good answer for addressing collective-action failures, particularly defection and free riding.

As noted, however, a super-strong player has established its own parallel security system, over many decades, since 1945. That system extends directly to the player's "posse"—NATO and a handful of others in Asia—but it also provides a much broader range of global public goods to many others as well, with the effect of reducing any real need by most players to test the UN collective security mechanisms. This has been framed as security global public goods, but this is far from the full extent of its provision. It is security in a narrow sense but more broadly the provision of global public goods—assurances that range from physical security to free trade in goods, whether those goods are Wal-Mart supplies from still-Communist China to oil that might proceed, in the flow of fungible global commodities, from Venezuela or Iran. Countries seem to have counted the costs of seeking to replace this parallel system with true collective security under the auspices of the United Nations and have not thus far been willing to pursue that risky alternative.

The capacities, expertise, and institutional experience that the United Nations is gradually developing through peacekeeping operations are essentially collective altruism, and in that sense they do not upset the security equilibrium between the United Nations and the United States.[1] Indeed, they further it insofar as they create a useful specialization and a division of labor in the provision of security to the world in different parts and ways. In many ways, this is a beneficial equilibrium, for however long it is able to last. It will last so long as great powers do not find reasons to take interests in the places (read: the assets) of genuinely "neutral" peacekeeping operations; so long as rich countries are willing to fund it and less rich countries willing to supply troops; to the extent that current delegitimizing scandals in the United Nations' peacekeeping procurement are cleaned up; and insofar as the United States remains willing both to fund and supply, at least in certain situations, essential infrastructure that it alone possesses—for example, the airlift capacity to move troops. American decline, under the guise of "multilateral engagement" in which the burdens of security will be "shared," as though it were mutual assistance rather than collective altruism, does not bode well for altruistic peacekeeping's hard-won successes. Such unwillingness to pay will have boomerang effects, less upon the United States at the United Nations. Rather, it will compound the perception that the hegemon is in decline and cannot afford modest expenditures for security for the worst-off, with losses in the legitimacy attributed to America's parallel hegemonic system, which will ironically be seen as merely power and less as authority. American conservatives beware; this thesis of this book is as little concerned with America's

1. Also, one hopes, the UN Peacebuilding Commission, which was one of the few useful outcomes of the UN reform process and which was established in 2005 for finding an institutional bridge for addressing postconflict issues, falls into this category.

standing with the United Nations as anyone, but what is at risk here is the legitimacy of America's own security system because it is accepted as legitimate because it is understood not merely to assert American power but to provide global public goods.

The existence of this dual and parallel security system should not leave aside, however, the other big security issue of the Security Council. This discussion has proceeded as if the fundamental problem with UN collective security were one of coordination and execution by a collectivity of its agreed-upon security goals—efficiency, in other words. But with increasing regularity, the issue is not collective-action failure but fundamental clashes of interest among the great powers on the nature of desirable action, collective or otherwise, if any. It is something of a comfort to treat the fundamental problem of the Security Council as being a failure of collective will to do something about which, in a cost-free, unlimited-resources world, everyone would agree. It is also something of a fantasy and likely to grow more so in the multipolar world of tomorrow.

What does multipolarity mean for the United Nations and for the US-UN relationship? Clearly, after all, the rise of new powers must have implications for the parallel security systems earlier described. The rise of new powers refers to at least three separate phenomena:

◆ *The rise of the "resource-extraction" autocracies.* These are driven primarily by oil but not necessarily limited to it. The obvious candidates are the Middle Eastern oil producers but also, of course, Russia, Venezuela, and a few others. Rises and falls in oil prices illustrate the general problem of a resource-extraction state's seeking to act as a great power on the strength of global commodities prices alone. The boom and bust nature of these autocracies in fact makes them more unstable and volatile as power players; still, a striking feature of current international politics is their willingness to band together and support one another, as a means of organizing against American hegemony. Autocratic at home and yet sometimes popular with national masses, dismissive of liberal democracy while perhaps adhering somewhat to democracy's bare forms (at least in the first couple of elections), anti-American even while bound to America and the rest of the parliamentary democracies by the commodities markets, aggressive abroad and with a strong sense of national grievances, they are destabilizing to the existing status quo and fully mean to be.

♦ *The rise of China, India, and Brazil as new production powers.* They are production powers rather than resource powers. They are, however, not just resource consuming or resource intensive in their economic growth but, as manufacturers (China especially), affirmatively *resource hungry* and energy intensive. They seek to sustain rates of growth to maintain internal stability but also to assert themselves in the world. (The differences between China, and India and Brazil, on other political metrics, of course, are immense.)[2] Increasingly one can add Brazil to this list,

2. India is a genuine and open democracy, to start with. Its economic growth has far more to do with the provision of services than China's manufacturing base does. It is far more a natural ally of the United States than a natural competitor, as China is. Brazil is also a special case of a rising economic power. Its economic power is driven far more by commodities than either India's or

though its commodity production remains vitally important. For all the reasons everyone today recognizes, of course, China essentially is its own category.

◆ *The empowerment of poor, sometimes unstable or failing states, with nuclear weapons.* These are, specifically, Pakistan, North Korea, and, seemingly soon enough, Iran. The nuclear weapon is not produced as a consequence of a rising economy but instead as a siphoning of resources from a declining economy. The most destabilizing scenario is a nuclear-armed failed or failing state.

This list has deliberately left aside that other compelling category—Islamism as an ideological and politicized transnational movement, whether as a set of directly terrorist groups or as a soft communal shelter therefor, particularly in failed states such as Somalia, Yemen, perhaps Nigeria soon, and elsewhere. This bulleted list deliberately focuses on states because, even if no good long-term solutions have been found, since 9/11 we are well aware of the transnationalist non-state-actor threat. But this intense focus has caused us to pay less attention to new threats to stability arising within the state system itself, which will certainly be visible—and frankly usefully so—at the United Nations.

If we are indeed moving toward a more multipolar world, in other words, the great-power conflicts promise to become

---

China's but not necessarily by minerals or hydrocarbons. This summary list is not intended to minimize profound differences between these rising economic powers. What they do share is that they all have enormous populations with considerable rates of economic growth but also considerably rising economic expectations. My list mingles these immensely different countries for a limited purpose.

more acute, not less. As David Rieff has pointed out, multipolarity is by definition competitive, not cooperative.[3] Moreover, issues over which the rising powers jostle sometimes are intensely ideological—what seem to the West sometimes inchoate national grievances and resentments carried abroad but which within the politics of a rising new power are concrete and unmistakable and perhaps (worse) nonnegotiable. Sometimes it is nationalism deliberately stoked at home coupled with a long-term sense of being deprived of a rightful place in the world. But in many other cases, the jostling is very much the competition over what, to the rich and self-satisfied West, look like frankly grubby commercial interests. China's willingness to protect Sudan during long periods at the Security Council, for example, is mostly about China's oil interests; so too is its willingness to sell the Gaddafi regime arms even as it acquiesced in a Security Council resolution authorizing military force against the Libyan regime. That is the nature of a more competitive world in which new rising powers are rising because they are unabashedly commercial powers.

Yet it would be a profound mistake to represent the rise of China in merely realist terms—the bouncing billiard balls of international relations. Alongside that indisputable element runs something else—the element that makes illiberal and undemocratic China potentially not just a great power in a multipolar world but a challenger to the liberal and democratic United States as hegemon. Hegemony is not

3. David Rieff, "Concerts and Silly Seasons," *Open Democracy*, February 23, 2007, *available at* http://www.opendemocracy.net /democracy-americanpower/concerts_4380.jsp.

simply a question of power but instead power conjoined with sufficient legitimacy that others internalize a certain tendency to follow it. They follow because they make not only a calculation of interest but also see a confluence of ideals, at least to a rough-and-ready degree. This is the power of legitimacy among nations. What makes this legitimacy striking, however, is that it depends in no small part upon the internal legitimacy of a regime—with its own people—and that internal legitimacy sends many important external signals to other players in the international sytem, including sufficient stability, reliability, consistency, trust and reliance interests. The dynamic of hegemony is not collective; a hegemon is, rather, a leader whom others are willing to follow because they trust the leader's interests and ideals to coincide sufficiently with theirs that they can trust the leader—because they trust it to follow its own interests. They are carried along in train. Internal legitimacy is very far from irrelevant to the process of the formation of expectations that result in the legitimacy among nations that, along with power, creates the conditions for hegemony.

One might conclude, from the discussion in much of this book and elsewhere, that China is simply a case of unrepentant interests, a hard realist out for only its own gain. That is so, but China is also driven by a powerful source of internal legitimacy—not human rights, not democracy, not liberalism, certainly, but simply by the legitimacy of the Party managing affairs to produce fantastic and yet steady economic growth and a perceptible increase in living standards inside China. The regime is legitimate because it produces that economic growth, and the Party leadership legitimate because it provides the coherence that the economic program requires, internally and externally, against many, many risks and uncertainties. Other countries, in the developing world especially, see that internal legitimacy and note that it offers certain things: economic growth, a warrant for centralized authority even in the midst of a global market economy, and an alternative basis of legitimacy that owes little to the global values to which the United Nations, and indeed much of the world, is supposedly committed (as discussed in chapter 6): human rights and liberal democracy. Obviously economic growth is good in order to make poor people richer; but if one is a developing world country (or these days, in some cases, even a developed world one), the combination of a claim to economic growth without liberal democracy and human rights, with the backing of a hegemon that is frankly indifferent to human rights conditions within your state— well, that is irresistible.

It is this attraction, not merely power alone, that makes China a risk to US hegemony. It is a model of illiberalism, hostile to democracy and human rights (or anyway willing radically to redefine them). The rise of China is not merely a question, in other words, of raising the possibilities of disorder, instability, and all the problems introduced by a multipolar world as envisioned by the realists. It is also a profound problem for the world's liberal idealists, who might imagine their visions to be universal. As it turns out, their visions are remarkably dependent upon the loose and undemanding hegemony of the United States to provide the sheltering sky for the presumably universal values of liberalism. Put another way, the discussion here about international security is far from disconnected from the discussion of values. Why? The system of international security that actually matters is a manifestation of hegemony and the settled expectations that it creates. But hegemony is a function not just of sufficient power but legitimacy as well, and legitimacy is a matter of sufficiently shared values undergirding shared interests.

Broadly speaking, as we have seen, there exist three possible models for the function of the Security Council:

♦ management committee of the UN collective security system

♦ concert of great powers

♦ talking shop of the nations

They are not mutually exclusive, but there is a built-in parsimony. Realistically, in a multipolar world, there is only a limited role for the Security Council as management committee of the UN collective security system model. It appealed to liberal internationalists in what turned out to be the historically unsustainable period of the 1990s—hence its appeal to Kofi Annan himself, whose invocation of it in his final speeches as secretary-general was more wistful than real. The fear is that the Obama administration has a sufficient number of nostalgics longing once again for those days of liberal internationalist hope and nurturing it through the invocation of multilateral engagement—abetted rather than opposed, weirdly, by New Liberal Realists believing that it is a useful internationalist language of engagement under cover of which, however, to stage an American retreat from presumably unsustainable hegemony. Whereas, in today's world, this management committee of the UN collective security system is only as feasibly broad as is the United Nations' altruistic security role—which is to say, limited to those increasingly rare situations in which important powers' interests are not in conflict with one another and the council can thus act as a whole. This category of altruism, already narrow, might become narrower still in a more resource-competitive, multipolar world.

The Security Council as a concert of rising powers and great powers is a model that corresponds principally to the even more rare situations of UN collective security as *true* mutual assistance, rather than altruism. The concert was most dramatically on display, of course, in the 1990 Iraq invasion of Kuwait and the first Gulf War. An area that today is perhaps amenable to the concert of nations through the Security Council is piracy off the coast of Somalia because the trade of so many nations is at risk, no matter what their other disputes. The possibility has become less and less likely as states discover that, even where common interest exists, they operate in such legally different spaces (How does one apply the human rights law as it works in London or Bonn on the high seas off Somalia? Whatever exactly did the Russians do with the ten Somali pirates they captured in 2010?[4]) that joint action becomes impossible. Perhaps the solution will turn out to be that preferred by the liberal internationalists—yet another UN tribunal—but much depends on how extensive, costly, and violent the pirates become, especially if states start to put more serious security pressure on them and their hostage-taking.

The irony is that the Western "powers" today are so paralyzed by their exquisite concerns for the rights of pirates

---

4. See "Freed Somali Pirates 'Probably Died'—Russian source," BBC News (May 11, 2010), *available at* http://news.bbc.co.uk/2/hi/8675978.stm.

that they cannot act effectively—and, indeed, do not really want to, preferring instead to wring their hands as a short-run, less costly alternative to action. It does not take very long for the world to realize that what expresses itself as too much legal purity to act is merely cover for lacking the security forces or will to act. Eventually, countries with equally large commercial shipping or oil import concerns and fewer scruples—China—act themselves and discover that, while a blue-water navy is expensive, such acts of "global public order" bring benefits that once accrued to the previous hegemon. The United States will, however, rue the day that the world notes that China is selfish, yes, but that it also brings crude order to disordered places that are important to it, such as the shipping lanes—and in so doing replaces the global public order so long brought about by the United States.[5] After all, that is what *hegemons* do. China will be much more

5. And so China, perhaps, concludes that it will have to act like a maritime power in defense of its own—but also indirectly everyone else's—commercial shipping, kills the pirates, razes their bases, hauls away their women as concubines, enslaves their children in IPad factories, and sows antipersonnel land mines in their fields—but then offers them a terrific deal on their undersea oil and mineral rights. It ignores the stern reports from Human Rights Watch, stonewalls the Security Council, and watches as the world both breathes a sigh of relief that someone did something and takes a deep breath in dismay at the party that did it.

The new strong horse signals its presence not by conquest but by the imposition of a rough public order on the high seas that the old strong horse used to enforce but had become unable to impose by reason of its insistence on a purely utopian rule of law, suitable for Oxford or Marin County, even for open ocean two hundred miles off Somalia. The act that signals China's hegemony, if it comes, will not be purely self-interested because pure self-interest is not what hegemony is about—it will be the imposition of a rough but reasonably effective public order mostly beneficial to it, but just enough beneficial to others that they will follow it as they used to follow the United States.

selfish and much less gentle. Piracy ought to be the most propitious immediate task for a concert of nations. But as the world becomes increasingly multipolar, it is far from clear that much scope exists for such concerted mutual aid.

The multipolar world that seems to be rising portends a Security Council that functions, in most important situations, *neither* as an agglomeration of great powers acting in sovereign concert *nor* as the "management committee of our fledgling global collective security system" in which institutions of governance superior to even the sovereign great powers have finally come about. A world in which new commercial powers are busily rooting about for resources is a world that is likely to *increase* the competitive material interests of the new powers, not to reduce them, and likely to convert situations that fifteen years ago might have been thought a matter of altruism in which no great power had much at stake into situations in which something big—money—really is at stake. The increasing commercial presence of China in Africa, in places where the rich Western powers cannot see a profit, has altered the material equation as to where the powers have merely *uninterests*, for example.

As a consequence, the fundamental role of the Security Council almost always becomes that of the talking shop of the nations. Only rhetorically and on special occasions will it be the management committee of collective security, and even less frequently the concert of nations. In times of genuine conflict and crisis among the great powers themselves, of course, a talking shop is always what the Security Council becomes, precisely as it was intended to be. The debates over Russian intervention in Georgia, or Kosovo's independence or, for that matter, the Iraq war are emblematic of the talking shop role of the Security Council—and in those terms, each of those debates was a *success* for the Security Council, not a failure.

Every one of these, after all, involved the deeply held, opposed interests of great powers—situations in which, as Kennedy observed, of course the interests of the great powers would sweep aside everything else but in which the most important global governance interest was merely that the great powers not walk away. Nor should this talking shop vision of the Security Council be written off as merely the rejection of true multilateralism in favor of pursuing "simultaneous" bilateral pure-power diplomacy in New York—great powers cutting their private deals, in dark side chambers in the side streets just off Turtle Bay. On the contrary, even as the pursuit of naked national interest, such diplomacy at the Security Council still has the virtue, at least by comparison to the alternatives, of being conducted relatively in public and in a setting in which other countries on the council are able to take part in the debate.

Even when reduced to pure-power politics, the Security Council is still far more transparent and open to diplomatic intervention by third parties than truly closed bilateral discussions of the kind that characterized much previous Westphalian diplomatic history. Consequently, in a competitive multipolar world, it is not merely in crisis that the Security Council becomes a talking shop, in which the United Nations and Security Council are invested with no greater aspiration than to serve as the place where great powers go to talk rather than fight. The Security Council becomes a talking shop among jostling powers much more of the time than that. It is, broadly speaking, a place for diplomacy—and that is all.

Or almost all, anyway: the Security Council also plays, as noted, one important operational role—UN peacekeeping operations. Peacekeeping is important in no small part because it is one area in which the United Nations actually does things (and often reasonably well) rather than simply talking. But the UN system, for even *attempting* to provide these actual (as distinguished from merely rhetorical) global public goods in security, persists largely because the United States and the world that takes its stability from US hegemony see it as the least costly system for enforcing minimum order in the hopeless world of failed and failing states.

These are places that the United States will not, and realistically cannot, hope to police directly. The abandonment of such countries by the US security umbrella leaves open a space for the provision of UN public goods in security and perhaps other things, even given the reflexive anti-Americanism built into the UN system overall. There is thus a point at which interest and idealism intersect in how the United States should engage with that UN collective security system. The United States should *want* the system to succeed in some places where the United States will not go—partly for its broadest interests but mostly on account of its ideals. This has three concrete consequences for US policy toward the United Nations and collective security.

First, the United States should invest heavily in, and pay its current budgetary share of UN peacekeeping operations (PKOs). Peacekeeping operations are one of the bright spots of the United Nations, an activity at which the United Nations has been doing successively better over the past fifteen years—particularly when combined with regional multilateral governance bodies in Africa and Latin America. They are still far from perfect. There has been massive corruption uncovered in UN peacekeeping operations, sexual crimes by peacekeeping troops, and ideological capture of the supposedly neutral UN mission in nearly anything related to Israel and places where, in the 1990s, peacekeeping was part of a humanitarian or even genocidal disaster—Rwanda and Bosnia, to start.[6] Yet however weighty these failures may be, they should not be permitted to overshadow the modest but accumulating successes of UN peacekeeping. American conservatives, in particular, need to understand the value that UN peacekeeping operations provide to the United States and its foreign policy.

The improving record of peacekeeping operations reflects improved doctrine at UN headquarters, improved professionalism and training of troops contributed by different countries, improved equipment and increased numbers, and above all increased funding. UN peacekeeping operations are funded on a budget that is outside of the regular assessed UN budget. It is voluntary in the sense that there is no formal Charter obligation to contribute to it. However, in order to avoid the problem of everyone's agreeing that someone else should pay for activities that all agree are a

6. Exemplified by this one, dating back to 2005, but never satisfactorily resolved. Claudia Rosett and George Russel, "Procurement Scandal: New Conflict of Interest in Annan's Inner Circle?," FoxNews.com (October 4, 2005), *available at* http://www.foxnews.com/story/0,2933,171216,00.html; Susan Notar, "Peacekeepers as Perpetrators: Sexual Exploitation and Abuse of Women and Children in the Democratic Republic of the Congo,"*American University Journal of Gender, Social Policy and Law* 14: 413–29; Zeid Ra'ad Zeid Al-Hussein, "The Zeid Report," UN General Assembly document A/59/710 (March 24, 2005), *available at* http://www.un.org/Depts/dpko/CDT /reforms.html.

good idea—as well as, crucially, to allow for advanced planning and development of missions that will run for several
years—peacekeeping operations have a voluntary but still
assessed and agreed-upon budget and schedule of individual
country contributions. And critically, the activity is under
the control of the Security Council, rather than the General
Assembly.

Second, as an indispensable adjunct to peacekeeping, the
United States should support and invest in "peace-building"
operations through the United Nations. This follows logically, inexorably in fact, from the successes of, and the investment in, the peacekeeping. One of the very few, but also one
of the most important, positive outcomes of the 2005 UN
reform process is found in the summit's "Final Outcome
Document" adopted by the General Assembly—creation
of a Peacebuilding Commission through concurrent resolutions of the General Assembly and Security Council.[7] The
commission is a UN intergovernmental advisory body whose
mission is to bring together crucial actors in the international
community in support of countries that are undergoing
transition from armed conflict to peace, to find strategies to
preserve peace in those countries, and to rebuild economic,
social, civil society, governmental, and other functions of
postconflict reconstruction that go beyond simply the provision of troops to monitor a ceasefire. It is a role eminently
suited to the nature of the United Nations' legitimacy: to
engage in nation building in a way that requires not merely
humanitarian *neutrality* but the willingness to assert basic
human rights and legal, political, and other values in ways

7. UN Summit 2005, "Final Outcome Document."

that are beyond the neutrality of merely "not taking sides" in armed conflict.

The United States is very rarely able to assert that kind of legitimacy, alone and solely on its own say-so, in the failed-state and postconflict zones. It has not really been able to do so in either Afghanistan or Iraq solely on its own, and it is even less able to do so in still more difficult places, such as Congo. What both the United States and the United Nations have learned out of their respective adventures in nation building over the past eight years is that security matters—it matters for its own sake, and it matters because in the absence of a minimum *tranquillitis ordinis*, nothing else good can happen either. Justice and peace both matter, but underlying each is first achieving a certain level of order out of the Hobbesian chaos.

UN legitimacy in these postconflict, peace-building, nation-building affairs and places is far from complete. For one, the assertion of legitimacy as a nation-building actor in Geneva or New York is not the same as legitimacy on the ground with an unconvinced local population. For another, the legitimacy that flows from the neutral provision of humanitarian assistance is altogether different from the legitimacy of postconflict peace building. Peace building involves nation building and reconstruction of social, political, and state institutions, and that work often requires not strict neutrality but the commitment to political values that might indeed be contested, even violently. Nonetheless, emergency humanitarian aid is not usually so contested, and the United Nations is able to carry out these activities in many situations and places in a way that neither the United States nor any individual state alone could hope to do. In making commitments to such situations, the UN agencies tasked with such work must necessarily maintain an independent weight and role to support that UN legitimacy, even at the cost of a certain amount of friction with the United States and its political goals.

Third, beyond political, diplomatic, and financial support, the United States, deliberately acting in its role of dominant military player within the system of UN collective security, should find ways to assist the practical and logistical requirements of both peacekeeping and postconflict peace building as well. The issue is not necessarily money. It might be in-kind capability, such as transportation, logistical "lift" capability, technologically advanced intelligence, and other assets that are realistically available only through the United States. As a general policy, limited of course by both resource constraints and competing priorities and existing wars, the United States needs to give serious consideration to ways in which it can provide in-kind assistance as appropriate and feasible. These principles apply as well to peace-building missions.

Yet both peacekeeping and peace-building missions are the exception for the Security Council, which by and large will be about not action, but *talk*. And the possibility of a multipolar world of rising new powers raises a very particular legal and diplomatic issue with respect to that function: If the Security Council is going to be the talking shop of the competitive great powers, then should it not be the talking shop of the *actual* great powers, rather than the great powers of 1945?

By nearly every measure—population, influence, even on some measures military might—the Security Council's five permanent members are unrepresentative of the world.[8] Whatever the justifications that existed in 1945 for giving permanent member status to today's five holders of that status, a Security Council today without India, for example, or any large, powerful country in Africa or Latin America as permanent members, is more than passing strange, not to mention infuriating to whole sectors of the world population. The Security Council P5 is not especially a collection of the great powers anymore, let alone a collection of *all* the great powers.

The arguments for reform of the Security Council's membership are powerful on the rationale by which the Security Council was created in the first place: to keep the great powers in the tent. Arguments against reform are mostly pure realpolitik. Permanent, veto-wielding members simply will not agree to drop existing members or even necessarily to add new ones with the veto. Other arguments against membership reform are pragmatic in nature. The United States took the position during most of the 2005 UN reform debates, for example, that however unrepresentative the Security Council is today, the only mechanism of change would inevitably be *expansion*—which would quickly turn the Security Council into an ineffective mass, incapable of making any important decisions. The status quo, however unsatisfactory, was still preferable. The United States later shifted its position to expansion in various ways, but its principal concern throughout has been to maintain effectiveness at the Security Council.

8. See Kennedy, *Parliament of Man*, 51 (describing the conundrum of the UN Security Council).

Even imagining that countries could agree in principle to expand the tent to include all of the modern great powers, it is not so easy to establish who counts as a great power. Countries able to project military power and contribute military assets, and not merely money, to collective security? Not Germany, despite its wealth, and only questionably Brazil or any other Latin American power—and Brazil's neighbors have no interest in seeing Brazil develop those capabilities, however useful they might be to the Security Council. Countries that are stable and legitimate? Nigeria is a big question mark; better to go with South Africa, unless one's priority were, as it perhaps should be, UN peacekeeping-troop contributions in which the African Union's troops have been a steadily improving force. Nuclear powers? Consider the incentives *that* would create. Regional representatives? But powerful regional actors are as likely to be seen as threats to others in a given region as they are to be seen as stabilizing, let alone representative.

More generally, the American security guarantee has allowed, even fostered, a separation of wealth from military power, and not just in Europe. Germany's remarkably insistent claim to a permanent Security Council seat solely on the basis of its moral virtue combined with its economic power and financial contributions to the United Nations, but with no military to speak of, puts the gap between wealth and military capacity squarely on the table in establishing criteria for membership. What does it even mean to be a great power today? Is money enough?

Serious powers understand that the Security Council is the only truly special club. Kofi Annan, after years of courting and stroking the international NGOs as a way of getting around the problem of powerful states, understood as soon as 9/11 had occurred that the Security Council was his true interlocutor, constituency, and master. The result is that no country will give up a permanent seat on the only body that really matters. Although it is conceivable that France and Britain's permanent, veto-holding seats might someday be collapsed into a single EU seat, P5 status is currently a vital national matter of pride to each. Certainly no other member—Russia, China, or the United States—could imagine not being a permanent member with a veto. Reform therefore comes down to proposed forms of expansion, with varying privileges extended by the existing club: Permanent? Long-term? Veto-bearing? How many more members before the Security Council becomes a mini–General Assembly?

Though ultimately intractable, Security Council reform dominated the 2005 UN reform negotiations. This was especially so in the national debates that took place within claimant countries in the run-up to the General Assembly summit. Perusal of the national presses in India, Japan, Nigeria, Brazil, Germany, and others would do much to dispel any impression that national sentiment is not what it has been for the last hundred years. All that national sentiment was rallied against one of the United Nations' fundamental antinomies: a Security Council that is realistically a meeting ground of the great powers but also representative of the world, in line with *realist* global governance. And, added to that, is the question of how to have a mechanism of change for something apparently set in stone. Justifiably dismayed and concerned that UN reform negotiations were turning into a single-minded focus upon an unresolvable issue, Kofi Annan (to his credit) repeatedly urged the main players in UN reform to leave this question aside in favor of more urgent questions that could be resolved, a request that was, however, only partly and grudgingly honored.

But the main antagonist in this argument was not (and is not) the United States. Its place on the Security Council is beyond question, and it is thus in the rare position of being a relatively neutral, "honest broker" on the issue. The US concern for the effectiveness, above any other consideration, of the Security Council is real—an argument the United States does seem to realize, however, cuts several different directions in the reform debate. The heated disputes arose instead from the lesser and declining military powers, France and Britain, as against the clamors of Japan, India, Nigeria, Brazil, and even economically powerful but demilitarized Germany. Yet suppose that the existing P5 had agreed, by some miracle, to accept an alteration. What then? In real life, Japan's claim is checked by China; India's by Pakistan; Brazil's possibly by its jealous Latin American neighbors, Argentina and Mexico; Germany's by, well, *everyone* in global recoil at a third EU permanent member. And, alas, it is far from inconceivable that in the next decade or two, Nigeria might fall into grave civil war.

Yet whatever its ultimate membership, the UN Security Council can authorize and perform many missions congenial to United States desires in places in the world in which the United States is unlikely to operate directly—and at a lower cost than any other realistic means of effectuating those missions. Thus, consistent engagement with the Security Council only makes sense. But successful engagement requires a clear understanding of the differences between the US security guarantee, UN collective security as a mutual benefit activity, and UN collective security as an exercise in altruism. It also requires US money and, in appropriate circumstances, logistical support in kind.

Engagement with the Security Council does not imply a more general default answer of US-UN relations, the autopilot of "always engage," meaning go along with what everyone else wants. The Security Council is profoundly different from other UN institutions. It is much smaller, for starters, and it does not operate by true consensus—so the United States wields a great deal more influence. It can always veto what it seriously does not like, and that veto is a real one, unlike the faux veto that every country supposedly holds in consensus talks. There is a stick, as well as a carrot, moreover, arguing for consistent US engagement with the Security Council: if the United States does not engage, someone else will. Recall the Korean War, which after all became technically a UN, rather than US, war only because the Soviet representative had boycotted the Security Council rather than remaining in the chamber using his veto.[9] Others will fill the void, if the United States disengages, and by doing so can claim the only power under the UN Charter to issue *binding* commands. Obviously, engagement means vastly more than merely showing up to vote. But full diplomatic engagement in the Security Council also only means something if the United States has a clear idea of what kind of institution the Security Council is—and that includes what the United States imagines it will become. Those expectations

9. Kennedy, *Parliament of Man*, 55–56.

about the future affect profoundly how the United States, and how other Security Council members and other actors, deal with it today.

There is much to regret if the move towards increasingly competitive great powers were to come to pass. Losers almost certainly would include places in which great-power indifference to local power politics would otherwise have permitted UN collective security to make a positive difference in the establishment and maintenance of basic order. Let us hope that these dynamics do not undermine the generally positive trend of UN peacekeeping or derail the possibilities of the UN Peacebuilding Commission. Losers might also include—likewise a gravely dismaying thought—current efforts toward enshrining the so-called "Responsibility to Protect" that would, under circumstances of grave and massive violations of human rights, permit under international law outside intervention to protect populations even against the wishes of a sovereign state. Proponents point to this doctrine's inclusion in the 2005 UN General Assembly final document on UN reform; skeptics point to the fact that the language refers to the authority of the Security Council and the dim view that P5 members China and Russia have taken toward such ideas in the recent past—in Sudan and Kosovo, for example. The ongoing Libyan venture is controversial for many important states.

A multipolar world could have the effect of making the Security Council more marginal, as other institutions respond to greater paralysis by questioning its authority. Glimmerings of this are already evident—for example, the quite remarkable European Court of Justice ruling that, the UN Charter notwithstanding, the Security Council's resolutions under its binding power are not binding after all. The supposedly mandatory authority of the Security Council turns out to be subject to the rulings of institutions such as the European Court of Justice itself, at least in Europe.[10] One may safely expect that a Security Council more driven by competitive great-power politics will generate more, and more insistent, legal reconstructions from without aimed at showing that the Security Council does not have final juridical word in international peace and security after all.

Whether or not negotiations undertaken in 2010 among states-party to the International Criminal Court (ICC) finally result in the ICC actively taking up trials for the "crime of aggression," for example, it is clear that important players are dreaming up mechanisms by which to get around the authority of the Security Council. One might have thought, after all, that if the Charter was committed to a single political proposition in the real world, it is that "aggression"—a threat to international peace and security—is above all committed to the *political* decision of the Security Council and nowhere else. It certainly cannot be a *juridical* judgment that, considered historically, is one step even beyond the mad utopianism of the League of Nations and Kellogg-Briand Pact that the 1945 Dumbarton Oaks negotiators knew instinctively they above all had to avoid. But in a more complicated, more variegated, multipolar world, it seems, other parties and states seek ways to "contract around" the Security Council. In the brave new multipolar world, the Security Council may

10. *Kadi v. Council of the European Union (C-402/05 P)* and *Al Barakaat International Foundation v. Council of the European Union (C-415/05 P)* 2008 WL 4056300, [2008] 3 C.M.L.R. 41.

prove an ever less functional institution, in the broad sense of pragmatic diplomatic realism, than it is even today in tandem with the United States' parallel hegemonic security system.

Nonetheless, in the case of the Security Council, the United States should always engage. The veto offers an ability to shape and "de-shape" the agenda and ensures that the United States not become trapped in the mire of serial, consensus negotiations in which negotiation becomes an end in itself. This result carries particular salience under the condition that the United States is (still) the global provider of global public goods, first in security but also in many other things. It bears noting, however, that, important as the veto in the Security Council is, the Council still operates by majority vote and is thus somewhat at the mercy of who happens to be sitting on it at any given point in time. One naturally tends to think of the Security Council as a negotiating chamber only of the permanent members, but in fact it is larger than that. The United States is sometimes unable to muster sufficient votes on a majority basis for initiatives it seeks to carry forward, quite apart from the threat of P5 veto.

Once past international security and the Security Council, however, we now turn to other specific parts and functions of the United Nations in order to set out the basic heuristics for addressing US interactions with them. The full range of possible ways of engagement are on the table, and the United Nations itself is sliced into constituent functions—not according to its endlessly looping tables of organization and reporting authority but instead according to particular US interests and values. As we shall see, "always engage"—the rule applicable to the Security Council—applies almost *nowhere* else at the United Nations.

A NOTE ON LIBYA

At this writing, the Gaddafi regime in Libya has fallen to the rebels backed by NATO air assets, but Gaddafi is still at large; though the immediate outcome is not in doubt, it is far too early to seek to interpret this episode definitively. However, this much can be ventured within the conceptual scheme offered in this book.

The Obama administration was sharply criticized by some in the United States for failing to lead the NATO coalition in a way that, presumably, the NATO coalition should go to war—which is to say, falling in behind the hegemonic leader. That the United States declined to lead—chose to "lead from behind," in the famous phrase—was taken by some on the American right (as well as, it seems fair to say, by some of America's less-than-friends, notably Syria's Assad) as evidence of the Obama administration's embrace of American decline and desire to abandon American hegemony. This seems to me wrong, at least on initial evaluation.

Instead, a more plausible account is that the Libyan adventure falls, according to the categories offered in this discussion, somewhere between pure altruism and the concert of nations. There was no obvious interest of the United States at stake and not an overwhelming one—military attack—for NATO allies. The motivation seemed to be altruism—an altruism ratcheted up by very particular members of the global elite class, including the French public intellectual

Bernard-Henri Lévy; Obama's close foreign policy adviser, Harvard academic turned National Security Council senior staffer Samantha Power; and former diplomatic envoy to Africa turned US ambassador to the United Nations Susan Rice. On the argument of this book, that is not enough to get to the hegemon sending its own forces to make war; at most it merits spending money to outsource the fighting to other forces. Outsourced not, as ordinarily the case, to African Union troops, but instead to France and Britain.

The motivation was sufficiently driven by these foreign policy elites, in other words, to push l'affaire Libya into the category of concert of nations, in which the leading Western military powers would actually go to war themselves and not simply outsource it to UN peacekeeping operations. In the event, politics pushed the intervention into a mixed category between these two—altruism in which the problem was seen as the United Nations', or at least someone else's, and not that of the US hegemonic security system, on the one hand, and a genuine concert of nations, or at least a concert of NATO nations, in which the US would naturally lead, on the other. The Obama administration placed the United States in almost exactly the role in which the theory of this book would predict—involved but not leading, a supplier of drones but not of military personnel, the ultimate quartermaster resupplying NATO forces with ammunition, but finally not seeing a reason to do anything other lead from behind.

On the argument of this book, and assuming that one had reasons to engage at all, this seems to be exactly what the situation required. This was not about US hegemonic interests; they were not at issue; some notion of human rights and UN values and collective security were, instead. In this case, the US had no reason to get involved, and if it did so, no reason to lead. This reasoning holds up, however, even on the terms of this theory, only insofar as the NATO-rebel coalition was not in serious risk of losing (or perhaps of entering a permanently protracted stalemate), which, because it had become a NATO operation, would have risked hegemonic reputation.

The legitimacy of the Libyan intervention depended in significant part on at least the momentary blessings of the Arab League. The Arab League is in a difficult strategic position, in its desire to remain in the graces of Arab populations at a time of multiple popular uprisings against autocratic states. Nowhere will its calculations matter more than regarding Syria, whose President Assad, at this writing, slaughters more and more civilians. There are calls for investigations to be conducted by the League itself and for reports and monitorings by the Human Rights Council. If any of these monitoring efforts come to pass, there will be calls to see in this a vindication of the Human Rights Council and US participation in it. This would be a mistake. Whatever comes to pass within the Human Rights Council (or the Arab League) reflects not some deep or objective commitment to human rights or accurately reporting on them, but instead merely transitory calculations by Arab and allied states at the Human Rights Council and the UN, seeking to find ways, not to protect human rights as such, but to stay on the good side of Arab populations. When these transitory interests shift, so will the performance of the Human Rights Council. The place where the US can—and, to give due credit, is making a positive difference to outcomes at this writing—is the Security Council.

5 SOMETIMES ENGAGE:
Internal UN Management and the General Secretariat, the Buyout of the UN-that-Works, and the Containment of the UN-that-Doesn't

The United Nations does not cost the United States a lot of money. Members of Congress may complain about spending money that could be spent remedying water pollution in rural Montana, for example, on UN bureaucrats who hate the United States. But US payments to the United Nations would not be paid over to domestic spending (comparisons to domestic spending are always inapposite), nor would foregoing such payments reduce the deficit. This is so even in these straitened times, however contrary that might be to the current stance of American fiscal conservatives. So the first lesson for the United States regarding money, management, and internal control of the United Nations is—*still*, even today—don't sweat the small stuff. There are many reasons for the United States to be concerned about how much it pays, whom it pays, what happens to the money, and whether and how much of it reaches its intended use. But these should be concerns over managerial efficiency at the United Nations itself, on the one hand, and concerns about leveraging the use of material resources to bring about institutional political outcomes congenial to the United States, on the other. The amount of money in total is not that large—and it is not the issue, even in these times of fiscal stress.

How much money is at issue?[1] The total official budget of the United Nations—meaning the budget of required membership dues assessed by the General Assembly as prescribed by the UN Charter—was about $1.9 billion in 2005.[2] The two-year budget cycle proposed by Secretary-General Ban for 2009 is $4.89 billion (with proposed add-ons that would bring it up to at least $5.4 billion).[3] The US share of that amount is 22 percent, down from 25 percent prior to 2001. For the regular operating budget, its assessed dues ran about $395 million out of the $1.8 billion budget in 2006. It also paid assessed contributions of about $500 million for UN specialized agencies—25 percent of the total budget. And it paid $1.3 billion out of the United Nations' $5 billion budget for PKOs—about 26 percent. There has been upward pressure, but not extraordinarily so, in the budget cycles since.

1. If one takes all the various UN agencies and organs, including ones that are part of the UN family, at least on paper, but effectively self-financed through voluntary contributions and self-run, the figure is roughly $20 billion annually. But that figure includes many agencies and functions that are not really about the political and governance issues at hand. This estimate is Jussi M. Hanhimaki's in *The United Nations: A Very Short Introduction* (New York: Oxford University Press, 2008), 45; it is in my estimation about right.

2. This figure is from the UN public relations page on the budget: "Is the United Nations Good Value for the Money?," *Image and Reality: Questions and Answers about the UN* (June 30, 2006), *available at* http://www.un.org /geninfo/ir/index.asp?id=150. See note 6 for why I have opted to have the figures in this chapter range across so many years. It is to emphasize their relative stability and the stability of the arguements I make about them.

3. Neil MacFarquhar, "Money Fights Are Brewing at the United Nations as Its Budget Season Heats Up," *New York Times*, November 8, 2009, A16.

Let us be clear from the beginning of this discussion. My own sympathies have long been to cut the UN budget in Washington; but given that the institution will not wither away because the US cuts a few hundred million to a billion dollars to the United Nations, the argument of this book is to be ruthlessly rational in how much and where to spend on the United Nations. Every interest group in Washington says the same thing—our activities are special; don't cut us—and only those making tradeoffs against different kinds of budgetary priorities can decide what to spend money on. A certain amount of spending on the United Nations, even in the form of mandatory dues that go to payoffs to countries and overpaid international civil servants and sometimes straight-up corruption, is what it takes to be the hegemon. It is the buy-in. If China were to take over these relatively modest payments, reaping the rewards of reputation and prestige as the indispensable player, the United States would be very, very sorry—in strategic terms, this would be the equivalent of a Chinese carrier group in the Pacific.

So. The assessed amount of the regular operating budget is the only "mandatory" Charter contribution. The other fees are assessed, in the sense that members make binding multilateral commitments, but the commitments are not strictly Charter-binding. Without agreed assessments for multilateral operations, such as PKOs, however, individual countries would hesitate to contribute, not knowing whether they would be the only ones to do so. Since the United States strongly and correctly supports many of the specialized agencies and their functions, as well as PKOs, the assessment system is a useful one for those purposes.

The regular operating budget of the United Nations, controlled under the Charter by the General Assembly, is a different matter. The United States pays the highest percentage for the regular operating budget; the top ten countries together pay about 76 percent of it.[4] The bottom half of countries in the world pay essentially nothing. For 2005, the forty-seven countries "contributing at the minimum rate were assessed $14,360 each."[5] Given the enormous disparities in wealth, these differences are not unfair. But fairness aside, the fact that the bottom half pays nothing while the top ten countries pay three-quarters cannot help but skew the incentives of the United Nations, its budget, its staff, and its member states. In an organization in which the General Assembly sets the budget assessments, the nonpaying but voting majority has an endless temptation to impose ever-higher assessments on the paying minority.

Despite that temptation, however, these budgetary issues are not that big a problem for other large countries. The EU countries taken collectively pay some 37 percent, considerably more than the United States, yet they never seem to get too upset at the cost of the United Nations. On the other hand, they almost never get upset about managerial issues within the United Nations, about patronage or mismanagement or corruption. They also typically pay on time, never threaten boycotts of UN dues, usually do not fall into arrears and, for that matter, they pay at the beginning of the fiscal

4. As of 2005, the top ten countries in regular assessed contributions were US (22 percent), Japan (19.47), Germany (8.66), UK (6.13), France (6.03), Italy (4.89), Canada (2.81), Spain (2.52), China (2.05), and Mexico (1.88). "Is the United Nations Good Value for the Money?"

5. "Is the United Nations Good Value for the Money?"

year, as countries are supposed to do, rather than at the end, as the United States does. Shouldn't the United States simply follow the EU, and other rich countries, and quit nagging the organization over managerial issues? Why not just pay up, pay on time, pay what is voted, and quit fighting over the details?

The introduction to this book noted that if ways of understanding the United Nations include both the idealist lens of liberal internationalism and the realist lens of standard international-relations sovereign interests, then a third way is simply to follow the money. Look inside the United Nations. Examine the organization according to its internal material interests, incentives and disincentives. In economic terms, it is a "public choice" approach to understanding an organization according to its internal incentive structure. It is one often unfamiliar to diplomats and lawyers—and, at least as applied to the actual United Nations, often even to political scientists because, with respect to an organization as materially and resource complicated as the United Nations and all its assorted entities, one has to be willing to read technical budgetary statements, basic accounting and fiscal statements for complicated public governmental entities and nonprofit organizations. This is frankly not very compelling for most people, particularly in international relations, but—well, follow the money. So, having sifted through these statements in the course of performing expert technical work for a US-UN reform task force a few years ago, we can ask, What is learned from the internal governance structures, budget and management structures of the United Nations?

The first is that differences are enormous between how the United States sees paying UN dues and how the EU

members or many others in the world see UN dues. Leave
aside the vast majority that pay very little. The difference in
attitude even just between the United States and the EU
arises from their very different conceptions of what UN dues
represent. In that sense, "following the money" tells something important about the grand values—and antinomies—
of the United Nations. Indeed, it is an antinomy baked into
the United Nations, yet another deep contradiction, all its
own. For big UN contributors apart from the United States,
UN dues are, first, an investment in reputation in the international community, a way of showing that a country is in
good standing and respects its peers in the international
community. They also represent a kind of down payment,
second, on the future ideal of global governance. In that
sense, it is the *fact* of the contribution that matters, and it
would be almost churlish to ask how the money was used or,
worse still, to ask for an accounting.

For the United States, by contrast, the future ideal of
global governance is not of obvious value—neither as a prob-
able outcome nor as a desirable one. Partly in consequence,
the United States sees its contributions, even those mandated
as dues, as something for which it is owed some level of fiduciary care in the present. Not insignificantly, the United
States believes it has an obligation, on behalf of its own people
but also on behalf of others with less leverage, to seek what
amounts to little more than a standard corporate accounting.[6] Not even that much, in fact—the US government over

6. Throughout this discussion, I have deliberately used figures that range
across years from the mid-2000s until today. The point is that whatever the
exact numbers in any given UN budget cycle, they are roughly in these ranges
over half a decade or more. They are relatively stable indicators of the amounts

decades has long since given up on the idea of something as correct as corporate accounting as simply hopeless at the United Nations. On the basis of my own personal experience studying UN management (and writing as someone with experience in management of international NGOs with sizable economic resources), I have never encountered an organization imbued top to bottom with quite so alternatingly dismissive and evasive an attitude toward basic fiscal accountability. That reaction is in line with the general assessment of leading outside experts, particularly the American ones.

The problem is not fundamentally with the senior offices of the secretary-general. It, indeed, "gets it," even if many of the senior leadership do not have sufficient knowledge to manage the issue or even to manage the experts who should manage the issue. The problem lies in so many other places in the organization(s). Everyone protects everyone else. States protect their own nationals within the bureaucracy ferociously. The UN employee union is (on top of being one of the most generous salary and pension systems in the developed world, let alone the rest) more protective and subject to less countervailing pressure than nearly any other public employee union. At bottom, no one actually believes in accountability. If one thinks that these attitudes toward fiscal resources are not reflective of, or condition, the rest of the work of the United Nations, one would be profoundly mistaken. The reader will observe that with a couple of exceptions, this chapter does not offer a parade of scandals and incidents of corruption, mismanagement, waste, and the like.

---

of money the UN spends on various activities. For the high-altitude purposes of this discussion, this is sufficient to show the general amounts and trends.

This is not because they do not occur—on the contrary, they occur so routinely and with so little oversight or accountability that it would be pointless to try and track them in this kind of policy essay. The mainstream US press largely overlooks them. The leading US press's standards of accountability for the United Nations are like those of the European governments, long since concluding that reporting on corruption and waste in any detail or attention does the United Nations as an institution more damage than the editorial board of the *New York Times* would ideally like to do. A handful of bloggers and watchdogs do the work—Claudia Rosett and the Inner City Press, especially—and the mainstream press mostly ignores it.

If this sounds scolding or moralizing toward the European governments, well, it is not an endorsement of American standards in all this. Swiss or German or Nordic standards of financial rectitude would be better than American—but for important reasons, the standards that all those countries would insist upon in their own institutions never seem to be important to them at the United Nations. The reason is deeply tied to the fundamental conception of UN dues as an offering to the future of global governance, in the hands of its UN priests; and one does not ask the church, much less God, for an accounting. If one thinks that these considerations do not affect the internal bureaucratic culture of the organization, one should think again. I have not, in my experience in the world of international organizations public and nongovernmental, encountered an organization with less of a sense among its staff—and in this criticism I *do* include the senior leadership—of a genuine fiduciary regard for the resources made available to it. The attitude is not fiduciary, it is not a sense of stewardship—it is pure institutional entitlement with a large dangling question of why there isn't more.

On the other hand, American attitudes seem utterly hypocritical, particularly to other large contributor states. The regular eruptions in which the US Congress has simply declined to pay dues that are, from a formal international legal standpoint, simple treaty obligations, do not persuade anyone of US fiscal rectitude. In any case, congressional refusals to pay amounts due are rarely about managerial effectiveness; they are much more commonly, over the years, values-based objections to certain expenditures. One of the few exceptions was the most recent US threat to withhold UN dues, this one from Ambassador Bolton in 2005. It was genuinely performance-based, though it was aimed at the member-states of the United Nations, rather than the UN bureaucracy as a managerial issue. The Bush administration threatened to break consensus on ratification of the UN budget, taking the view that perhaps dues ought to be paid out on a schedule linked to the actual completion of an agreed-upon portion of the agreed-upon tasks of UN reform.[7] The proposal caused near-apoplexy at UN headquarters and among other large state donors. It smacked apparently a little too much of linking pay to performance. The threat did not

7. John Bolton, *Surrender Is Not an Option: Defending America at the United Nations and Abroad* (New York: Threshold-Simon & Schuster, 2007), 239–45. It bears noting that Bolton disagrees with the opening assessment of this chapter that the amounts of money at issue are not greatly significant in absolute terms. This is relevant in part because Bolton is highly experienced with the inner workings of UN budgets, fiscal accountability, and all the rest that diplomats frequently gloss over.

get very far, in any event. And predictably—no doubt for
many different reasons—very little of the UN reform agenda
has been completed or even undertaken.

The recent introduction in 2011 of a bill in Congress on
UN funding is unusual in that it marries concerns about
values issues—US funding of the Human Rights Council—
to fiscal management concerns. Each is indeed a legitimate
source of concern for the United States; yet quite apart
from the inability for very many such bills to go forward
in Congress, only rarely can Congress use its power of the
purse to induce positive changes in an administration's dealings with the United Nations, and almost never can it induce
changes, positive or not, at the United Nations itself. The
political reality is that dealings with the United Nations
are very much in the hands of the executive, at least when
it comes to the actual money, separate from public hearings
and other forms of political pressure.

Over the long term, the US approach to UN funding has
always carried, and even under the Obama administration
continues to carry, an irreducible demand upon the organization for fiduciary obligation and performance with respect to
accountability for its and others' funds. It is an expectation
that is not found to anywhere near the same degree in the
language or behavior of any other significant UN contributor. Even if the dollar amounts are relatively small, it matters
to the United States whether the money is effectively spent
or not; whether it disappears into personal corruption or into
officially approved but frankly unnecessary salary increases
for already highly paid secretariat staff; or whether it furthers
US interests or instead furthers the agendas of anti–United
States actors in the international system. These all remain

important questions to the United States, even if the amount of money is relatively small.

Bolton wearily remarked at one moment in his tenure as UN ambassador that the process of UN reform is never really done.[8] In nothing perhaps does this apply more completely than in the matter of UN internal management and governance. As the Iraq oil-for-food scandal erupted in 2003, the Annan secretariat realized that merely taking umbrage at serious allegations, and much evidence, of both personal corruption and institutional nonaccountability would not fly—for once. The United States, at that point, was paying serious attention as the documents of Saddam's immense program of kickbacks and rigged oil contracts (to obtain money for the regime that was intended to go to impoverished Iraqis and also to purchase influence in the West to ratchet down UN sanctions) emerged from Iraq after the US invasion.

It is true that other countries, to the extent that they expressed dismay, mostly did not see it as the scandal that the United States saw. Other countries understood the kickbacks, bribes, and general winking at the putatively illegal oil trading as part of an "informal" relaxing of sanctions that, it was supposed, would eventually result in a more formal relenting of sanctions. Under intense US pressure, Annan appointed the highly regarded former Federal Reserve chairman Paul Volcker to head an investigation. Volcker and his staff issued a series of carefully worded reports that ultimately confirmed much of the alleged corruption and exposed more while leaving (just barely) room

8. Bolton, 239. As Bolton said, "Reform is not a one-night stand."

for Annan to hang on.[9] And hang on he did. And in the
usual cycle of UN permanent crisis-stasis, the whole scandal has been quite forgotten and swept away.[10] Indeed,
there has been little if any accountability for the oil-for-
food scandal of a sort that might, in the years following
it, have improved internal management of the United
Nations. Down to today, the United Nations has not only

9. A convenient summary version of the reports can be found in a book
by Volcker's aides: Jeffrey A. Meyer and Mark G. Califano, *Good Intentions
Corrupted: The Oil-for-Food Scandal and the Threat to the U.N.* (Based on the
Reports of the Independent Inquiry Committee, Paul A. Volcker, Chair) (New
York: Public Affairs, Perseus, 2006).

10. The entire affair exposed one of the peculiar gaps in the UN
system—it is so insulated from accountability that there is no clear mechanism
even for filing criminal charges against its personnel for embezzlement or other
serious financial crimes. Governments protect their own no matter what, and
there is no accepted jurisdiction, apart from governments disciplining their own
nationals, for addressing crimes within the UN itself.

The well-respected then-district attorney of Manhattan, Robert
Morgenthau, eventually initiated investigations that resulted in a guilty plea
from one UN official, Alexander Yakovlev, and the (hasty) departure of another,
Benon Sevan, to his native Cyprus. These legal moves were uneasily tolerated
by the UN (which is to say, tolerated by a panicked Kofi Annan under grave
pressures for his own role in the oil-for-food scandal). But they do not have a
clear international-law basis, given the extraordinary circumstances of a New
York state prosecutor taking the position that because the UN headquarters (or
at least the persons involved) was located in New York and key elements of the
fraud apparently took place there, New York courts could exercise jurisdiction.

Although private companies and individuals have been successfully pros-
ecuted by the US government for the oil-for-food legal violations, in the years
since the scandal, the UN has simply ignored it as a matter of internal accountability. An internal UN staff-grievance panel later ruled that the UN was
responsible for Sevan's legal fees, for example. Morgenthau's personal reputation and the enormous political pressure on Annan created a result unlikely to
be duplicated, given the strength of the UN employee union and the general
desire to ensure that no court, anywhere in the world, has clear jurisdiction even
over basic fraud and embezzlement when it takes place within the institution
of the UN.

no effective mechanisms for addressing serious corruption, the internal structure of the organization facilitates cover-ups of both personal corruption and institutional misfeasance. This is owed in large part to a widespread belief at the United Nations and among its elite constituents that it did nothing, or at any rate very little, wrong in the oil-for-food scandal, and this was a put-up job by the United States and the Bush administration. Volcker, most recently an economic adviser to Barack Obama, would surely have had little incentive to go on a vendetta on behalf of the Bush administration, and in fact the language of his reports was carefully crafted to avoid even the appearance of one; they were the more damning for that. But few people read them and few people cared.

The United Nations has, to be sure, a system of internal auditors and, in principle, internal fiscal controls. They are as baroque in their complexity as they are ineffectual in practice. The system has evolved over time by adding one layer of "oversight" and "accountability" on top of another, usually in response to pressure from the United States, finding ways to circumvent and evade what was last put in place, and sometimes simply undoing layers of controls once the heat is off. The long history of failed attempts to maintain some kind of fiscal accountability at the United Nations points to several systemic managerial issues, none of which is really fixable at the fundamental level.

First, there is no genuine top-down management authority at the United Nations; the secretary-general has only limited power. Annan complained that he had far less managerial authority than people associated with his title. In this, he was entirely correct, and it is a great weakness of the

organization.[11] A managerial reform on which Annan and
the United States thoroughly agreed was the creation of a
new executive position at the top of the secretariat, a chief
operating officer who would be responsible for internal management, with genuine power to act within the organization,
and reporting to the secretary-general directly. Unsurprisingly, given how many private fiefdoms within the bureaucracy this might upset, as well as member states, the proposal
went nowhere.

Second, from an internal control standpoint, the United
Nations is not really a single organization but instead a
whole array of agencies, organs, and separate institutions.
The major entities each have their own control sections, and
they are not necessarily obligated to share information on
waste, corruption, or investigations with the member states.
For a long period of time, even the audits of a particular
UN unit undertaken by the central inspectors were paid for
by the unit itself—with obvious consequences for the incentives of inspectors to identify possible problems. This is the
"United Nations of baronies"—competitive and cooperating

11. Hence, the secretary-general (and by extension all the secretariat) is the
servant of the member states, a high-level minister to their needs who is titular
head of a large bureaucracy but still not truly an executive. The secretary-general
is named in the UN Charter as the "chief administrative officer" of the United
Nations, but in fact the secretary-general is not a true CEO—because, after all,
being a CEO means in the first place being able to hire and fire. The bureaucracy and the member states—jealous of their privileges, protective of their
rent-seeking behaviors over available resources, and unhappy with any American
effort to demand even the routine accountability that any industrialized nation's
government would demand of its offices or any corporation would consider
mundane—give a high-minded sniff, if no longer precisely at the very concept
of accountability, then at actual practices of accountability that might involve
actual accountability.

fiefdoms, whose entities and chiefs jealously guard their privileges and largesse in the form of appointments, staffing, budgets, and any resources that might pass their way. In addition, powerful states (and these are not necessarily the largest, richest, or dues-paying ones) protect their nationals in the UN civil service. In many ways, the smaller and poorer the state, the more incentives to enable its nationals in their rent-seeking. At moments when internal bureaucratic control is the most needed, the institution collapses back into the model of a mere "servant" of the member states.[12]

The need for the United States to press for managerial accountability at the United Nations is as abiding a principle of US policy toward the United Nations as can be found. If the United States does not do it, no one else will. It is true that bad things happen in any institution; the United Nations is striking because of its lack of credible systems to address them.[13] Even when action is undertaken in the first

12. Following the oil-for-food scandal and the emergence shortly thereafter of evidence of massive fraud in peacekeeping procurement, a special office specifically for procurement fraud was established within one of the UN's accountability watchdogs, the Office of Internal Oversight Services (OIOS) under the direction of an American ex–federal prosecutor with experience in financial crime. It has been under relentless pressure to be shut down by governments— Russia and Singapore, for example—whose nationals are under investigation, and it is unclear at this writing whether or how much of its work will even be completed. The historical precedents of auditing and fiscal control suggest that very little will take place, and in any case information derived will not be acted on.

13. The lack of interest in so much as knowing about corruption and rent-seeking and money scandals at the UN is pervasive in the mainstream American press, let alone elsewhere in the world. Two indispensable sources of information about UN mismanagement and money scandals are, first, the reporting by Claudia Rosett, journalist-in-residence at the Foundation for the Defense of Democracies and, second, investigative reporting by the independent Inner City Press (http://www.innercitypress.com).

instance, it nonetheless turns out to be ineffective—often because whatever gets announced as a "consequence" is quietly reversed by some internal body or decision later on. It would be more accurate to describe the system of "controls" at the United Nations not as ordinary bureaucratic controls but instead as the enforcement of a *preexisting* division of the spoils. Theft, embezzlement, fraud, corruption, bribery, kickbacks, patronage, overpayments of expenses, institutional rent-seeking, waste, inefficiency, lack of fiscal controls, unaccountability, diversion and conversion of institutional resources—these things at the United Nations have consequences for people in the real world, usually for an undefined mass of very poor people who lack voice. They ought to have consequences for the United Nations as well, and only US pressure will make sure that they do.

The United Nations has fixed costs—costs of keeping the system going that have to be paid no matter what. And the United States has an interest in making its regular apportioned payments, not out of any special affinity for the United Nations, but simply because the United Nations performs many practical functions that the United States wants to see performed. While these fixed costs are not especially expensive in absolute terms, they are monumentally inefficient, quite apart from issues of corruption, fraud, and illegality. In the 2009 UN budget negotiations, for example, attention focused (even in the *New York Times*) on the fiscally stunning figure of $2,473 per page of translation by the United Nations' in-house staff. This compares with $450 per page for translation by outside contractors. The United Nations justifies these costs on grounds that its in-house translators are on call for immediate work, yet the United Nations is years behind in document production, much of it widely recognized as unnecessary in any case.[14]

The largest portion of direct costs goes to staff salaries, and permanent staff salaries are generous in exactly the way one would expect of an organization committed to "parity" with the salaries of the most generous national civil services.[15] The United Nations has what amounts to a tenure system with one of the world's strongest unions; downsizing permanent staff is nearly impossible. The similarities to the Western European labor-market model are impossible to ignore, likewise the tendency to sclerosis—tenured senior staff with extraordinary salaries, benefits, and pensions, usually aging and not very productive alongside untenured junior staff who do much of the productive work. This leads to the hiring of some of the most productive and useful staff on insecure months-long contracts. Exercising internal discipline is likewise extraordinarily difficult, given the endless layers of review and the opportunities for quiet reversal of disciplinary sanctions.

The General Assembly for years simply saw the UN budget as an opportunity for poor nations to spend the money of rich nations. The effect was endless growth of the permanent

14. MacFarquhar, A16.

15. Joshua Muravchik notes, as of 2005, "Undersecretaries general are currently paid more than $250,000 per year—in other words, 40 percent more than a member of the U.S. cabinet. And there are so many of these 'USGs' that the undersecretary for management recently noted, 'It is not possible for all USGs to report to the Secretary-General.'" *The Future of the United Nations: Understanding the Past to Chart a Way Forward* (Washington, DC: AEI Press, 2005), 43, quoting United States House of Representatives, International Relations Committee, "Hearing on United Nations Reform," testimony of Catherine Bertini, May 19, 2005.

staff as a patronage perk of General Assembly "players." Over time, the rich, paying states have negotiated new budgeting arrangements. The heart of them today is a consensus process that effectively grants a de facto veto to individual countries. This arrangement creates a measure of restraint on the part of those states in the General Assembly which spend other people's money, but it also requires a general willingness of the wealthy countries to make payments as agreed.

Inefficient, expensive, and badly managed as the organization is, the United Nations' fixed costs must still be covered if the United States wants to see the practical benefits. The United States should therefore understand its UN dues in the following, coolly self-interested, way.

The United States has a modest interest in maintaining its fundamental reputation as a member in good standing of the system. As a question of reputation, the United States should ordinarily pay its basic dues first and other voluntary amounts for particular purposes second. This is so *even if* it believes that the same money spent by one of the voluntarily funded, specialized agencies—the World Food Program or the World Health Organization, for example—would be more effectively used. It is also what it should do *even if* it believes that the United Nations as an overall organization will simply waste these resources. Reputation is purchased at the United Nations and, all other things equal, it is a valuable commodity obtained in part through basic UN dues.

These basic UN dues for the regular operating budget are best understood as a "hold-up premium" charged by the rent-seeking United Nations, as a cost on engaging in the more effective activities of global welfare. The dues are a tax that, while seeming to fall on the rich countries, instead falls indirectly on the global poor. They are an indirect opportunity-cost tax on more efficient opportunities for global welfare. They are not some noble payment into some selfless organization or an offering to a sacred god. Yet provided the costs do not rise unacceptably or become a question of fundamental US values, it is a tax worth paying by the United States. It should simply be clear with itself that it is mostly purchasing reputation and buy-in as a player from the UN-of-rent-seekers. US engagement with the United Nations here should aim at *containing* the regular operating budget and making sure it does not balloon, as it naturally would.

The most important category of funds provided by the United States to the United Nations is not regular dues, however. It is voluntary contributions to specialized UN agencies and funding for a few special functions, such as peacekeeping operations. One can roughly think of these funds as variable costs. The fundamental value-added of the United Nations as an organization lies with these specialized agencies and the work they perform on the margin. However necessary funding of the organization as a whole might be, in real life funding the United Nations' regular operating budget means funding many activities that are not just inefficient or wasteful but also deliberately and pointedly anti-American. Selective funding among variable activities is therefore an absolute requirement of long-term US policy. In the politicized UN world, the United States has a clear and compelling reason to favor voluntary funding of particular activities and to minimize contributions to the organization as a whole.

Some of the valuable activities of specialized UN agencies have already been identified, and there are many more. The World Food Program (WFP), for example, is the "largest food-aid program in the world . . . and in 2003 reached a record 110 million people."[16] The WFP relies "entirely on voluntary contributions" but is generally regarded as an efficient and well-run agency, having the "largest budget of any major UN agency or programme—as well as the smallest headquarters staff and lowest overhead." The United Nations is right to tout the efficiency and effectiveness of the program. The United States makes major contributions, but in an era of rising global food-price inflation it could usefully make more. The same is true of the Food and Agricultural Organization, whose Food Security Program will certainly increase in importance in coming years with tighter global food supplies and higher commodity prices.

UN agencies often play an important coordinating, multi-lateral standard-setting role—frequently in apparently mundane but cumulatively important technical activities. One of the historically most successful international agencies ever to exist, for example, is the International Telecommunications Union (ITU), which dates back to 1865. It has set international technical standards for telecommunications for over 150 years, and today it has taken an important role in radio frequency allocations and satellite orbital positioning. The International Maritime Organization, for another example, has coordinated treaty efforts to control accidents and oil spills at sea as well as pollution from ships. There are many such examples, often unsung, and the United States has strongly supported and should continue to support and fund these agencies for obvious practical reasons. Sometimes their

16. United Nations, *Basic Facts about the United Nations* (New York: United Nations Department of Public Information, 2004), 177.

relationship to the institutional United Nations is close as a political, budgetary, and operational matter; other times, it is much more distant, to the point that the United Nations might better be understood as having "licensed" its "brand." In practical terms, the United Nations does quite a lot of licensing and branding. In the case of an organization with a strong and desirable sense of internal mission and esprit de corps, one might be concerned that it was weakening itself by licensing itself; in the case of the United Nations, almost entirely the opposite is true.

Some of these agencies are stand-alone operations that collect funds from member states in order to pursue their activities. In other cases, the agencies serve as forums for multilateral regulatory networks. The United States properly seeks multilateral coordination and appropriate levels of regulation agreed upon by sovereigns. These efforts need not founder on the kinds of collective-action failures that tend to doom collective security; the calculations of costs and benefits among sovereigns often, although not always, will tend to favor some level of regulatory agreement. Robust multilateralism, even multilateral regulation that limits US behavior—particularly in economic, trade, global finance, and environmental issues—can be of enormous benefit to the United States.[17]

17. As the World Trade Organization has long shown in matters of trade. The issues implicit in this "robust multilateralism" are costs and benefits, sovereign agreement and collective-action enforcement to limit free riding. Crucial to the cost-benefit analysis is seeing each of these strictly on its own terms, rather than as part of a larger and forward-looking agenda of political global governance. Counting benefits so as to include the presumed future agenda of global governance creates a considerable problem. Justifying multilateralism on the basis not of current costs and benefits but of the marvelous future biases decision making toward accepting unacceptable costs and bad tradeoffs in the present.

Although many of the agencies that deserve considerable, even increased, US voluntary funding are technical agencies, this is not always the case. As discussed in the previous chapter, peacekeeping is a prime example of a successful *political* activity at the United Nations; if properly developed, the Peacebuilding Commission might prove similarly useful. For that matter, the thoroughly political international tribunals—whether that be the ad hoc tribunals for gradually phasing out Yugoslavia or Rwanda or Sierra Leone or elsewhere or the International Criminal Court—are examples of political activities that sometimes deserve US fiscal support, and sometimes do not. It is also true that tribunals always believe they must go on and on, always believe that they need more resources; others have to make decisions about resource trade-offs, because they cannot do it themselves.

But in any event, the tribunal system is an example of the UN licensing and branding otherwise independent institutions. Those of a liberal internationalist bent at some point have to consider whether it is a bug or a feature that an increasing range of institutions are essentially branded by the United Nations, but that is mostly it. That, after all, describes important features of the ICC, though it has a direct connection to the core United Nations through, among other things, referrals from the Security Council. The intense interest of international-law academics and others in these institutions is owed in no small part to the fact that they are much, much more amenable to the influence of academic and NGO outsiders, in large part because their resources are not funneled through the accounts of the rent-seeking United Nations.

But even technical-expert organizations are not inherently immune from politicization and corruption. The World

Health Organization (WHO) today enjoys a good reputation, for example, in an era of feared pandemics and other issues of global disease. But the WHO underwent an ugly and damaging politicization in the 1980s, when Japan, as a matter of national pride, insisted on backing and protecting a WHO executive director who was obviously corrupt and bent on turning the organization into a personal fiefdom of corruption, personal influence, and rent-seeking.

The very characteristic that makes these agencies attractive for voluntary funding is that they have a certain amount of independence. In the hands of a competent and dedicated director, this can result in valuable work that the United States should support with strong resourcing. On the other hand, this is precisely the feature that makes an agency particularly susceptible to corruption. The "barons" of the UN agencies are truly barons—powerful agency heads who are largely unconstrained by the secretariat. Some have the backing of powerful member states or are protected by the general procedures of the General Assembly and its entrenched processes. Sometimes they are backed by the United States, sometimes not; sometimes the barony is a good way of getting good work done, while other times it simply leads to ineffectual work and corruption. There is no general rule, apart from a view that the fewer resources committed over to the general United Nations without triggering a Charter crisis, the better.

And the bad United Nations agencies are not just corrupt or incompetent—inefficacious or inefficient. They are also frequently politicized in a general sense and anti-American in a particular sense. Sometimes the anti-Americanism is only too sincere, as in the infamous "new information order" of twenty-five years ago by the United Nations Educational, Scientific, and Cultural Organization (UNESCO) that caused the Reagan administration to pull out of the organization altogether. But sometimes, too, it serves in part as a means of neutralizing American managerial criticism that might otherwise interfere with incompetence, bad management, rent-seeking, patronage, or corruption. In either case, politicization of UN agencies is almost always a function of the single least impressive institution of the UN system: the General Assembly.

Political legitimacy and the claim to be an international organization both require that the United Nations have a General Assembly—an assembly of all member states of the world in a single body organized under the principle of one nation, one vote. The United Nations' founders sought to remedy the collective security problems of the League of Nations and its general assembly of states by creating the Security Council as a meeting place of great powers specifically to deal with "threats to international peace and security." But they left most other things to the General Assembly to address.[18]

Proximity of the General Assembly to the budget and to the personnel-appointment processes of the United Nations ensures patronage and rent-seeking by member states. The patronage system starts innocuously enough with provisions

18. This includes the dues-based budget of the UN as well as either an approval or recommendation concerning the budgets of some of the leading agencies (different specialized agencies can be part of the UN for budgetary purposes in widely differing ways or, as in the case of the Bretton Woods financial institutions such as the World Bank or the International Monetary Fund, not at all).

of the Charter mandating that, although, on the one hand, the paramount consideration in employing UN staff is to be the "highest standards of efficiency, competence, and integrity," due regard shall be paid, on the other, to "recruiting staff on as wide a geographical basis as possible." This is scarcely surprising, even unavoidable, in an organization whose legitimacy is based in large part upon its universality. But the effect upon efficiency, competence, and integrity is corrosive and has been from the beginning. Member states jealously guard their access to the hiring process.

Beyond the staffing issues of patronage, however, the entire General Assembly system of voting and taking of resolutions is built around two general behaviors. First, member states vote as part of their regional blocs on many crucial issues—especially on matters related to distributing the largesse and appointments of the organization. Ban Ki-moon is secretary-general today, in the first place, because it was "Asia's turn"; after that, only because the United States and other powerful states signed off. The same general principle applies to a great many decisions taken by the General Assembly or by some subset committee or subcommittee thereof. Regional bloc voting has been identified by every serious observer of the United Nations as a major impediment to creating a workable method of decision making. However, it reduces conflict among members and to a considerable extent ensures lock-step operations. This is not an undesirable feature, to be sure, insofar as more activity on the part of the General Assembly generally implies greater overall damage to US interests. Bloc voting thus contributes much to the UN-in-equilibrium. It ensures that many decisions that would otherwise be deeply contested are instead settled on the arbitrary basis "of my turn now, your turn next." There is no substance here about which to complain.

Second, most member states vote in the General Assembly and its committees and suborgans as members of some ideological group: the Group of 77, the Nonaligned Movement (NAM), or the Islamic conference, for example. There is a largely notional group of aligned democracies, but, in actual behavior, many of the democratic states vote with the developing world blocs, and, since hitting a high point around 2006 or so, it has declined in visibility. This tendency arose during the Cold War, originally among countries—almost all from the developing world—that at least nominally tilted toward neither superpower in the Cold War. As a voting bloc in the General Assembly, this group has grown to some 130 or so countries that can be depended upon to vote loosely as a bloc on a wide range of issues. The leaders of the NAM and Group of 77 are some of the most virulently anti-American in the world; Cuba and Gaddafi's Libya, for example, assiduously long cultivated relationships to maintain leadership of these blocs and, through them, leadership in UN activities and organs.

Yet there is a remarkable disconnect between voting behavior of countries in the General Assembly, where bloc voting by region and ideological group reigns, and those countries' foreign relations with the United States in the real world. The reason for this is simple and, from the standpoint of the whole of US foreign policy, quite rational. Most of the issues taken up by the United Nations for votes are so remote from actual US relations with the countries in question that it is not worth the expenditure of diplomatic capital to get these states to vote with the United States in the United Nations.

To be clear, the United States incurs real costs by treating the United Nations and real life as separate domains in this way. The discourse and mood and fashions of the "international community" centered around the United Nations do have a much greater long-run impact on the United States in both domestic and foreign policy than might be apparent in any particular instance. This approach, therefore, has the distinct disadvantage of discounting far more than it should the effect of that diffuse, long-term international discourse that seems to be nothing but talk in New York or Geneva. At the same time, if the United States were to permit intercourse between the United Nations and the United States' real diplomacy in all the capitals of the world, it would have to be willing to pay something in the real world to extract support in the UN world.

The General Assembly is the playpen of the nations. A recent General Assembly president was elected from Gaddafi's Libya; its previous president was from Nicaragua. Each was elected in large part on agendas of anti-Americanism and enthusiasm for political authoritarianism and was procedurally ensured by bloc regional voting and the endorsement of ideological groupings. The lesson for the United States is simple: the closer an entity or activity of the United Nations is to the control of the General Assembly, the less likely it is to be effective at its stated purpose and the more likely it is to be driven by patronage, rent-seeking, corruption, and straight-up anti-Americanism. The policy corollary for the United States is equally simple: the United States should ordinarily seek to contain the General Assembly and its directly controlled appendages—their budgets, their mandates, and their operations.

At the same time, the United States should use its funding to effect what amounts to a management-led *buyout* of those agencies that are efficient and effective, through the influence and control it can exert through voluntary funding. The United States should seek a buyout of the UN-that-works and containment of the UN-that-doesn't.

This is not as nefarious or cynical as it sounds. It is precisely what the Western European donor nations and private philanthropic donors have been doing for many years. My personal experience working with organizations that have done exactly that for decades without thinking themselves any less liberal internationalist and progressive makes the policy an obvious one to me. In the actual funding doctrines of their national aid agencies, of course, they refer to it as good management practice, not as buying control, but that is indirectly what it amounts to. It is a policy the United States would do well to emulate with respect to the agencies of the United Nations that it believes are effective.

The intention is for voluntary funding to become sufficiently large, and the useful agencies sufficiently dependent upon it, that it has positive effects on staffing and governance. At some point, voluntary funding that emphasizes accountability and effectiveness can help create a shift within the bureaucratic culture of the agency itself. This is the final and most important meaning of control—using voluntary funding to assist in remaking the internal culture of the organization.[19]

---

19. The best European national aid agencies, those among the Nordic countries, especially, follow these policies without fanfare in the development field, simply as part of what they regard as best practices. US government aid agencies—United States Aid for International Development (USAID)—could learn from them in this regard.

This kind of buyout requires much more than money; one perhaps needs to take a lesson from the world of private equity and venture capital. It requires slow, patient, understated, internally oriented engagement. It can only work with the agencies furthest removed from the crippling culture of the General Assembly and its fetid, complex, practically tribal division of bureaucratic resources—those agencies that are responsive to cultural signals arising from voluntary outside funding. It is not a long list of UN organs and agencies that fit this profile, and there are many, many opportunities to go wrong on the long march to value.[20]

There are other dangers, too. While the United States attempts a buyout of these agencies, the agencies' internal cultures will militate towards a sort of reverse buyout: the capture of US resources without supporting US missions or goals. What is more, in seeking to contain other parts of the United Nations through budgetary contributions, the United States needs to be aware that it and the developed-world democracies are not the only states with resources should they choose to use them. Indeed, members of Congress who think that cutting off UN funding is cost free need to understand that the United States is not the only source of funds, just a relatively reliable one. The United

---

20. Moreover, it would be a profound mistake to imagine that the obstacles lie wholly (or even mostly) on the UN agency side of things. US efforts in these matters display attention deficit disorder for bureaucracies. It is not news that many US aid programs often have little follow-through and little of the institutional patience that is required, over years and years, to remake agencies through the attractions of voluntary funding. The US State Department, USAID, and all the other involved US government agencies are their own complex ecosystem of tribes, clans, and kinship groups—not infrequently mired in deep bureaucratic struggles with one another.

States needs to be careful that it does not so constrain—or cut off—the resources it offers that other states, ones hostile to the United States and its interests, step up and capture the funding process instead. The "resource authoritarians," for example, or the rich countries of the Islamic conference, are capable of putting up large resources.

How big an impediment this threat of counterfunding, a hostile counteroffer, is in any individual case can be hard to assess in practice. And such strategies link closely to an understanding of the United Nations increasingly as a brand that licenses itself to agencies with money. All that said, US policy should be to let engagement vary by function and part of the United Nations, with the deepest form of engagement being a buyout of parts and functions of the United Nations, using voluntary funding as a means of influencing attitudes and culture within UN agencies.

With respect to the secretary-general and the UN senior leadership, the watchword is, always engage, albeit in highly particularized fashion, issue by issue. But engagement also means both supporting the secretary-general on issues of strengthening the executive and management functions of the office—while being willing to lobby, pressure, complain, and threaten in order to keep up pressure so that fiscal accountability means something. As for other UN agencies, the answer is, sometimes engage, sometimes engage with lots of money, sometimes contain, and sometimes—but very rarely—put America's dues-capital on strike. Finally, as touching the General Assembly, the word is containment and nothing more, in money, dues and, really, every other way.

6 PARALLEL ENGAGEMENT:
International Development and Global Human Welfare

Certain institutions of the United Nations—the Security Council most notably—are ones with which the United States should always engage. Certain institutions of the United Nations—the UN-of-parts—are ones with which the United States should selectively engage, buying out the effective parts and starving the bad of funds. And there are times when the appropriate strategy is something we might call "parallel engagement," that is, unilateral United States activity alongside the United Nations' efforts, on the same theme, but done by the United States on its own terms and in its own way.

When the United States engages with the United Nations or its parts, we ordinarily conceive of that engagement as reflecting a common policy or a working together toward some common end or contributing resources to it so that the United Nations can do it on all our behalf. This conception of engagement contains an important ambiguity, however, that goes to the heart of the expectations that the United States and the United Nations have of each other.

The United Nations typically imagines the best arrangement for engagement as one in which the United States simply hands over resources to the United Nations or offers to
do things involving the expenditure of resources in ways
that the United Nations chooses and even directs. The
United Nations might conceivably have good reasons for
expending resources in this way, though it is not very often
in the development arena and usually corresponds to a limited range of activities of its organs, such as vaccination programs or food aid. It thinks it can do the best job with the
funds, for example—a belief that the United Nations has
the best comparative advantage in choosing, managing, and
directing. Or UN officials might believe that the particular
common policy or goal can only be achieved by pooling,
under common UN direction, resources together—akin to
the need of businesses to raise large pools of capital for large
projects. This might partly reflect a belief that the particular goal requires a large amount of coordinated, commonly
invested resources being pooled together in order to achieve
a large-scale end, such as building a gigantic dam or some
similar capital-intensive project. But it must also involve a
further belief about who is best able to control and manage that project and hence should be the locus for pooling
the funds. The non-self-interested argument for the United
Nations is conceivable and true under particular circumstances, but beyond that requires heroic assumptions about
the United Nations' abilities. Unsurprisingly, the United
Nations and its agencies nonetheless tend to believe that
they are the best location for funds and their administration
in development.

Just as unsurprisingly, donor countries have mixed feelings about that. The United Nations' chief donor countries—and not just the United States—all things being equal, prefer to retain control over their own assets, even when they share a common goal and even when they are willing to cooperate toward a common goal. Many of them, including the United States, do put considerable sums directly into UN coffers. At the same time, they both face pressure from the United Nations to put in more and yet have a strong sense that possibly the best thing they could do with the money is to do the activity themselves (or pay some NGO to do it). The United States feels that tug especially keenly and is typically more willing to say so than more circumspect donor countries, but it is far from alone in its ambivalence. Put another way, yet another ambiguity in the meaning of "engagement" with multilateral institutions is whether it means engaging through the United Nations or engaging in the same kind of activity, toward roughly the same end, but doing it oneself and not ceding either operational control or resources for the activity to the United Nations.

This ambiguity in the meaning of engagement toward common ends and policies matters a great deal as we turn to questions of global human welfare—matters of international economic growth and development, the environment and climate change, health and pandemic disease, natural disaster relief, and other aspects of human development and well-being. The problem for the United States is to ask itself pragmatically whether, even if it *shares* the policy goal, it best serves that goal by acting according to a UN plan—or whether in some circumstances it would serve that goal better by acting in *parallel* with the United Nations.[1] In nothing is this question so important as in global human welfare and international development. This is to ask basic questions of efficiency toward a broadly shared goal—where there is little reason to think that the United Nations will do it effectively or well, and where, in any case, there is serious disagreement as to how the overall problem should be approached in the first place.

Look, we are good people and we want our governments to help relieve global poverty—and we still want that, even in these difficult economic times. We want UN agencies to do their part. We want to pool our rich-world contributions to Christian Children's Aid and Oxfam and know that they help girls in Africa to get schooling or help to staff AIDS clinics or to provide bed nets against malaria. We want—some skepticism here, granted—to contribute to Bono's causes to make sure the attention of the rich world remains focused upon the world's poorest poor. It would also be nice if someone—not us—would speak out against stoning women, too, but that might raise sensitive religious questions, so although (or maybe because) no one could question that we're against it . . . let's not. But hooray for Kiva!

Unfortunately, there remains a central, unavoidable, harsh truth at the core of international development, development aid and assistance, and economic growth. Whether we call them the poorest of the global poor, the bottom billion,

---

1. The concept of "parallel" here is not quite the same as that offered in the discussion of parallel security systems in chapter 3. In the case of international development and global human welfare under discussion in this chapter, "parallel" refers to sharing a goal but being willing to engage in parallel activities to get there.

the bottom fifth, or anything else, they have a specific rela-tionship to the global economy and to globalization: they are superfluous to it. They lack the skills to take part in the global economy even at the bottom. They are too poor, too unskilled—even to exploit.

The economically superfluous poor contrast with what we might call the global reserve army of labor or perhaps the world's working poor: the billions across China and else-where who toil in manufacturing for the rest of the world. They labor for low wages in textiles or fish farming or maqui-ladoras, assembling electronics or mining. It is their rise into the ranks of the global money economy that accounts for the remarkable fall in overall global poverty. Programs of inter-national development cannot be credited with that transfor-mation. Gains for the reserve army of global labor, rather, come from trade and investment. China's economy, India's, and those of other places in Asia or that of Brazil point the way. Although critiques of this standard model of trade, export, and foreign investment abound, the United States and, indeed, parts of the United Nations itself have embraced it. But that model is fundamentally about the global work-ing poor—those already connected, or gradually being con-nected, to the global economy—through, in seemingly every case, the mediation of a *national* government that, whatever its other problems, has figured out that economic growth is a necessary condition for legitimacy among the very poor but that sovereignty is also a means for leveraging growth.

But what, then, about that bottom fifth, the ones super-fluous to globalization? How should the United Nations, or anyone else, address development for them? And how should US policy interact with the United Nations on the question?

In principle, the task of international development should be to draw the poorest of the poor up into some niche of the global market economy. In that sense, there is no sharp divide between the poorest poor and the working poor of the world. In practical terms, however, there are great differences, and those differences pose an important and fundamental question: Does development as an activity exist in order simply to minister to the immediate needs, or even the long-run needs, of a group of poor who will perhaps never join the world economy as producers? In that case, international development is fundamentally about global income transfer and efficient provision of social services. Note that this view of international development—transferring income to the poorest poor and providing social services—is comfortable to many developed-world social planners, since it is simply the Western welfare state writ grander. At the same time, there is not enough money in the world to do this, even over the short term, so it is something of a nonstarter. It is also something of a no-no to declare as a policy; hence some people who in fact think that income transfer is, or should be, the policy say something else.

The alternative vision of international development, by contrast, imagines gradually ratcheting up the productive power of the world's poorest people, so that over time, they or their children, or someone's children can eventually join the global economy. What the alternative vision of development as development, not merely income transfer (and, to be clear, development, not income transfer as such, is the standard model), leaves unanswered is the role of the sovereign state. The success stories have all been mediated by a sovereign state that has figured out sufficiently that leveraging economic growth has to take priority over extracting whatever already exists through economic rents or, worse, eating society's seed corn.

The failures in every case have featured the failure of state institutions and governance, whatever else went right or wrong; every international development program, activity, or intervention has to decide, explicitly or implicitly, what role it assigns institutions of the state. In the case of the largest programs, the ones with the most money, biggest-scale impact, or widest diffusion within a society, those establishing the program have to take a position on whether and how to incorporate the state into the process; on whether to seek to influence the state by improving its governance so to improve the institutions that indirectly condition economic growth and investment; and on how to address the state in the areas in which the state insists on maintaining a role. This is the question at the heart of debates of "official development assistance" given directly from government or international agency to governments. It is likewise the question at the heart of heated arguments over whether it is worth investing in capital improvements that will not be maintained because the government lacks the governance capacity to do so. And it is likewise the question at the heart of policy standoffs between the United States and the United Nations over whether aid should flow to governments that respond to incentives to improve governance or instead should flow to the places with the most need—in large part, *because* their governance is so bad.

It is not simply a matter of public relations that the goal of international development is offered as human development to empower the world's poorest to improve their economic status by improving their opportunities and ability both to produce and consume. Improvement in their condition can be helped by resources from the developed world, of course, but real, long-term, permanent income gains for these people, gains that translate to human development improvements, can only come as they are gradually able to join larger economic life, to take advantage of globalization so as to leverage their initially modest endowments. This is the insight, for example, of the microfinance movement globally.

The trouble is that although we have a pretty good idea of how a working-poor society can move up the wealth curve, we have very little idea of how to get to that starting point.

How, in other words, does one get a society to the point that it is a matter of the working poor rather than those left out altogether? While those on the bottom share the condition of extreme poverty, their circumstances beyond that are heterogeneous. In many of the worst cases, they suffer from civil war and the traumas of post–civil war—conflict, now or in the past, is the clearest indicator of deep trouble.[2] In other instances, they suffer from failed or failing states. In still others, the problems are endemic failures of governance and political institutions that make private capital flows difficult to sustain—at least those capital flows that produce jobs and wealth and, eventually, inflows of reasonable taxes into the coffers of reasonably honest governments. Places where AIDS is widespread pose other problems; likewise malaria and other diseases. Whatever the particular etiology, it is overwhelmingly unlikely that the world's poorest societies could find ways out of these daunting problems on

2. Provision of fundamental welfare services needs distinguishing from the provision of humanitarian services as relief aid in cases of war, postwar, and natural disaster. War, postconflict aid, and natural disaster each pose very different questions about assistance.

their own. They cannot get onto the virtuous cycle of upward investment, either public or private.

Despite the common development goal of getting these societies onto the ladder, there exists no agreement on what the role of international development aid should be, or anyway how it should be done. This might seem surprising, since the total flows of global resources over the past few decades to international development have been stunning, amounts in the trillions of dollars. Those trillions have been spent in one failed paradigm after another, and there is very little reason to think that it has done much of anything in the sense of long-term, economically sustainable improvements for the world's poorest people. Global poverty has been substantially reduced—there has been a shift in people from the poorest of the poor to the global working poor—but that success cannot be attributed to global aid programs. It has everything to do instead with the successes of particular societies in clawing their way up into the global economy. Development assistance has had very little to do with the successes of China or South Korea.

I do not mean to argue here for abandoning development programs. To the contrary, the poorest societies and poorest people are not going to find a way out of the cul-de-sac by themselves, so development matters, even if it has failed depressingly over past decades.[3] It is also the

3. Although we should not discount in the least the chastened experience of economist Abhijit Banerjee: "It is not clear to us that the best way to get growth is to do growth policy of any form. Perhaps making growth happen is ultimately beyond our control." "Big Answers for Big Questions: The Presumption of Growth Policy," in Jessica Cohen and William Easterly, eds., *What Works in Development: Thinking Big and Thinking Small* (Washington, DC: Brookings Institution Press, 2009), 207. Maybe development does *not* matter.

case that certain important successes have been had at the
global level—for example, in public health, related to certain infectious diseases; we should not see only the persistence of malaria and HIV. Yet the failures indicate that the
fundamental intellectual bases of development matter, too,
because the deployment of millions and billions of dollars
will depend upon them. Reduced to caricature, we have been
offered two competing paradigms for development over the
course of the last fifteen years. The first, the one associated
with Columbia University's Jeffrey Sachs, forms the basis
of the United Nations' still-current, if somewhat tattered,
development strategy, the Millennium Development Goals
(MDGs).

The key feature of the Sachs-MDG approach is that it
proposed to spend enormous sums of money in a relatively
short number of years—under Sachs's plans, starting from
$65 billion in 2002 and rising to between $135 billion to
$195 billion annually by 2015. In a period of paradoxically
straitened national budgets and yet, on account of bailouts
and stimulus, of a defining-down of what billions and trillions of dollars mean, $200 billion annually might not sound
like much; a fraction of what governments have tossed around
since 2008. But it is enormous on its own terms and as a
question of spending at the microlevel in development—the
township, village, urban slum—given the structural difficulties in absorbing such funding efficiently. The second key feature of the Sachs plan, as expressed in the MDGs, was that
spending money should be under the direction, if not actually flow through the accounts, of the United Nations. The
United Nations would provide not just coordination among
donors but be able to take information from the local scene

and evaluate it so as to be able to direct global funding in the tens and hundreds of billions of dollars.

The competing paradigm, associated with New York University's William Easterly, begins with a skeptical observation about the repeated failures of well-intentioned aid programs. But rather than counsel despair, Easterly instead counsels a long-term approach that assumes that aid is usable only at the "retail" level and must be dripped into individual, heterogeneous, dispersed projects—rather than seeking, as the Sachs plan seems to do, to alter the fundamental terms of life among the poor by spending vast amounts of money in a short time.[4] Where Sachs seeks to flood the arteries of the system at the large-diameter aid pipes, Easterly says that such resources cannot work their way through to the tiny capillaries in which very poor people actually work and live. So much money so quickly will inevitably swamp the existing systems, get diverted into many bad things, and thereby create their own bad incentives and distort prices and incentives at the local level, he argues. Moreover, Easterly warns,

4. Easterly set out his critique of the development aid most sharply in *The White Man's Burden: Why the West's Efforts to Aid the Rest Have Done So Much Ill and So Little Good* (New York: Penguin, 2006). Easterly, formerly with the World Bank, is especially critical of what he regards as the messianism of top-down solutions for global poverty and, of course, he has Sachs particularly in mind. Easterly characterizes those advocating such top-down approaches as "Planners" and contrasts them with what he calls "Searchers"—those seeking bottom-up solutions to particular and discrete problems. He notes the failures that have always attended large-scale (for whole countries or even many countries, for example, rather than particular locales), top-down, centrally planned, capital-intensive development efforts across the whole history of international development since 1945. His positive program endorses local, discrete and particular, small-scale efforts to deal with issues and problems on a piecemeal and opportunistic basis.

it is not possible for this activity to be directed from the top down.[5]

Does the disagreement matter? The United Nations' Sachs-drafted plan called upon the world to double-down the bet on official development aid run through UN agencies. Not surprisingly, UN agencies, the ones that would handle this global stimulus, agree. That is the essence of the Millennium Development Goals from the perspective of those who would administer and control the flow of aid. The United Nations enthusiastically signed on—not just to the MDGs as overall development goals but, in addition, to the many detailed targets and subsidiary schedules that Sachs and his UN team elaborated like so many Soviet-era Five Year Plans. The rich countries of Europe likewise enthusiastically joined the call. So did many other countries, rich and poor alike.

In addition to the still-current MDG program, which dates back to 2000, the official international doctrines of UN development rely on a much older funding formula:

5. There are other ways to distinguish the two approaches. Sachs's fast ramping up of vast sums of official development aid annually might be thought to resemble the "big bang" policy for jump-starting capitalism in post-Communist countries that first brought Sachs to public attention. Or it might be thought to be a massive global fiscal stimulus aimed at the poorest societies, aimed at jumping them permanently to a higher equilibrium. It might be conceived in terms very different from Easterly's top-down versus bottom-up critique. One might also see the distinction between Sachs and Easterly as whether one focuses on the arterial system, as Sachs does, in getting enough blood through the system or, instead, one focuses, as Easterly does, on the capillaries and points out that the failures are really at that very local level—and the problems are slightly different and require slightly different solutions, local level solutions in every case. To use another metaphor, Easterly argues that what matters is the last mile—without knowing how to overcome that gap, case by case, none of the rest gets where it needs to go.

the so-called 0.7 percent gross domestic product doctrine. It is not especially visible in current circumstances of cratering rich-world budgets, but its very longevity as an idea is instructive. The distillation of this UN mantra is that developed countries should contribute a minimum of 0.7 percent of their gross domestic product in the form of official development assistance (ODA) to the developing world. The actual percentage derives from a conference in the 1960s and has no formal methodological basis behind it. Why 0.7 percent, rather than 1.0 percent or 0.2 percent or anything else? There is no reason, no serious argument that this is the amount of money that will best promote development without retarding growth in the developed world. Perhaps even more importantly, nobody offers much basis for believing that ODA, rather than mechanisms such as private investment or NGO charitable flows, will best aid developing governments in the first place. Nonetheless, the figure has achieved near cult status as a measure of international goodness and virtue, as it were, and developed-world countries have felt obliged to sign aboard as a matter of reputation, quite irrespective of whether they actually reach such levels of ODA or not. Only a handful, the small Nordic countries, have ever approached it in practice.

More typically, states promise the 0.7 percent figure as a goal or target and then fail to live up it. With respect to the MDGs, Secretary-General Ban has observed on multiple occasions during the past four years that countries have failed to deliver more than a modest fraction of what they promised under the MDGs, and that was even before the current economic crisis. The MDG funding gap today is so large that it is hard at this point to see what remains of the targets and schedules developed by the United Nations Development Programme (UNDP). Nearly a decade after adoption of the MDGs, with so much fanfare and so much diplomatic pressure on holdouts like the United States, they turn out merely to follow the usual pattern of grand and expensive initiatives coming to naught. Indeed, the picture in 2011 looks as though it has shifted with regard to grand development plans at the United Nations, without quite saying so, yet again. The economic crisis of the developed countries has laid low the plans of a decade ago, but even without economic crisis, they would have followed the pattern of promise and defection that was already well underway for the MDGs even by the mid-2000s. As for 0.7 percent—well, it seems downright quaint in today's economic climate, but the likelihood is that it will be revived as a basis for ODA discussions sometime down the road, if only because it is rhetorically too tempting to abandon. The MDGs produced enormous promises and, utterly according to predictive theory, very little delivery. They are dead in the water and will never be revived, even as they continue to be debated. Rich countries have discovered that they are not so rich, and growth rates in the not-so-global recovery have featured the rising powers, China most of all, certainly not Europe.

Even before the global crash of 2008, however, the fashionable developed world had grown tired of poverty. The poor are so intractably poor, and for a nearly endless series of almost village-level reasons, poverty is fixable seemingly at the lowest level and subject to so many confounding contingencies, from civil war to a new virus. The fashionable developed world had decided instead that the "new" new thing would be climate change. Among other things, climate change offered an apparently vastly more orderly world of emitted molecules whose production and sequestration could be managed by a marginalist economist's dream of carbon markets with two tradeable factors, carbon and money. It was all so technocratically tidy—governments regulating gigantic markets consisting of businesses and corporations, who would then pass along the revised terms of production to their customers, and the carbon-reducing results would naturally spread across the world's consumers and their lifestyles. Unlike the entrenched poverty of the bottom 20 percent in all their micro messiness, carbon regulation required far less need to deal quite so directly with very, very poor people in their villages or slums. Governments regulating markets would operate on global consumers as though by invisible hands. That caricature matters, certainly, and is not the only or perhaps even the most important factor in this shift in the priorities of global elites of the developed world, but the shift itself was certainly there over the course of a dozen years.

The UN community, with its nearly infallible antennae for the Next Big International Thing, saw an opportunity and took it enthusiastically. The formerly hidden secretary-general, Ban Ki-moon, embraced the cause and took it as an opportunity to appear in the public eye, preaching something that was not very different from platitudes of world peace. Brilliant environmental economists put their heads together and concluded that, with a little tweaking, a monumental climate change regime could manage to overcome the collective-action problems of both carbon regulation *and* the United Nations that had never been overcome before on either matter—and on a scale that dwarfed pretty much everything else. Notably, few of these environmentalists truly understood the agenda of the United Nations, *as* the United Nations and with the United Nations' special history. As a consequence, they did not seem to have understood how much the United Nations depends on the cycle of stasis-enforced-by-crisis, punctuated equilibrium producing an orgy of rent-seeking and then deliverables dribbling off to—nothing.

The Copenhagen conference on climate change duly took place in 2009, followed by the conference in Cancun, followed by another conference in Durban in 2011. Leave aside the deal from the climate change activists' standpoint; it will be some time, in fact, before the actual diplomatic details are reliably known.[6] Considered merely from a *development* perspective, however, it can already be seen that it was regarded by states at the negotiations as simply the latest historical reason on which to justify massive transfer payments from rich world to poor world. Embodying, however, a distinctive set of distortions related to climate change policy—from the standpoint of development alone, without any special regime for climate change—the "green" policies of developing alternative energy in places lacking electricity, clean water, sanitation, and other services, were clearly distorting and intended to be. Moreover, from a development standpoint, the deal—unclear and at this point dead anyway—seemed to favor, at a minimum, transfers of aid directly to governments. Whether a good idea or bad, or dependent upon particular circumstances, from a development perspec-

6. An important early scholarly account is that given by a highly regarded academic environmental lawyer, Daniel Bodansky in "The Copenhagen Climate Change Conference: A Post-Mortem," *American Journal of International Law* 104, no. 2 (April 2010): 230–40.

tive, the preference for resources to governments, versus other development actors, thereby adopted a strong position on a deeply contested issue in the whole matter of development assistance. The de facto shift of the "global" policy on development aid at the United Nations, away from emphasis on the MDGs to whatever was supposed to come out of Copenhagen through the lens of climate change, was not without highly distorting preferences, in other words, at least as seen from the standpoint of development.

In the meantime, the MDGs march gamely on. No one has said they do not exist or no longer matter or should not command many, many more press conferences. It is just, like so much of the United Nations, they go on marching, but marching in place. They are trapped in a cul-de-sac in which the funding will be minimal, targets will not even be laughably approached, and an aid policy highly dependent on ramping up a vast amount of spending globally in a short period of time through a series of command and control Five Year Plans will not have the resources even to be truly underway on its original benchmarks. The MDGs march along—zombified.

That is the United Nations. The environmentalists at Copenhagen do not seem to have understood that the "unique legitimacy" of the United Nations means that it corrupts whatever sources of authority it touches, uses them up and spits them out. Whatever the exact state of climate science, the marriage of the authority of science and the authority of the United Nations plainly corrupted a non-negligible number of the climate scientists. Not, let us be clear, that it took very much to sway scientists who were offered what appeared to them levers by which to direct global economic policy *and* win Nobel prizes. They were corrupted—but also taken for suckers, from the standpoint of the United Nations' permanent and immutable political interests in what it is supposed to become in tomorrow's dream world. The United Nations said—Ban Ki-moon said—if we do not address global warming, the planet will collapse in a puddle of cosmic ice cream. And perhaps it will—but meanwhile, the institution of the United Nations will move on to some other issue offering new sources of rent-seeking and new hopes for governance authority accreted to the United Nations. If regulation of the global economy through climate change offers that, outstanding; if it peters out, okay, time to find something else. The constant here is not what the environmentalists, assuming theirs was the only permanent agenda, seemed to have believed. Although the climate change issue will march along—for nothing ever truly goes away at the United Nations—the reality is that it is already wearing itself out at the United Nations, even if it has some play yet, because it no longer seems to offer enough possibilities of money or political governance. The United Nations will gradually shift to some new issue in the perennial cycle of punctuated UN equilibrium. What then of the United States and its development policies?

The United States holds to an eclectic development policy. It has a reasonably clear view about how to help the global working poor, which amounts in essence to foreign direct investment and open trade. (On the other hand, when it comes to the most important of those categories, open agricultural trade, it violates nearly all its own principles—as does Europe.) But when it comes to the economically superfluous poor, the United States takes an eclectic view. It funds many different things in fact. The truth is, the rest of the wealthy world is no different, but they talk differently about it. Where many wealthy donor countries show similar eclecticism in how they act in fact—while holding with a straight face at the United Nations to how they are committed to the MDGs and the 0.7 percent target and a standard set of platitudes—the United States is unusual in that it is willing to commit to this eclecticism officially. That might perhaps have changed under the Obama administration, committed as it is to multilateralism for its own sake, arguably even at the expense of the best policy. But so far it has not changed; the administration's focus on domestic issues has overshadowed those concerns, at least as far as big-picture strategy goes. The United States has a strategy on development, of course—but it is called "multilateral engagement" and working with our partners within the constraints of our resources.

It is also quite true that America's wars in Iraq and Afghanistan have sucked up a vast amount of development aid dollars—some of which have been extracted from what might have been other priorities in the poor world and others of which are simply built into counterinsurgency, nation-building war, intrinsic to the military budget. From a strictly development standpoint, however, whatever the security benefits obtain at this moment or while the United States is present in Afghanistan's villages, US development aid investment there will be largely, if not wholly, lost after US ground troops are drawn down. It was predicated upon reasonably stable governance structures; the Taliban will not have quite the same ideas about schools for girls as was originally intended. So long as so much of the US aid community and budget is tied to war-related efforts, however, the constraints on other development priorities, strategies, and concepts elsewhere in the world are significant. Add to that budget pressures from the general economic situation, and it is fair to say that, although Obama officials, or any future administration's development officials for the foreseeable future, must talk bravely about essential priorities in a tough environment (hence the heightened importance of targeted, effective aid), retrenchment is on the table, not creative uses of new resources.

Looking globally over the last several decades, however, rather than strictly to war-related US development aid, the United States has endorsed and acted on policies that appear sometimes Sachs-like and sometimes Easterly-like. On the one hand, it backs large-scale infrastructure projects run as official aid through governments. The United States hands over large sums to global public health programs of obvious value and which have shown technocratic efficiency at the United Nations—for vaccination, for example. The same is true of many other basic public development goods, such as education and health.

Because the United States is willing to go off on its own, however, its behavior raises difficulties as far as the United Nations is concerned. The first is whether and to what extent the United States acknowledges the United Nations as having a quasi-governance role in this broad area. This has a political legitimacy aspect to it, as well as a practical who-controls-the-resources aspect. Hence the intense preoccupation of the United Nations, its various organs and officials, and many other countries invested in UN governance in the development area to press the United States to join and pool its resources in these supposedly common activities. On the one hand, whether UN officials believe their own arguments as fully as their vehemence suggests, they take US independence to be undermining their own efforts and as an affront to UN governance on these matters. On the other hand, despite its eclectic policies, the United States also strongly argues three interrelated propositions:

♦ bottom-up aid models are better than globally top—read UN—down models;

♦ aid models focused on governance structures (for example, corruption) have more important long-term effects on development to create conditions for investment and private business; and

♦ rewarding with more aid the countries that create good governance is a better plan than (in effect) incentivizing poor governance when the worse off get more aid.

The United States has often funded development bilaterally on the basis of these general propositions, and properly so. Again, it acts no differently from other developed-world aid agencies in so doing, except in its refusal to simply simultaneously go along with official views of why the United Nations should set the goals, agendas, and targets. And perhaps it does act differently, at least in its public relations, in its hard-nosed, economics 101 view that governments, like people, are capable of responding to good and bad incentives; this is a departure from the canons of important parts of the so-called aid industry. These heterodoxies cause friction with the United Nations because, as with so many areas of the United Nations' agendas, the issue is never simply "the issue" but always tied up with a larger vision of the United Nations gradually assuming a greater governance role. This was on pointed display in the shifting US position on the MDGs in the 2005 UN reform negotiations.

Joining the negotiations over the final reform language late in the process, the Bush administration's ambassador, John Bolton, adamantly refused to go along with the MDGs and, more importantly, with their implementing targets and schedules. Bolton, for example, refused to put the United States on record at the 2005 summit as agreeing to the 0.7 percent figure. This particularly infuriated other countries, which assumed that the United States had already agreed to this figure, under President Bush no less, at an earlier 2002 summit meeting in Monterrey, Mexico. And, to be sure, the United States had endorsed the MDGs as *goals* in the original 2000 UN summit that proposed them. It had then agreed, in the follow-up Monterrey Consensus—in language noteworthy, once again, for its careful but ultimately unhelpful ambiguity—that wealthy nations would "make concrete efforts towards the target of 0.7 percent gross national product (GNP) as ODA."

According to Bolton, however, the United States had never agreed to the detailed targets and schedules drawn up by UNDP and Sachs's team. Nor, for that matter, did it take the text of the Monterrey Consensus to mean that the United States intended, or had committed itself, actually to ramp up to 0.7 percent ODA. In his UN memoir, Bolton acknowledges that the United States, at the time of the 2005 UN reform negotiations, had indeed supported the MDGs as they were stated in the original 2000 Millennium Summit—that is, as broad goals. Yet Sachs, he writes, had subsequently "created quantitative measures for the goals, which were never accepted by [the] heads of state." Both the original goals and the UNDP's quantitative measures and targets were often referred to as the MDGs, Bolton says, thus giving the impression that the United States and other states had accepted UNDP's targets. In the 2005 "Final Outcome Document," according to Bolton, the MDGs were defined to be "MDGs according to *our* understanding of the term. So defined, we endorsed them."[7] Others present in those negotiations will likely have a different account of the US position. But inevitably, the United States was excoriated, and Bolton bitterly attacked, for failing to follow the global "consensus." Finally, Secretary of State Rice intervened under great pressure from US allies and allowed for a compromise formula that constituted yet another of those artful, but not necessarily useful, ambiguities of the United Nations.

This little story, from the ancient history of 2005, matters mostly because it, or something very like it, will happen again; it is, as much as anything, a story about the risks of buying into consensus as a process. As to the substance, the United States, its aid agencies, and its development professionals do *not* really believe the full global consensus as urged upon the United States in the 2005 negotiations. They did not believe it then, under the Bush administration, and they do not believe it now, under the Obama administration. For that matter, it is doubtful that the "full global consensus" really believes the "full global consensus" either. How many aid professionals really believe the 0.7 percent figure should be defended on its own merits? Some of them might well believe that the United States should greatly increase its

7. Bolton, 210.

overall official aid expenditures, but the actual 0.7 percent figure remains as arbitrary as ever—and sillier than ever, in economic conditions that will define the next several generations.

But the crucial, long-term point is a different one about
process. The United States went as far as it did under the
Bush administration, not because it believed in the integrity of the position but because the Bush administration
concluded that going along in some fashion would be better
because of *other*, unrelated diplomatic goals. As noted in the
discussion of consensus negotiations, the negotiating result
not infrequently is not a lowest-common-denominator outcome but instead a tradeoff of positions on unrelated matters. The tradeoffs at that moment were mostly relations with
allies and ultimately went back to the issue of support for the
Iraq and Afghanistan wars.

Similarly, if the Obama administration goes along with
the global consensus on development, or were to make (at
this point, highly unlikely, because largely irrelevant) concrete positive commitments regarding the MDGs, it would
likewise do so not because it is truly convinced that the (evap-
orating) consensus is right but because it would be trading
off a relatively minor card in relation to other goals: issues of
security, Group of 20 negotiations, or all manner of unrelated things. That is an understandable diplomatic choice. It
might even be the right one given the *whole* picture of US
foreign policy concerns. But, at least as far as international
development and global human welfare goes—the poorest
of the poor—it is not a principled one, no more so under
Obama than Bush.

US government development policy draws something
from the large-scale, top-down approach, especially with

regard to public health issues. It sponsors, for example, global efforts to eradicate polio and malaria, areas in which long-standing international public health protocols have proven to be highly effective. Sub-Saharan Africa was a particular concern of the Bush administration and AIDS policy most of all. Even sharp critics of that administration give it considerable credit for a policy on AIDS that incorporated top-down elements with bottom-up ones, and placed great emphasis on follow-through and execution. It has been a highly successful policy and one that the Obama administration should build upon—or, more precisely, take care not inadvertently to dismantle, just as congressional fiscal hawks should take care not to dismantle it today, either. The United States has supported many other programs that are directly about public infrastructure in the underlying conditions of economic growth—primary and, particularly, girls' education, basic health, and other goods that are typically public in nature.

But many other US government policies have been much closer in spirit to the Easterly bottom-up approach to development. They have focused on the institutional, political, and social conditions necessary to support the private investments that lead to job creation and permanent long-term income gains. Nowhere is this more evident than in the Bush administration's bilateral aid program, the Millennium Challenge Account, created in 2004, for the express purpose of promoting foreign aid to countries that meet certain institutional and governance criteria that would, in the view of the program's designers, both promote long-term gains from aid and incentivize better governance. Regular foreign assistance efforts have the effect, the theory goes, of rewarding bad governance behavior with development aid aimed at alleviating the suffering caused in part by poor governance. The Millennium Challenge Account program, by contrast, sought to reward countries that could be shown to be making progress on a range of governance indicators, including corruption, the rule of law, economic liberty, human rights, and others.

The program has been controversial in some quarters, with many conservative organizations, such as the Heritage Foundation, praising this incentives-based approach, and many liberal voices, such as the *New York Times* editorial page, attacking it. The liberal complaint is that it has not been willing to hand out aid unless the basic criteria are met—with the effect that it does not hand out aid fast enough. As the *New York Times* complained in 2005, the "account has yet to pay out a dime."[8] In a program specifically designed to establish incentives for governments to receive aid through governance improvements, criticism over the failure merely to shovel money out the door fast enough would appear entirely to miss the point. Moreover, the program's premise that economic growth bears some broad connection to such things as the rule of law and human rights is scarcely an unknown thesis in mainstream development economics. Nonetheless, over the last several years, the United States has responded to criticism by relaxing some of the criteria in some instances while still seeking to preserve an incentives-based program.

From the standpoint of overall UN-US relations on the issue of development, therefore, the Millennium Challenge

8. Editorial, "America's Promises," *New York Times*, January 28, 2005, *available at* http://www.nytimes.com/2005/01/28/opinion/28fri1.html.

Account program (run through a special US government vehicle, the Millennium Challenge Corporation) was viewed at its inception with suspicion and dismay at the United Nations and by many other rich countries. For these purposes, it does not much matter whether it is effective or not; it is a symbol of disrespecting the consensus. The suspicion resulted in large part from the fact that the United States, in this question of incentives and governance, went its own way and not the way of the international community as organized by the United Nations, through UNDP and the MDGs. It proceeded bilaterally, according to its own criteria, and using its own money.

Today, the controversies are muted because the developed world is, in a word, broke—expectations of aid budgets have only to go down, for the United States as well as other rich donors. The baseline is now in flux, and the arguments over the best approach to development at this very moment take a backseat to more fundamental questions of how much aid budgets of the wealthy nations will be cut—and whether countries such as China (or, more bluntly, China) will step into the gap. Indications are that China will rebrand some of its mercantilism and investment in raw materials in the developing world, particularly Africa, as "aid." The debate is shifting already to whether and in what ways this constitutes a new and better development model or whether this is simply a form of multinational exploitation from a country to whom apparently no one can say no.

But that leaves the question of United States development policy and its relation to the United Nations. The United States' breaking UN consensus on how to spend money on

development and international aid is supposed by some to
be a problem. But why, exactly? When should the United
States allow the funds dedicated to fighting extreme global
poverty to be dedicated to supposedly consensus activities
or to something else? And when should it allow its funds to
be routed through the United Nations? This is to ask under
what circumstances central planning and control, beyond
coordination, make sense. Three conditions ought to be
met before central planning, control of global development
policy, and material resources might conceivably be justified:

♦ there must be genuine agreement on how best to approach
  the problem at hand;

♦ it must be truly necessary, in order to solve the problem, to
  have all the resources controlled and coordinated together
  in a large, planned operation; and

♦ central planning must be the only way to avoid wasteful duplication and operations working at costly cross-
  purposes.

If we do not have general agreement on what policy should
be, however, then parties pursuing their own methods and
programs are not really working at cross-purposes, at least
so far as can be known. Rather, they are conducting experiments on what works and what does not. Such experiments
are not wasteful until one has answered the underlying question. And we have not yet done that. While there is obviously
a global consensus on the need to address the poverty of the
world's poorest people, there is no agreement in substance as
to what to do, what approaches to take, or how to actually

achieve this goal. Certainly, there is no agreement at the level of operational detail, governance, funding, or deployment of resources that the United States has ever agreed to.

Moreover, to judge by actual state behavior, other states do not agree with the consensus either; they certainly have not offered up aid in pursuit of those year-by-year targets as though they actually believed that they were the obvious way forward. But more importantly, if one leaves aside the usual problems of easy promises and incomplete delivery and actually reads what leaders, experts, researchers, and the development community say, there is no consensus as to means among them, either. While a consensus does emerge, certainly it was never a consensus on the MDGs in their targets and schedules, even when they were still relevant and in vogue. It is, rather, merely a consensus that something must be done.

The UN leadership, from Annan to Ban and beyond, can confuse this consensus with the actual substance of the UN agendas, whether that be 0.7 or the MDGs or anything else, but this is not really how the international community acts. The experts were cautious in committing themselves to the MDGs as the exclusive means of going forward, the thing to which everyone's global ODA resources ought to be largely devoted. The experts hesitated to commit to that proposition for the sensible reason that no one really knew if it would work as planned. Nothing else ever has, after all. In that case, parallel activities are not only justified, whether by the United States or others, but efficient because they allow evidence to gather as to which of competing approaches works best and in what particular ground-level conditions.

This is, in any case, what the national aid agencies of leading donor states tend to do anyway, in practical terms—they might commit more to the UN programs than the US does but less than one might imagine, believing correctly that they are better able to judge and monitor efficient uses of their aid money. The US is much less an outlier in practice than the public debate during the last decade might lead one to think.

The United Nations, however, has every self-interested reason to contend that resources should flow to it. It is thus hard to take its substantive judgments too seriously. And leaders of states who have so earnestly signed on in speeches and statements to the United Nations' programs do not reveal any special knowledge of what programs propose to do; their national aid agencies are much more nuanced in their dealings with UN programs than the sweeping press conference statements of leaders at summits would suggest. The 2005 Group of 8 summit at Gleneagles, where Tony Blair and confreres proposed to "make poverty history" seems like another era, utterly remote from our world of 2011. Commitment is presumably sincere even today, but it remains a commitment to the idea of *doing something* and, perhaps further but more weakly, the idea that this is the plan we have, so we should commit to it.

And frankly, between the global financial meltdown and the nanosecond attention span of the fashionistas of the international community, global poverty is not just "yesterday"—*yesterday* was climate change, even if no one quite knows what today's cause will be. Global poverty is the day before yesterday. As this is written, the MDGs are being shoved down the memory hole by the collective bureaucratic consciousness.

Not by a wicked and indifferent US government but by the United Nations itself, as it probes and scratches for its next adventure in rent-seeking. Read the collective mind of the United Nations, restlessly searching for the next It-Girl of global policy. Its message about global poverty is just this, an exquisitely mixed sense of hope and dread: "China's rich and it's undemocratic and *it* knows what to do with poor people."

7 DISENGAGE AND OBSTRUCT:
The UN-of-Values and the Human Rights Council

Presidential administrations are always tugged by idealism and interest in foreign affairs because, well, that's America. Sometimes the idealism is more globalist and sometimes it is more sovereigntist, and likewise the varieties of interests—there are liberal and conservative varieties of each. The Obama administration, at least to outsiders, has seemed more polarized than most, between a particularly florid liberal internationalism, on the one hand, and a New Liberal Realism, on the other, that is particularly fervid because, in part, it sees itself as reacting to that *other* idealism in American foreign policy, the neoconservativism that predominated in the first Bush administration.

On the one hand, therefore, there is a profound idealist belief that the United Nations has ways to sift out cooperation from competition among states, through the universal solvent of international law and institutions and that the collective-action problems inherent in multilateralism can be solved. Idealism can overcome interest, or even idealism *is* interest—and it can overcome in a very particular fashion, by getting people to sign documents and assent to words on paper. On the other hand, there is realism pushing in the opposite direction. It does not really matter what pieces of multilateral paper are produced, or what documents or treaties a state signs, or even whether it does or not, because interests will win the day and a state can, if it wants, almost always refuse to do something that it committed to do merely on paper. Save in the very special area of trade—largely outside the United Nations' remit in any case—there is no enforcement.

This is a very peculiar realism, however, because it counsels two opposing things. Don't believe the words on paper, yours or anyone else's. But should this make one chary or sanguine about signing things? The Obama administration has seemed to be of the view that we should be of good cheer, downright insouciant about agreeing to things on paper, because pieces of paper do not really matter, except as reflecting or as not reflecting one's current interests. One might as well sign anything one likes, this realism urges, because it does not make any difference down the road. So the idealist and the realist come to share their contentment in signing multilateral documents—in one case out of hope for their effectiveness, and in the other case out of indifference to the same.

This caricature helps show how apparently incompatible extremes can come to the same strategic conclusion. And both the caricature and the strategic convergence help convey the role of "values"—words, after all—in shaping the US relationship to the United Nations. Social relations at the United Nations—meaning here the general background assumptions of discussion among states, missions, bureaucrats, diplomats, and other actors—have a strong if quiet impact in shaping the terms of argument and negotiation and the composition of political agendas. Words on paper matter, in part, because of hard calculations of serial political reputation and trust. They matter as much or more because they are the currency of diplomacy and international organizations and law that shape the agendas for what is to be discussed. Will it be climate change or Iran or North Korea or African poverty or the UN mission in the Congo or nonproliferation? Reality does intrude to reshape the terms of discussion, certainly, but rarely completely—the beginning point of discussion, which typically begins with assumptions about certain values and relationships, retain an influence even as realpolitik conditions the conversation. The values that establish the terms of thinking around an issue are often enormously influential and not infrequently decisive in setting boundaries of acceptable thought within the political society that constitutes the United Nations and its international community. Framing matters. This occurred in the run-up to the 2005 UN reform summit, and it occurred with respect to the Copenhagen climate change conference as well. It will happen in successive issues down the road as they are brought to the multilateral hothouse of the United Nations. Values at the United Nations matter, and they matter particularly to the United States as a player that acts explicitly from both interests and ideals.

Unfortunately for the United States, values at the United Nations all too frequently run contrary to US values, not to mention US interests. This is so in ways that are frankly unreformable and likely to grow in frequency over time, particularly if the United States continues its current course of decline under cover of multilateralism. Engagement in values exercises at the United Nations is often a profound and eminently *foreseeable* mistake for the United States. The best policy heuristic for the United States in most of the values debates at the United Nations, therefore, is generally to abstain from getting involved and quite often to obstruct the effort. Let's not bury the lede: many of the things said in this book with respect to US-UN relations, to this point, are unlikely to be disputed by the Obama administration— "We're doing that, just with slightly less neoconservative language, thanks"—and so trivialized in various ways—"Yawn, you're imagining a strawman controversy."

But where the rubber meets the road for what the Obama administration has been desperate to do *differently* from the preceding administration is found here, in the realm of UN values—human rights, moral standards and ideals of behavior at the United Nations. It has been eager to engage in all the venues and conversations that the Bush administration stepped away from. It has been aggressive about wanting to show itself and show the face of America in forums of dubious legitimacy, starting with the Human Rights Council and, until forced out by domestic politics, Durban II. This is leaving aside forums of much harder realism, such as the Security Council, in which it has also indulged idealistic symbolism— a nuclear-free world—while offering the United States, its friends and allies and even merely enemies-of-my-enemy, no answer to an Iranian nuke. Whereas values statements and symbols are seen as down payments on future exercises of political will, the consequences of these signals emerge in many unanticipated ways.

There are two profound relationships that arise from the treatment of values in multilateral forums. The first is that the rest of the multilateral world—lacking good proxies of long-term political willpower—will anticipate at least some significant future behaviors on the basis of today's values assertions, and, if they are weak multilateral bromides that signal an inward focus and indifference to hegemonic leadership, that will be noted. Values matter to that signal. The second is that the values that matter not only to the United States, but also to other democratic sovereigns committed to human rights (in some broad-church sense, regardless of disputes among themselves and with the United States over the values' meaning and definition) shelter under the umbrella of US hegemony. This offends the pride of universalism—but, paradoxically, "universal" values, at least of the kind that the United States and its kindred idealists treasure, are possible only because of a rough-and-ready shell of American hegemony, not power alone, precisely, but hegemony of a kind that mingles power with a roughly shared set of ideals.

If, by contrast, one yearns for American decline and the rise of a new, post-American-hegemony world of cooperative great powers in peace and harmony, think again—the human rights universalism of the last twenty years has been an epiphenomenon of American hegemony. If this fades, the human rights universalists fade with it. A multipolar world is competitive and more aggressively Westphalian, not less. Countries whose general engagement with both the universalist project and American hegemony was not before in question are already making other plans. That Brazil would be in commercial discussions with Iran is not surprising; the overtly political tone of its current discussions is.

But the Obama administration thinks it manages to avoid the horns of these apparent dilemmas by adopting the double-take sketched above. Its liberal internationalists believe that the United States, and the world, can have the multilateralism—not only without these consequences but with many, many positive returns. Its New Liberal Realists presumably do not believe that for a moment—they believe the far more realistic proposition that multilateralism *is* strategic withdrawal by another name and that this is the Kissingerian good. The New Liberal Realists instead believe in insouciance, that it does not finally matter what one sets one's name to in the process because one can always walk away.

They cannot both be right; the reasoning is mutually exclusive. Yet they have reached the same strategic conclusion—entering forums and conversations about fundamental values is gain, not loss. Which will it be? The answer matters if the piece of paper under discussion concerns, for example, fundamental rights of free speech and expression or other matters of domestic constitutional importance. As Eric Posner has noted, one reason why the "transnationalist" legal position is able to maintain such a prominent place as against resurgent liberal realism is that it is not fundamentally about relations in and with the world—it is primarily a legal tool for seeking to alter legal debates *within* the United States, to bring supposed international law and obligations to bear on domestic legal issues and upon domestic democratic processes. In that case, perhaps the contradiction between the liberal internationalists and the New Liberal Realists is not so pronounced—they seek to affect different spheres, divided between domestic and foreign policy.

In any case, the Obama administration seems to believe its single strategic answer on largely inconsistent grounds clever. But it is too clever by half. The reason why the United States should not engage with forums that, on their own terms, propose to negotiate fundamental values in the name of universal human rights is simple: many of the values that the United Nations and its forums might propose to negotiate are not negotiable for the United States. Much of the argument over such venues as the Human Rights Council are that simple. It matters that the Human Rights Council is a corrupt forum, populated by many of the worst abusers, dominated by them and their agendas, and that the United States should not grant it legitimacy. But even if the HRC consisted of the purest of states, many of the matters that might be taken up there are not actually in the power of the United States government to negotiate because they belong to the people of the United States through their Constitution—to them and them alone.

Granted, it is not always true that international negotiations involve deep human-values issues and therefore are beyond negotiation by the United States because of its own constitutional processes. Sometimes these are very important matters. For example, the United States should get involved directly in negotiations over human trafficking, which, after all, does implicate deep values. But such cases are the exceptions. The United States should be deeply wary of any presumption of engagement that would have it involved in negotiating, for example, over free expression—a very live subject in UN forums these days. No simple rule can distinguish the negotiable from the nonnegotiable in every circumstance in advance. But if an issue goes to a core value of the United States in ways that run to its internal democratic behaviors so as to propose that its internal processes might be overturned by outsiders—including but certainly not limited to its constitutional matters—then it is a clear mistake even to join discussions, even less so, obviously, when discussions are with those that dominate the Human Rights Council.

This does not mean keeping silent. To the contrary, the United States should articulate and seek to press, as policy and action, its values in many different venues, outside of the institutional United Nations or in those forums of the United Nations in which negotiation of those values is not the game. But it should take care about joining values processes that are about negotiation—and virtually never those that effectively propose to negotiate core "American" values by recasting them as "global" values. By recasting them as "universal" and "global," the ironic effect is to put things that Americans thought beyond negotiation up for negotiation with the rest of the world, worse still in a rolling-text, consensus-based negotiation. As a general rule of thumb, the United States should never engage with any of these things.

Unfortunately, the UN processes frame values debates in a manner that tempts the United States to be a player in consensus processes. It also makes the debates at once seem innocuous (because who is not in favor of baby seals or promoting global religious toleration?) and unthreatening (because none of this is truly binding) and appealing to in-built US moralism (because, of course, the United States of America has something important to say about human rights and democracy). It is hard to say no at the front end. This is so if one has committed oneself to a view, as the Obama administration has done, that engagement is a good thing for its own sake.

This is also particularly so for those who believe instinctively that US and UN values significantly or even mostly overlap and can come together in negotiations reflecting good will. They are, alas, quite wrong about this much of the time. The Bush administration had few such idealists; the Obama administration has many, though, under Secretary Clinton, fewer than at the beginning. But engagement here *also* tempts the realists, who see in values negotiations at the United Nations a cheap way of buying off various constituencies, both domestic and international, with little more than talk. None of it is binding, and, compared with the verities of interests, who cares? Curiously, the Bush administration had fewer of these realists than one might have thought. To the contrary, a large part of the Bush administration's refusal to engage and its reputation for obstruction derived from its belief that words actually mattered a lot, and therefore it would hoard them and offer them up accordingly. The Obama administration's promiscuity with words is well known; at some point it will have said everything that anyone would like to hear to everyone, and then what? Irrespective of which administration indulges in this sort of thinking, however, it is dangerous and hubristic.

The United Nations does not lack for values. On the contrary, the United Nations has a long list of values, things that it says are politically, morally, and legally good, or matters of human rights. They are not all obviously or necessarily consistent with one another, and disagreements crop up frequently. Intervention to prevent mass slaughter by a regime is good, but so is the territorial integrity of member states. Children's rights are important, and there is a treaty to prove it, but so are the family laws of shari'a, providing many Muslim states a basis for a treaty reservation to bypass much of the children's rights convention. Over the six decades since promulgation of the Charter in 1945, categories of values have multiplied and reproduced, evolved and mutated, until the UN system positively teems with values and assertions of the many things and propositions for which the United Nations supposedly stands. Many of these values the United States shares—which, the United States should also be clear, does not mean they are matters of "rights." But not a small number the United States does not share and should not endorse. Some the United States should affirmatively oppose. And their number is growing, not shrinking, over time.

Although the universal human rights of individuals as a concept was present at the United Nations' founding, for much of its existence, the real driver of institutional values has been not human rights but international peace. Human rights was present at the birth of the United Nations, not just in the Charter, but also in the Universal Declaration of Human Rights and, later, in the International Covenant on Civil and Political Rights and the International Covenant on Economic, Social, and Cultural Rights, which, taken altogether, are often described as the "international bill of rights." Once the Cold War was underway in earnest by the late 1940s and early '50s, however, world peace was the fundamental ideal for which public opinion in the United States and Western Europe looked to the United Nations. Dreams of a world government and the other apparatus of popular idealism about the United Nations in that period were largely about a peaceful world, one free of nuclear weapons and the threat of nuclear Armageddon. To the extent that human rights was a subject, it was typically a kind of adjunct to the main project of international peace, the rule of law by-product of a peaceful world under a world government.

The other main driver of values at the United Nations, which began bubbling up in the 1950s and then exploded with the wars of national liberation and decolonialization of the 1960s and '70s, was the self-determination of peoples. Although this could be understood as a matter of human rights, it was independently declared as a value in the Charter, a matter of the rights of a *group*, and it harkened back to a conceptually distinct category of thought that dated back at least to Woodrow Wilson's famous Fourteen Points. With the United Nations frozen through the Cold War with respect not only to material interests of the East-West superpowers but with respect to values as well, the Third World groupings at the United Nations—the Nonaligned Movement and subsequently the Group of 77—came to dominate values discussions at the General Assembly and its appendages.

For the new states, the United Nations was a natural place to make their claims, a place to gain legitimacy and recognition, and a forum for making their voices heard as the emergent majority of states. And the United States did not start out as a necessary, natural target for these new movements. Unlike Britain or France, it did not have a long history of overseas imperialism or extensive imperial claims of territory. Indeed, successive US governments generally had been unsympathetic to European imperialism. Yet over time, the

United States, along with Israel, became the target of anti-imperialist and anticolonialist ideology. This continues to the present day.

Human rights as a specific expression of the paramount values of the United Nations goes back to the latter years of the Cold War. Human rights gradually achieved "apex" status over the older universal ideals such as world peace—but only with a certain degree of difficulty. Human rights as a value, in contrast to international peace and security, challenges territorial sovereignty and the assumption that states could not be called to account for conduct within their borders. While human rights values had been immensely useful to the anti-colonial cause, once national liberation had been achieved, the interests and perceptions of the new states and their rulers, often despotic and sometimes genocidal, shifted to favor the perquisites of sovereignty. What is more, it was far from clear that the claims of human rights always assisted the messy compromises of achieving peace. The slogan of the human rights movement, "No Justice, No Peace," represented a quasi-religious, determinedly Kantian absolutism asserted as an empirical thesis for which there was, and is, little evidence.

Nevertheless, over time, human rights gradually took hold not just as *a* value but as *the* primary, apex language of values at the United Nations. The triumph of human rights as values at the institution was largely completed after 1990, in what appeared to many at the time as the permanent victory of liberal democracy in the struggle of political ideals. Many leading democracies incorporated human rights as part of their formal foreign policy apparatus, the United States included. This was the time of dreaming of a New World Order, a time of optimism for the view of history that animated many liberal internationalists: history as the forward movement toward more enlightened forms of governance and eventually establishing governance over the anarchy of sovereign nation-states. An idealized United Nations was understood as the vehicle for these hopes; the contradictions of these visions only gradually emerged.

Human rights discourse allows those who wield it to speak categorically. It offers a language of political mobilization that, in principle, brooks no opposition. After all, in traditional liberal political terms, a right in its purest expression is both a trump and a shield. Considerations of consequences, utility, and power cannot overcome a successful invocation of rights; that is why rights are important in liberalism.

The problem with a successful language of political mobilization, however, is that everyone wants to use it, particularly if, in principle, it admits of no opposition. In addition to embracing the traditional liberal-bourgeois political rights of individuals, however, the core underlying UN documents also embrace cultural, social, and economic rights. Cultural and social rights are group rights that can easily be in profound opposition to an individual's rights—when, say, taking a child away from a parent, for example, to ensure that it is raised in the group culture or religion. Economic rights, for their part, involve aspirations and decisions of economic policy that are not amenable to categorical provision. A state can decide as of today that it will not torture people, and it can, if it wills, be 100 percent effective in its decision. It will have a more difficult time deciding categorically that it will double salaries across the board and end poverty today and give everyone a five-week paid summer vacation and retirement at full pay at age 52.

Nevertheless, the United Nations has seen the growth of rights as a language for everything anyone might think important or want. The United Nations and its organs, its member states and the world of NGOs, speak and write and demand a promiscuous list of categoricals—bewildering in their complexity, unclear in their derivation, and unshakeable in their self-confidence. There are civil and political rights, rights to the self-determination of peoples, economic rights and social rights and community rights, rights against slavery and the trafficking in persons, rights of individuals, rights of groups, women's rights, children's rights, gay rights, rights of the disabled, the indigenous, the immigrants, the refugees, and the migrants; there are rights of combatants and noncombatants in armed conflict, of prisoners and detained persons, rights against torture and inhumane treatment and police brutality and extrajudicial execution and disappearance, rights to food, health, medicine, and education, rights to land, rights to gender, racial, ethnic, and religious equality, rights of civil society to freely organize, rights to peace and international security, rights against genocide and crimes against humanity, rights against international aggression, rights to territorial integrity of states, rights of democracy and exercising the consent of the governed, the rights of traditional societies to their customs even if not so democratic, the right of respect for religion, the right of free expression—and oh so many more.

If everything is a right, then nothing is a right—not really. The rhetoric of rights has become so flexible that it can cover any claimed social good. When you call some good a right, however, what you are really saying is that this thing should jump the queue over other claimed social goods and take priority. That is, after all, the point—to say that these special things cannot, or should not, be denied, *relative to* other social claims. But as political philosopher Michael Walzer presciently remarked in the early 1980s, at the beginning of this process, "The effort to produce a complete account of justice or a defense of equality by multiplying rights soon makes a farce of what it multiplies. To say of whatever we think people ought to have they have a right to have it is not to say very much. Men and women do indeed have rights beyond life and liberty, but these do not follow from our common humanity; they follow from shared conceptions of social goods; they are local and particular in character."[1]

Over the long term, everyone has learned the rhetorical "rights" move, even those representing theocratic despotisms such as Saudi Arabia and Iran. And as the scope of topics has inexorably widened, this language of political motivation has simultaneously weakened. Not every rights claim can be treated as inviolable trump, after all. And in political processes at the United Nations, clashes that might once have been presented as debates over interests suitable for compromise have become matters of rights that cannot be altered. The language of rights, from the vantage point of the United Nations and its member states, is at once mobilizing and immobilizing. It is another feature of the UN-in-stasis.

One way of dealing with the intellectual, and inevitably political, contradictions is simply to decide not to deal with them. One senior human rights NGO leader on whom I pressed this issue some years ago finally responded with some exasperation that it *was* a merely political venture, so I should

---

1. Michael Walzer, *Spheres of Justice: A Defense of Pluralism and Equality* (New York: Basic Books, 1983), xv.

just get used to it. A human right, he said, is not a component of some preexisting list. Rather, it is simply whatever *in retrospect* the human rights community has succeeded in making a right, using the mechanisms of international forums and the language of political mobilization.

The polite way to describe this is as an evolutionary conception of rights. But "serial absolutism" might be a better name. Categorical, absolute, nonnegotiable political positions today—but quite possibly replaced with new, equally categorical, nonnegotiable positions tomorrow. It is far from a complete free-for-all, however, because, as with all political processes, it is skewed to favor some over others. The NRA fares less well among the global bourgeoisie of the United Nations than does Amnesty International.

The United States has a serious interest in preserving the objective, universal, deep but therefore—of necessity—*limited* character of rights. Progress does not consist of multiplying rights. One reason for the American interest is that its own internal political community is founded upon rights, rights in the limited but profound sense, not merely as a strategic and expedient political language. Both for its own place in the world, as well as for the integrity of its own political language, the United States needs to be clear with the world about its own language and conception of rights. And that conception is bourgeois, liberal, and rooted in the pursuit of happiness, yes (and also in Lockean concepts of liberty of property and the ability to alienate it, which is to say, the rights attaching to market relationships among freely consenting individuals). The American conception of rights remains meaningful—because it generates some outcomes but not others and because it is not infinitely flexible and indeterminate. But it will not long remain so, even for the Americans, if successive governments of the United States treat the language of human rights, in its dealings with others, as a merely strategic language.

Moreover, the United States really *does* believe in the concept of universal rights for the world. That does not necessarily mean sending in the Marines or undertaking to liberate Iraq from Saddam. The United States is in the process of learning that culture matters rather more than American foreign policy neoconservatives in the Bush administration thought. In that regard, at this writing, it would not be responsible to try and predict where the Arab Spring revolutions will finally come out—whether liberal or illiberal, it is impossible today to say. But if it is a mistake today to deploy them to support the arguments of this book, similarly, it is too early to deploy them to refute its arguments, too. But in any case, the United States has a moral duty to itself and others to ensure at a bare minimum that the language of Enlightenment human rights at least be preserved for others in the world, as a category of meaning, to use on their own behalf. The United States cannot do this by adopting a get-along-go-along attitude toward the proliferating assertions of rights made in world bodies.

This is an exceedingly unfashionable view of both rights and the role of the United States, not just outside the United States but, let us acknowledge, inside the Obama administration, too—whether among its liberal internationalists or its New Liberal Realists. It conjures up an intellectual world long past and understandings of rights that were arguably out of date even at the time of Eleanor Roosevelt. But the content of rights at the United Nations is changing again—changing from the strategic language of liberalism into a strategic language profoundly and dismayingly different, an illiberal language of, among other things, global religious communalism. Strategically inclined, postmodern progressives, for whom the language of human rights was long currency for them alone to spend, inflate, and deflate, are likely to find that the language of rights has somehow transformed itself into an illiberal language, one whose ends they do not finally share. Why? Because they wasted and despoiled it when it was theirs. Rights only mean anything when they are deep and narrow.

These understandings condition what the United States should aim to achieve in choosing to participate or not in symbolic forums of world political institutions in which the core issues are values and rights. Precisely because these are issues of symbolism, they are the issues on which the pure decision to engage or not to engage matters the most. If the United States merely goes along—whether for cynically realist reasons or for improvidently idealistic ones—it corrupts its own use of the language of liberal rights, and it contributes to depriving others of that language.

Because the United States regards rights—conceived in a deep and, therefore, limited fashion—as universal, it is quite willing to use them as a mechanism for criticizing other countries. This willingness is always qualified by realpolitik and will sometimes exempt friends and allies and sometimes even exempt enemies. There is no question that the United States' use of the language of rights has been conditioned by its calculations of interest. During the late Cold War, Ronald Reagan's UN ambassador, Jeane Kirkpatrick, tried to resolve the discrepancy by arguing that a purely evenhanded human rights standard was highly unlikely to move totalitarian US enemies; it might, however, *undermine* less-than-totalitarian but still brutal and unattractive US friends. It might even move them into even worse human rights conditions of Soviet-style communism.

Kirkpatrick's argument was not really one from realism, as it was often portrayed, but instead an argument from idealism, premised on the virtue of the attainable second best ideal over the unattainable, and finally more damaging *because* unattained, ideal. Mixed arguments from both idealism and realism also sometimes crop up. They include the claim that the maintenance of a general level of global security, including through unattractive but necessary friends, is better than disorder—and quite possibly a necessary condition for achieving human rights gains. Regardless of the form of argument, realpolitik remains unapologetically on the table, and no less so in the Obama administration than in any other. Consider only the current State Department's general unwillingness, for example, directly to criticize China's human rights record.

Yet despite its inconsistency in the willingness to criticize human rights, and with respect to whom, the United States has as its basic attitude that human rights *are* universal and that they *should* be pressed, where politically prudent, upon other countries. Moreover, the US government has long made a sizable commitment to monitoring and producing an account of human rights, country by country, around the world. The State Department's annual human rights reports have had occasional distortions throughout the years, but overall they are understood by the human rights community to be a useful, and reasonably fair, annual account of human rights worldwide.

The United States also accepts that under some circumstances there can even be a right—and perhaps even a narrow
obligation—to intervene by force to stop or prevent massive
human rights abuses. That was its view in Bosnia and later
in Kosovo, and as this is being written, in Libya, too. This is
subject to many realist constraints, but the principle has been
accepted that there exists some right and responsibility to protect populations even from their own governments. Overall,
the view of the United States at least since the 1970s has been
that human rights are an expression of American values—
something the United States ideally, if not always in practice,
ought to carry outward in its dealings with the world.

But "outward to the world" does not necessarily mean "to
international institutions such as the UN" and still less "in
thrall to them." The world is not federal and US sovereignty is justified by its popular liberal democracy, account-
able inwardly to its people. To the contrary, one of the core
features of the US view of human rights is that it ideally—
with whatever realist caveats—ought primarily to condition
bilateral state-to-state relations. Human rights as a practical
policy, the US view contends, has greatest effect not through
grand multilateral institutions but instead in the weight that
the United States can bring to bear in its total relationship
with a given state. As policy, human rights does best when it
consists of geopolitical realism in the form of political pressure brought to bear in the name of universal human rights
idealism—multilateralism through institutions at most provides weakly shared universal values and commitments as a
backdrop for that political pressure.

What is more, the human rights vision the United States
carries outward to the world is bifurcated; it reserves for itself

policymaking latitude, as for other self-governing democratic sovereignties. It takes its own democratic processes seriously even when it shows little patience when "internal" sovereign standards are invoked by human rights abusing nations. This is seen around the world as the United States invoking a double standard—and that perception is not entirely unfair. It is, however, right. The fundamental notion of international law—the sovereign equality of states—is a useful rule in some circumstances but not when it requires lumping together for purposes of "values" the states that have the liberal, democratic rule of law and the ones that do not. In referring to a double standard, I am not talking here just about all the issues of counterterrorism—detention, interrogation, torture and abuse, and rendition—on which the United States is quite willing to invoke its own internal standards and ignore other internationally accepted ones. The issue is not even limited to nonterrorism concerns that important parts of the world see as US human rights abuses—most notably its continued embrace of the death penalty. Potent though those sources of controversy over the US stance may be, alone they would not produce the deep unhappiness that substantial numbers at the United Nations, in Europe, and in the international human rights community have long felt toward the United States on human rights, long predating the war on terror.

The broad issue is that even as the United States presses other countries to abide by many external, international standards of human rights, it also insists on abiding by its own internal standards as generated by its own internal democratic processes. This is not just true of the death penalty and counterterrorism but of many issues—international children's rights, for example, immigration and asylum law, and a great deal else besides. But the United States operates on a double standard only if one believes that international human rights is purely a matter of international law—meaning that the view of what human rights are, how they shall be understood, and how they shall be applied belongs, in the final analysis, to international bodies, institutions, organizations, belongs, in other words, to the United Nations.[2]

The United States has never—including today under the Obama administration—accepted this view of human rights and internal US standards. The US view of itself as a political community, expressed in its constitutional order, says plainly that, so far as rights internal to the United States are concerned, the US Constitution is supreme—and the US willingness to put its standards first is not limited to constitutional matters either. So, yes, insofar as one's legal conception of human rights is that they are binding *as interpreted by bodies outside the United States*, the United States does indeed adopt a double standard. It holds its constitution supreme with respect to its territory and political order,

---

2. The argument made on behalf of the "universal" authority of the UN wrongly conflates "universal" with "international." It assumes that international bodies are impartial and disinterested, because they are not territorially based but does not consider the only too likely possibility that international bodies have interests and partialities of their own—precisely the list of partialities and interests that one would attribute to institutions and people who are not tied to a particular territory. Upon making this observation at a human rights conference some years ago, I was told in somewhat shocked tones that this kind of skepticism would make me a "moral relativist." But in fact it is not an argument from moral relativism. Not all skepticism about rights arises from relativism. One can, for example, be skeptical not about rights as such but about this particular claim of right. Or, as I suggest here, one can accept the notion of objective human rights while being skeptical as to who should be able to definitively and finally interpret and pronounce the content of those rights. It is skepticism not as to the *existence* of rights but as to who shall pronounce them.

and that fact does not stop it from using human rights as a language, strategy, and device for the promotion of what it regards as universal values elsewhere in the world. One can, therefore, understand the anger. The US position sounds like not merely a double standard but a naked assertion of democratic sovereignty over universality to boot.

Yet the criticism is fundamentally mistaken—not the noting of the double standard, which is in some sense real, but in the belief that the double standard arises out of an assertion of sovereignty as such. The real justification of the US position is that when it comes to human rights, the United States, to reiterate, does *not hold to the formal equality of states.* The United Nations does so, and no doubt it must. But the United States, for purposes of the universal content of human rights, does not consider all states as its moral equals. It divides the world into the liberal democracies that have substantive possession of the rule of law and everyone else.

The United States is happy to accord members of the former group the same status of self-rule as it claims for itself. To be sure, not all countries in that position *want* to exercise that function, because they envision the role of international institutions differently from the manner in which the United States conceives it. But the United States affords them that latitude, whether they then choose to delegate it to the United Nations or not. And the overall effect is that, with respect to itself and other functioning liberal democracies, the United States regards the enforcement of international human rights not as a direct function of the United Nations or any other international body—unless such a country chooses to be so governed. And while some functioning liberal democracies choose to do so in varying degrees, the United States does not.

But framing an issue as a matter of rights potentially has subtle consequences for this dynamic. That is, it tends to shift the authorized adjudicator and decision maker concerning those rights. When complex social claims are at issue, the United States looks principally to its own majoritarian democratic processes for decisions. Fundamental decisions about the common good it presumes to be in the remit of the legislature; that presumption can be overcome, but the starting point is popular self-government through legislation. Yet the now-standard move of human rights advocates, to frame all these contradictory and inconsistent issues as matters of international human rights, has implications for *who* is lawfully authorized to decide the issue. Human rights, in political terms, is less about *what* than about *who* has authority finally to settle claims.

International human rights thus becomes a mechanism by which these actors attempt an end run around domestic legislatures—and the things that the US Congress, as well as the individual states, have enacted as law. Advocates engage in an untiring effort to persuade courts inside or outside the United States to enforce international human rights treaties and to use treaty language, interpretations, and standards that come from outside the US domestic system. Very often, this amounts to NGO advocates' seeking a second bite at the apple of controlling political outcomes. They seek to get from international human rights and its forums results they could not get from democratic, law-governed domestic processes. The crucial step is not only to shift the substantive rule from domestic law to international human rights law but also to shift the decision maker from legislature to courts by reframing policy questions as matters of international human rights law.

The attempt to end-run internal democratic processes has been discussed at great length by conservative America writers. John Bolton, for example, described this legal-political move in the late 1990s. Civil society, the glorified term for NGO advocates, he wrote, "seeks to re-argue its preferred issues, by trying to leverage political power from outside of the democratic polities where they have been unsuccessful politically. This 'outside' political power may well, over the long term, leave them in a stronger domestic position than their opponents, who have neither access to nor allies beyond their own countries. In effect, therefore, 'civil society' attempts to renegotiate the basic constitutional issue of democracies—who governs?—to its own advantage."[3]

He is quite correct. When Bolton wrote, the issues contested in this fashion with respect to the United States included (among others) the death penalty, the Kyoto Protocol and climate change, and other environmental issues. The list has only expanded since then, particularly since 9/11 and the Bush administration's war-on-terror policies. But the criticism of the end run does not always come from the right. Jed Rubenfeld—no one's idea of a conservative—frames the issue as a clash of constitutional visions. The European vision of a constitution, he argues, is an expression of "universal, liberal, Enlightenment principles, whose authority is superior to that of all national politics, including democratic politics. This universal authority, residing in a normative domain above politics and nation-states, is what allows constitutional law, interpreted by unelected judges, to countermand all

3. John R. Bolton, "Is There Really 'Law' in International Affairs?," *Transnational Law and Contemporary Problems* 10, no. 1 (Spring 2000): 31.

governmental actions, including laws enacted by democratically elected legislators. From this perspective, it's reasonable
for international organizations and courts to frame constitutions, establish international human rights laws, interpret
these constitutions and laws, and, in general, create a system
of international law to govern nation-states."[4]

American constitutionalism is rooted, by utter contrast,
in popular sovereignty. As Rubenfeld notes, in the American
vision, a constitution ought to be made through a national
political community's "democratic process, because the
business of the constitution is to express *the polity's most
basic legal and political commitments*. These commitments
will include fundamental rights that majorities are not free
to violate, but the countermajoritarian rights are not therefore counterdemocratic. Rather, they are democratic because
they represent the nations's self-given law, enacted through
a democratic constitutional politics."[5] Those with political
agendas unlikely to receive the blessing of democratically
enacted law at the national level have every incentive to seek
the second bite of the apple. But it also bears noting that
they have every incentive as well to confer as much legal
and political legitimacy as possible on the processes and
actors that might vindicate their current claims of human
rights, which is to say, they have great incentive to heap
legitimacy upon the processes and actors of international law
and the institutions of the United Nations. They have great

4. Jed Rubenfeld, "The Two World Orders," *Wilson Quarterly*
(Autumn 2003): 26, *available at* http://www.wilsonquarterly.com/article
.cfm?AID=386.

5. Rubenfeld, 27.

incentives to favor the "international" for its own sake—
even if that might sometimes mean sacrificing the substance
of human rights in favor of "international" processes and
institutions.

In any case, UN institutions assiduously resist doing the
things that ordinarily confer legitimacy within democratic
polities. The General Assembly's main business oscillates
between waste and wickedness. The Copenhagen conference
was exhibit A in what the General Assembly is all about: rent-
seeking from the rich world. Not a few academics and intellectuals at Copenhagen found themselves repenting of their
earlier attachment to the legitimacy of the United Nations
as a body of "all the world"—suddenly thinking that an oli-
garchy of the leading countries needed, instead, to ignore
the sovereign equality of states and just get together and cut
a deal. It likely would have made little difference, for a long
list of reasons related to collective action even among the
oligarchs; and this discussion takes no position on the underlying merits of the scientific case. But the climate change
advocates' surprise would perhaps have been less had they
paid closer attention, long before Copenhagen, to the functioning of the General Assembly and its organs in matters of
values generally and, particularly, in human rights. For the
prototypical pattern is longer-running and more pronounced
in matters of human rights than in anything else.

Why is it, to start with, that the General Assembly has so
long rested in the hands of its worst members—the illiberal,
authoritarian, totalitarian, corrupt, decrepit states? Why is it
that, in 2009, the General Assembly president was an aged
radical expriest from Nicaragua whose revolution had failed
him but who had risen again on the platform of international

organizations? And why is it that its next president hailed from Gaddafi's Libya? The simple answer is that the worst actors on the world stage have the most to gain from command of the levers of the United Nations. The worse a country's behavior, the greater the return on protective investment at the General Assembly and its organs. It functions as a rent-extractor, on the one hand, and a protection racket, on the other. Containment is the watchword for the General Assembly.

This is not to say that the United States should always refuse to engage with the General Assembly as such. Its mandate and work, through the various standing committees and subcommittees, touch nearly everything at the United Nations and many things of importance to the United States. There are many particular bodies, committees, and organs that report to the General Assembly—entities and activities with which US engagement is prudent and principled. In some cases, they are functionally independent of the General Assembly. In other cases—the committee on disarmament, for example—the United States is able in many cases to have, if not quite success, certainly an outsize impact on policy. In such cases, the United States should nearly always engage. Nonetheless, engagement with a body whose principal currency is symbolism requires careful affirmative justification and judgment. The core incentive for the United States is to minimize the role and influence of the General Assembly.

Part of the extended mischief of the General Assembly takes place through the proliferation of UN conferences. The function of these extravagant and fantastically expensive events is to create a Potemkin village for the media, the internet, the world of image that there is a global society that comes together around an urgent policy topic: climate change, racism, or African poverty. It looks a little like a global constitutional convention around the topic, coming to understandings and agreements and statements designed to look very much like law, if not now then down the road. Why these massive UN road shows? Why not simply undertake these discussions, whatever their value, in the regular course of business at the United Nations? The answer is the creation of the illusion for the rest of the world that what is said is a function not of states and their faceless bureaucrats but the product of a "society."

UN conferences deliberately put state parties alongside NGOs, in concurrent and parallel meetings. They seek to convey to the global public the picture of politics based both on states and on a quasi-democratic global populace, represented by the NGOs and all the individual hangers-on. UN conferences seek to mobilize public pressure in the international community to the ends of political awareness and, often, the elaboration of "soft law" through pronouncements, final communiqués, declarations, and all manner of statements that aim to take on the quality of law in some forum.

The United States' position regarding UN conferences and the global circus that accompanies them should be simply to decline to participate—no matter what the issue—and in the course of many such forums, such as the Durban conferences, active opposition. The United States stands to gain very little, if anything, from these media extravaganzas under the best of conditions. And anything that it might gain from engagement on the issue it can achieve in other forums while subjecting itself to much less pressure from what landmines activist and Nobel prizewinner Jody Williams once described as the NGOs united together as "a superpower."[6] The entire hothouse environment of senior government officials, UN senior leadership, NGOs, advocacy intellectuals and academics, and the traveling street theatre ensures that outcomes will be less restrained than desirable. Copenhagen must have convinced at least some global *bien-pensant* thinkers that global conferences are not a good way to pursue serious, lasting policy. It is a losing ground for the United States, and the United States should simply announce that it is not going to participate in *any* of them.

The assumption underlying the UN conferences is either that the planetary elite needs to go on a little retreat, as it were, to consider some abstraction like racism, in order to come back with some presumably shared moral resolve, as though the peoples and nations of the planet were all part of some shared religious communion or that there is some extraordinary crisis—climate change being only the most recent—that requires bypassing the ordinary UN processes in order to get a deal. Either way, it says a great deal about the almost entirely imaginary global society that is presumably governed by the United Nations. It also says a great deal about the utter failure of ordinary processes at the United Nations to deal with anything. The United States should simply announce that it will take whatever money it might have spent on these conferences and spend it instead on AIDS, malaria, and education in Africa, and challenge other countries to do the same. A policy of active disengagement,

6. William Korey, *NGOs and the Universal Declaration of Human Rights* (New York: Palgrave-MacMillan, 2001), p. 27, quoting Jody Williams.

delegitimization, and obstruction would serve US interests far better than has the engagement of both the current and former administrations.

This same policy makes sense as well for that most prominent—and odious—of the various dependencies of the General Assembly dealing with UN values and human rights: the Human Rights Council (HRC).[7] Over the course of several decades, the predecessor to today's council, the Human Rights Commission, gradually became a club of the world's worst human rights abusers: Libya, Cuba, Iran, and Saudi Arabia all gravitated toward the then-Human Rights Commission. It gradually took on two roles—first, exempting its own members from human rights inquiry at the United Nations and, second, denouncing Israel. The time and effort invested by human rights abusers in taking control of the United Nations' supposedly premier human rights body rose in tandem with the increased attention to human rights throughout the 1990s.

By the time of Kofi Annan's 2005 UN reform initiative, everyone save the abusers had concluded that the Human Rights Commission should either be reformed under a new name or simply abolished. The reformers included Annan himself, the self-consciously virtuous nations of Europe, the United States, and the NGOs. This was the considered opinion of the leading editorial pages—the *New York Times* and the *Economist*, for example. As with so many other UN issues,

7. As to the possibility that the HRC, with support from the US, might play a salutary role in reporting on human rights abuses in Libya, or conceivably, Syria, this mistakes a temporary, transient interest of worried Arab States vis-à-vis restive populations, not some newly-discovered commitment to neutral principle.

however, the majority of nations of the world vacillated, saying in speeches that they favored reform but, in the General Assembly, continuing to confirm the same worst-abuser states.

Annan's reform proposals set out new criteria for membership on a smaller Human Rights Council. Crucially, these included mechanisms to avoid, as much as possible, bloc and regional voting; requirements for supermajorities to gain election so as to ensure that the world's real democracies would have a voice; a requirement that each member submit to substantive human rights review; and other mechanisms. Annan's proposals may well have eventually resulted in capture once again by the world's abusers. He sought a procedural means to ensure a certain substantive outcome, after all, and a considerable number of the member states who would have to enforce the result would inevitably seek to undermine those means.

In the event, however, Annan could not secure backing even for reform proposals that he at the outset had regarded as grave compromises. Countries that had no direct interest in supporting the worst human rights abusers lined up in the General Assembly, as ever, behind them to torpedo Annan's already watered-down proposals. The United States, at Bolton's direction, had pressed for even tougher reforms, but those of course went nowhere. Bolton's legion critics blamed him for torpedoing Annan's plan, but then blaming Bolton was the convenient default position on which all UN parties could always agree.

Annan, seeing defeat, then backed off to a new, even weaker compromise position—one that formally abolished the Human Rights Commission and replaced it with today's Human Rights Council. The new plan allowed him to salvage some claim of success. The price of his saving face, however, was giving up virtually any significant procedural or substantive change that might have made a difference to the performance of the HRC going forward. The human rights NGOs offered a disgraceful policy performance of support for the farcical "compromise" that demonstrated mostly their preference for procedural "internationalism" for its own sake over the substance of human rights; the incident at least had the virtue of clarifying Human Rights Watch's otherwise opaque ideology of the relative priority of internationalism and the substance of rights. The United States, at Bolton's insistence, held out for Annan's original position, and when that failed, the United States announced that it would not put itself forward for membership on the new HRC. This was widely denounced as a combination of US whining and bullying— once again, another version of the insistence that even on issues of symbolic participation and fundamental human rights values, the United States must always engage and has only to gain and nothing to lose thereby. This was, and is, specious nonsense.

The results today are every bit as dismal as Bolton predicted, indeed worse. The HRC is again dominated and led by the abusers. Indeed, their dominance never for a moment stopped. It has issued more reports on Israel in a three-year period than on all other 191 member states combined. It has headed off criticism of Sudan over Darfur and over a long list of other gravely serious human rights situations. Its general strategy has been to shift away from attention to individual countries—excepting, of course, Israel—in favor of pursuing thematic issues of human rights and UN values: development, health, the environment as abstract matters of human rights, for example. These issues members can discuss in the abstract without implicating particular states.

The HRC's motley majority of authoritarians, abusers, unfree states, and autocrats would not even consider issues of the abuses relevant to its own members while nonetheless finding time for the member from Sri Lanka to issue a call for the United Kingdom to hold a referendum on the apparently burning issue of its undemocratic monarchy. Within just a few months of the new HRC's beginning its work, even the *New York Times* editorial board concluded with some vehemence that the new body had proven to be worse than no change at all. The *New York Times* editorial view notwithstanding, the HRC is the body to which the Obama administration meekly petitioned, and obtained membership for the United States. It is a move that has been widely applauded by those for whom engagement is its own virtue and its own reward. The US ambassador to the Human Rights Council seems to spend her days defending the council and the houses of playing cards that the US spends its time building there: look, we got a sentence not wholly hostile out of x country, and country y agreed to water down the latest anti-Israel screed by an adjective or two, and so on.[8] A statement mildly in favor of gay rights excites Ambassador Eileen Donahoe, less for its content than for her ability to point at it and say, "The Human Rights Council is not all bad!"[9] Well, all in all, it is.

8. Eileen Donahoe, "Fighting the Good Fight," *New York Times, International Herald Tribune*, September 13, 2010, *available at* http://www.nytimes.com/2010/09/14/opinion/14iht-eddonahoe.html.

9. US Department of State, Briefing on Lesbian, Gay, Bisexual, and Transgender (LGBT) Resolution at UN Human Rights Council, June 17, 2011, *available at* http://www.state.gov/p/io/rm/2011/166470.htm.

The fundamental issue is, and should be, why is the United States even there? and the answer is, it should not be.

Historian of the human rights movement Samuel Moyn— no conservative, certainly—suggests that the Obama administration's approach to human rights is to emphasize that all countries are sinners, and what separates us in such venues as the Human Rights Council is a matter of degree, not kind.[10] This is right, but an approach to human rights that emphasizes that the United States' human rights failings, or, for that matter, Sweden's or Costa Rica's, are not really all that different from those of Syria, Iran, North Korea, and above all China, is not one that takes seriously the idea that countries have to face strong bilateral pressure to change. It is mostly about confessing US sins, in any case, in a misguided and, as ever, doomed-to-failure bid to ingratiate the United States into world opinion by abasing itself. The rest of the world takes signals from this—and they have little to do with human rights and a lot to do with whether the United States intends to play its rough-and-ready role as provider of basic public goods. This is one of the many problems with embracing a view that violation of human rights is a matter of weak sinners, all; the message taken by much of the world is weakness, and not just about human rights.

It is right that the United States state clearly its views about its own human rights compliance; it has done a bad thing for the cause of human rights for actual individuals around the world, however, if it is unable to distinguish between degrees and absolute kinds of violations. In any case, this kind of

10. Samuel Moyn, "Human Rights in History," *Nation*, August 11, 2010, *available at* http://www.thenation.com/article/153993/human-rights-history.

"weak sinner" language lasts only until the United States decides that force might have to be used—and suddenly the language shifts over to moral absolutes. The rest of the world might be forgiven for thinking that the decision to use force comes first, and the moral absolutes come afterward.

There are parts of the United Nations' human rights bureaucracy that are not all bad and to some extent, at least, independent of the member states that make up the membership. Some of the human rights special rapporteurs on particular issues do their jobs faithfully as independent and impartial experts, as do some of the independent commissions of inquiry. It is important for Americans to understand just how vital to various global situations these activities can be—particularly those that deal directly with country situations, such as those in Sudan, Guatemala, Burundi and others. The so-called "thematic" special rapporteurs, who deal not with country-specific situations but broad topics such as education, food, adequate housing, etc., can sometimes be much more problematic, in that they largely set their own agendas in relation to human rights. Sometimes the person appointed as special rapporteur is troubling; unsurprisingly, these have mostly to do with Israel. Princeton professor Richard Falk, for example, a special rapporteur on Israel-Palestine, was appointed despite having publicly expressed questions as to whether the Bush administration might have known about the 2001 attacks ahead of time; more recently he sent around on the Web a cartoon easily seen as anti-Semitic.[11]

11. The US government called for Falk's removal. See United States Mission to the United Nations and Other International Organizations in Geneva, "U.S. Urges UN High Commissioner for Human Rights to Condemn Falk's 'Hateful Speech,'" July 8, 2011, *available at* http://geneva.usmission

The leading controversy over rapporteurs and their missions and reports has concerned South African jurist Richard Goldstone's report on the Gaza war. From the original one-sided nature of the council's mandate to Goldstone's methods for gathering facts and witnesses, the report could scarcely be said to constitute an objective or factually accurate document or to provide adequate legal grounds for its conclusions asserting Israeli war crimes. This did not stop the NGO advocates from whipping up a diverse coalition of HRC member states to ensure that this deeply flawed report was duly reported out, however. Remarkably, Goldstone has seemingly repudiated important parts of his own report; unremarkably, that has had little impact on the use of the report itself.

In some cases, it makes sense for the United States to cooperate—to an extent—with a UN human rights rapporteur. The Obama administration, for example, ought to provide the UN special rapporteur on extrajudicial execution with a robust defense of the legality of the US program of targeted killing in the war on terror, rather than simply stonewalling; starting with the observation it has already made, however, that though the US government will defend its policies, the requests of the special rapporteur exceed its mandate. The United States should make equally clear, however, that it concedes no legal consequences for it or its government officials irrespective of a rapporteur report and that the rapporteur's views of international law merit any special deference. In other cases, such as the UN special rapporteur

---

.gov/2011/07/08/u-s-urges-un-high-commissioner-for-human-rights-to
-condemn-falk's-"hateful-speech".

on human rights and counterterrorism, the special rapporteur received considerable cooperation from the State
Department but, as the US government noted, had obviously
begun from a legal conclusion quite at odds with either the
Bush administration's (or the Obama administration's) view.
The special rapporteur started from the view that there was
an irreducible human rights obligation to try or release all
detainees—an absolutist position that, however popular with
advocacy groups, has no grounding in law as understood by
the United States. There is no point in dealing with rapporteurs or processes that are stacked in advance.

There is no good reason why the United States needs to be
on the Human Rights Council in order to support the limited
amount of good work done by a small number of expert func-
tionaries who function within the United Nations' human
rights agencies.[12] The harm vastly outweighs the benefits. The
United States' ability to create or curtail policy, as a single
member in a sea of bloc voting, is minimal. And the argument that the United States somehow "has to be" a member
of the HRC in order to engage in diplomacy, or more "effectively" engage in diplomacy around human rights issues, is
flatly untrue. The United States can *always* be a diplomatic
player when it wants to be, member or not. That is not a matter of membership but of what political capital it is willing
to expend. Does anyone think that the United States cannot
throw its political weight around if it really wants to do so or
raise costs to countries for doing things at the United Nations

12. This discussion glosses over the technical details of differences between
the Human Rights Council, the Office of the High Commissioner for Human
Rights, and various other agencies of the UN not needed for this discussion.

if it really wants to? The problem is, rather, that the United States does not want to expend the political capital in the real world in order to affect what goes on in the hothouse of the United Nations. And what the United States *cannot* take back, once having joined, is the legitimacy that its presence conveys.

This legitimation will not trouble the liberal internationalist idealist eager to see the United States subsume its sovereignty to the sovereign equality of states and subordinate its democracy to global institutions and law. Such a person will discern a humble America, not a weak one—and a deservedly humbled America, at that. Nor will it trouble the New Liberal Realists, who will see an America that does not stand on symbols and ceremony about human rights moralism in order to show that America knows its newly humble place in the world. This New Liberal Realist America does not worry overmuch about the internal quality of regimes when they are newly wealthy and powerful and when America owes them trillions. The New Liberal Realists get directly to the realist nub of the matter: of course one talks with one's enemies, without messing with pretexts and preconditions, because they are the only ones truly worth talking to. It is a badge of honor, in the realist calculation—an indication of political heroism and courage, not pusillanimity—for the Obama administration *not* to hide behind pretexts of human rights, authoritarianism, totalitarianism, and general wickedness as reasons not to engage.

There are profound downsides to this realist policy, however, whether undertaken at the United Nations or in bilateral relations. One is that, as has been increasingly observed, despots have taken the measure of the American administration and do not fear it. Apparently, they do not understand the difference between a humble and a weak America. They see the American eagerness to always engage, not as a sign of American self-confidence, but as exploitable weakness and as a signal of American desire to withdraw via multilateralism. A second is that, in the necessarily complicated dance between the United States and repressive regimes and their restive populations, the policy of always engage favors the regime. Whatever the precise and appropriate message to a justly rebellious populace such as that in Iran, systematic engagement with the regime disfavors the popular resistance with whom America's values and interests finally lie. Has the United States learned this lesson today in dealing with Syria's Assad and his restive population, who at this writing are being slaughtered by Syrian forces? The Obama administration, to its credit, has stepped away from Assad—better late than never—and American diplomats in that country have bravely continued to travel to the besieged towns. It is too early to know what will come of this; or whether this represents a late-term lesson that always engage with despots is a bad heuristic.

The language of human rights will not go away at the United Nations; the rhetoric of the categorical imperative is too enticing to leave behind. But it will be rivaled over time, perhaps, by new languages of values and by the revival of old ones, perhaps in the categorical language of rights and perhaps not. These alternatives include a resurrection of the ideals of world peace and, particularly, nuclear disarmament. They include climate change and economic development and the proclaimed justice of transfer payments from the rich world to the poor world. The striking feature of these new languages of values, however, is that they seriously curtail any need to point at any country or regime in particular as being bad or evil or wicked (excepting, of course, the United States and Israel). A move toward such nonaccusatory language was precisely what President Obama announced in his UN appearances in September 2009; the new forms of values espoused by the United States at the United Nations would focus on shared concerns and not matters that might require serious judgment of good and evil. Moral judgment was so neoconservative and Bush administration. The United States could not hope to judge until some day it got its own house in order.

The wave of the future appears to be a deemphasizing of pressure by the United States and any other great power for human rights compliance. Europe consists less and less of great powers, or even powers. It is even more turned in upon itself and its aging population than, so far, the United States even proposes to be; even as it talks gamely of global constitutionalism and governance through multilateral institutions, its attention is upon itself, consuming itself and its social capital and its seed corn. The rising powers—China, India, Brazil, and so on—are more keen on appropriating the language of human rights for the legitimacy of their policies of economic growth and poverty reduction internally and less keen on using national power as a source of pressure against other states to honor them. The old system established certain partly universal, partly international mechanisms for determining who should be called out for human rights violations—and then to a very large degree depended upon the willingness of powerful states to make things happen. It has broken down in all sorts of ways, starting with the lessened willingness of great powers to engage in that kind of pressure and the suggestion that bodies like international tribunals can do the job instead—a proposition remarkably sanguine at best.

Moreover, the new values ascendant at the United Nations feed into mechanisms of engagement and multilateralism that conspicuously require little actual commitment apart from the long-shot possibility of massive payoffs to the developing world. The new multilateralism rests remarkably lightly on sovereign shoulders, including above all—it cannot enough be said—the United States. The Obama administration does not seem unhappy with this, far from it; sovereign "owner-ship" of obligations to press for human rights for others in the world is all burden and no benefit, it seems. But the new multilateralism also rests remarkably lightly upon the shoul-ders of the United Nations, which is to say that if and when a true humanitarian or human rights crisis happens—genocide redux—all of it is likely to turn out to have been kabuki. No one will step up, no one will bear responsibility; the hege-mon has retired, and the point of intersection between UN collective security and UN values—responsibility at least to prevent genocide—nonexistent.

Shall we raise Libya as a counterexample? Apart from being too soon prudently to draw conclusions, the most obvi-ous answer is that Britain and France could barely raise the air power necessary to the job, even with massive behind-the-scenes support plus drones from the United States, to avoid a stalemate and finally bring down Gaddafi; it is far from clear that they will ever dare try such a thing again, for fear of outright losing. It will not be long before the capacity to do so might be lost in large swaths of the world. This is presumably why Western humanitarian interventionists are offering strange new respect to the humanitarian virtues of drones. It will be drones, and not much else, that in the future might be the only developed-world armed forces available for undertaking responsibility to protect. It is better to have robots of war than nothing at all. In any case, in a world that is simultaneously more multilateral and multipolar, with more competitive and jostling great powers for whom the United Nations is a place for negotiation, humanitarian intervention is going to face many more hurdles there, in the Security Council, than in the easy days of the 1999 Kosovo war.

Needless to say, this multilateralist power vacuum is not a good thing for the cause of human rights, but neither is it good for the United States. It favors neither its values—obviously—but it also undermines its hard realist interests because of the profound signal to the world that the hegemon is no more. Hegemony is *never* just about power; it is about power that carries a certain legitimacy about certain baseline values and that carries enough others in its train because they trust the combination of its values and its power. To give up that legitimacy—which owes exactly zero to the United Nations—is to give up a vast amount of residual power. It is not the silliness of "smart power" as imagined by the Obama administration early-term theorists—imagining a world of power through multilateral institutions—but instead the residual power of legitimacy that arises when other countries as a matter of sufficiently shared internal values acquiesce and do not actively oppose the hegemon and even provide support both moral and material.

Meanwhile, the "hard" values and mechanisms of human rights are sliding away in favor of soft-focus values that put far fewer demands on anyone whose compliance with them would actually matter. As in the global security field, multilateral engagement over the hardness of human rights is actually mostly cover for American disengagement.

In short, the language of rights is not going away, but rights are being redefined at the United Nations in ways that recast certain fundamental ideals of the United Nations and pose fundamental issues for the United States. The evidence of fundamental change in the nature of values and rights at the United Nations, still tentative, is gradually accumulating. It has reached the point at which one can speculate about the gradual transformation of the values and human rights language of the United Nations from a vehicle mostly for international progressive politics into a vehicle—and this is a remarkable transformation, seen over the entire postwar period—for the binding expression of global religious communalism.

Free expression is the liberal canary in the UN mineshaft. The indications are not auspicious, and the Islamic conference—a bloc of Muslim states at the United Nations—and its allies have for several years been agitating at the Human Rights Council, at the two Durban conferences, and in other venues for language to protect religion from insult or offensive expression. The rhetoric for expressing these deeply illiberal sentiments is, however incongruously, impeccably the language of human rights. And the model for these provisions is likewise drawn impeccably from other measures sponsored by and endorsed by liberal and progressive human rights organizations—measures against hate speech; against incitement to racial, ethnic, or religious hatred; and other such carve-outs from the guarantees of free expression. These efforts recapitulate similar efforts at the national level. European and Asian countries often have sweeping laws against hate speech and incitement to ethnic or religious hatred that in practice often amount to laws against blasphemy. For its part, international human rights law does contain various exceptions to full expression, on incitement grounds—though these were traditionally interpreted narrowly and not as, in effect, an invitation to blasphemy laws.

At the United Nations, the Islamic bloc has pursued these agendas with much greater effect today than in earlier years. Most striking in this long-running campaign, however, has been the general paucity of response from the human rights community. Again, the marriage of politically progressive views on free expression and those of illiberal religionists is not a new phenomenon within national politics, but it is nonetheless striking and deeply disheartening to see the tepid (at best) support given by the leading human rights organizations to the defense of free expression. It is as though they feel, when pressed, that they must say something—but they have no deep commitment to it other than as a strategic political obligation. The days of these organizations' serving as robust defenders of free expression are long gone—and, as they pander to the new demographics, never to return. Sadly, funding in Saudi Arabia will also have that effect, of course.

This leaves, of course, America—ironically, the most religious of the large Western democracies—alone as the last bulwark of the rights of a pure secular liberalism that is ironically not really its own and defender of the free-expression rights of heretics, apostates, and blasphemers. The United States does the job that human rights organizations and all the machinery of human rights protection will not bestir themselves to do, partly for fear of giving offense to the increasingly aggressive global Muslim community and partly simply because the human rights community's heart is no longer in it.

What the struggle over free expression signifies is that human rights is no longer even a language that is unequivocally, in its substance, the language of freedom and liberty. It signifies that the self-appointed human rights community has only a nostalgic, historical, and contingent connection to rights in a secular liberal sense. This community retains that connection only when using rights as a progressive stick by which to attack democratic politics. The language and apparatus of liberal internationalism is gradually shifting at the United Nations—and, in this rare case, the United Nations is the epicenter of this change—toward something that we might call multicultural internationalism. And this multicultural internationalism is another name for global religious communalism. Human rights is no longer about individual human rights. Human rights are transformed into a global management tool by which various global elites seek to manage group relations, particularly among religious communities; global human rights organizations are this evolving universalism's service providers.

There is a model for this new order, but it is not the European Enlightenment. It is the world of the Ottoman Empire. It was a relatively humane social and political order, in its way, a governance order of clear communal religious relations. And this sort of religious communalism as a global order is a worldview very congenial to many of the world's elites, particularly Muslim states at the United Nations. They do not see it as a step backwards but forwards, a relatively just and humane way of organizing global governance. There is no particular reason, after all, why global governance has to be organized according to liberal internationalism. And they have found, with considerable endorsement from the human rights community, ways to frame the call for global religious communalism as a matter of human rights. This might well be the tendency of the United Nations and its values on into the future. But three things it is not: secular, free, and liberal.

So the conclusions across these highly disparate topics— loosely related by a notion of "values" at the United Nations, but not much else—are these. First, the fundamental stance in dealing with the General Assembly should be containment of its material and spiritual resources—and open opposition and criticism on matters considered of importance. In that process, it is important at every turn to stress what the UN Charter says of the General Assembly—this being one of the key innovations of the United Nations over the League of Nations—that resolutions of the General Assembly are nonbinding. They are not "international law"; they have no status as anything other than a recommendation of the motley run of nations that have nothing to lose in letting the craziest parties run the forum.

Second, it is a very bad idea to indulge strategic ambiguity as a way of thinking the circle has been squared. The tendency to this in the Obama administration is strong, if only because its ideological apparatus is seemingly divided between the largely irreconcilable strands of liberal internationalist idealism and the New Liberal Realism. It therefore thinks it can trade off these symbolic issues against other issues, harder issues of hard realism and interest. It cannot. Strategic ambiguity merely signals weakness on these and much else and not merely to those who follow the strong horse but also to those who depend upon the legitimacy of hegemon, but only if it is around for the long run. They flee. They seek other arrangements, and why not?

The United States cannot win fights in these "values" forums—whether the HRC or the whole circus of international conferences or similar venues. This is in part because it cannot win in negotiation settings devoted to "consensus" and in part because, at the end of the day, not even the Obama administration can negotiate fundamental American values that run counter to its internal constitutional gift, its institutional and popular settlement. The United States is a democratic sovereign, committed to popular self-government, a "political community, without a political superior." There the matter rests. There is nothing to negotiate as to American fundamentals, and to enter such forums is to leave in humiliation, after having granted legitimacy where one should not. Third, the very notion of human rights is evolving in these multilateral forums at the United Nations and among the international NGOs, and the only long-term result of the United States following in train will be to deprive a language of historical and moral force of any deep, and thereby necessarily limited, meaning.

The much harder task is proactive delegitimation of processes and forums that, over time, propose to deprive the terms of human rights of meanings that have been built up with difficulty over long periods. The United States should not be looking to "engage" with these processes—on the contrary, it should reject, obstruct, object, disengage, and make engagement more costly for others. The virtue of this policy will only become clearer as the content of universal values at the United Nations comes ever more closely to be that of global religious communalism. Leave cheerleading for the conversion of human rights into a language of a revived Ottoman Empire to the human rights organizations, as they scurry to seek their self-aggrandizing yet unrequited places in this new communalist multilateralism of values. Perhaps they—and the states that go along with the new global communalism in place of liberal democratic values— can yet get themselves declared "defenders of the faith." The United States, for its part, has a more universal order of values—ironically, both *more* universal and yet an order *of its own*—which it is obliged to preserve, protect, and defend.

CONCLUSION

At the outset of the Obama administration, the world longed, it appeared, for an agreeable America. America longed to be agreeable. And why not? After all the harshness of the Bush years, the rest of the world apparently wanted an America that would set out on a listening tour. America was apparently eager to listen: smart diplomacy, smart power, reboot, reset. Above all, America wanted to reengage—with friends, allies, and especially enemies who wanted to talk or even if they did not. And America wanted to engage through everyone else's apparently favorite multilateral institutions for global sharing and caring. We were—we are—the new multilateralists, and the United Nations is a good place to show it.

The moment of easy listening soon passed. The world thought this meant the United States intended, more or less, to do its bidding; we meant, more or less, that we did not much intend to do anything at all. Friend and foe alike rapidly grew tired of talk that turned out not to mean anything. Our friends were frightened and unnerved—the Obama philosopher-kings were *serious* about all that smart stuff? Our allies looked nervously around for the strong horse they were used to following, the one that follows its interests but carries them along in train, and what they saw on the horizon was China. This emboldens them when they sit far away in Latin America or Europe but scares them the closer they are to the monolith in Asia and see the United States conspicuously fail to address security imbalances or offer believable assurances; the uncertainties finally push our allies around the Pacific rim to make their own accommodations. At some point, our Asian allies' anticipatory accommodations, in the absence of a credible presence of the United States, will make the bad dream of the Pacific come true. The United Nations seems very far away in the Spratly Islands; when the US Navy presence was greater and closer by, that was less of a worry than it is now.

But perhaps even the Obama administration grows tired of its own global catharsis, prostration, and confession of unilateral guilt, followed by assertions of weakness in the form of faux modest claims of multilateralism. The expressions of humility of the first days of the administration seem a little embarrassing even to it, now, and exhausting. And though it might want to give up the responsibilities of the security hegemon, it still wants to insist on the privileges of economic hegemony and world's reserve currency a little while longer. But still with us today, and in all likelihood throughout all the Obama years, is the strategic ambiguity of multilateralism: its too-clever insistence that it can be, whenever you like, both the device of coordination among proud sovereigns and yet also a forward-looking, expectation-based vanguard party for genuine global governance—American sovereignty when we want it and burden shifting off onto the United Nations and other multilateral forums when we want that, too, all under the same name of multilateralism This ambiguity provides a crucial ingredient for the Obama administration's never-ending quest, through a formulation of words, to have its cake and eat it, too.

But multilateralism also exhibits another form of strategic ambiguity—this one particularly focused upon today's urgent situation of the hegemon that apparently has grown tired of its calling. What happens when the hegemon decides that it wants to turn inward or when it embraces decline or when it decides that the parlous state of its domestic economy requires that it put on hold the issues of the previous ten years: foreign policy and war, terrorism and counterterrorism, the decay of NATO, fundamental security issues of the global order that for decades (even during the Cold War) had corresponded to the United States precisely because it stood outside collective security? What happens when it runs out of money and cannot borrow more from the rising masses of Asia because they do not believe the Obama administration's multi-trillion-dollar promises that Americans tomorrow will remain meekly indentured to pay off union and public pension benefits and baby boom health care today? The United States went on a grand listening tour and, it turns out, slept through it and dreamed about itself. What happens to order in the world and global public goods when America decides to focus itself upon its domestic policy and politics by announcing "multilateralism"—when America decides that what it needs most is a good global nap, as if saying, "wake us when we're over"?

America has enemies who, of course, would rejoice if the United States were to forsake its role as provider of hegemonic order, but what of America's friends and allies? During the brusqueness of the Bush years, friends and allies sometimes thought they wanted a weaker America, provided that it made itself weaker by spending itself down to providing important global public goods to friends, allies, and the world—global order today and a weaker America tomorrow. Friends and allies sometimes imagined, looking at the Bush administration, that they truly wanted an America ground downwards until it transmuted from hegemon into merely another powerful international player in a world of great powers, safely contained in multilateral institutions. Multilateral multipolarity would make the world better, safer, and more just. But friends and allies were kidding themselves, and by and large they are waking up to the dangers.[1] A multipolar world is competitive, not cooperative; more dangerous to everyone, not less dangerous, ever more a state of nature than an international society. And most of them wake up to reality when they contemplate what a world of hegemony under China would actually be. But they are also concluding that the Obama administration might possibly have managed, quite remarkably, in four short years to carry America past the tipping point where its hegemony will necessarily fade and fade away, and that largely as a consequence of its domestic, rather than foreign, policy. So those in the eastern Pacific think about how quickly they must make their deals with China; Turtle Bay is a very long way from the South

1. For example, Philip Stephens, "The Dangers of American Retreat," *Financial Times*, September 8, 2011; Max Boot, "Europeans Fret U.S. Won't Defend Them," *Commentary Magazine*, Contentions Blog, September 11, 2011, *available at* http://www.commentarymagazine.com/2011/09/11 /europeans-u-s-defense.

China Sea, and apparently Washington, too, grows ever farther distant.

What is more, America's friends and allies wonder, can
one trust a truly multilateral America? During the whole
postwar period, the deal has been this: one can trust an
America concerned *mostly* with its own interests and a *little*
with its ideals—so long as you see your own interests and
ideals roughly, unevenly, loosely running in America's train.
One might denounce it sometimes as a unilateralist, as a low-
cost way of trying to keep it in line and exercise some influence. One will insist that America go through all the forms
of mutual security, particularly in NATO, even though, just
beneath the surface appearances, we all know the deal. One
can trust an America that undiplomatically, rudely even,
declares its interests and its ideals, puts them first, and invites
others to go along with it. Multilateralism is great if it means
one can have some influence on the plans of America—but
only if one can still trust that America will carry out its plans,
because they are still *its* plans rather than those of a bunch of
unreliable partners.

But can one really trust an America that suddenly wants
to work the hardest, most intractable, hard-realism problems through the United Nations, an America that actually
believes that the multilateral processes of the Security Council
or even the General Assembly and its organs are any way to
pursue serious foreign policy, at least those issues not involving drone strikes? Can one really trust an America content to
be treated as just another of the big boys in the world—the
biggest, sure, "indispensable" even, but at the end of the day,
just another player? And when America positively *insists* on
being treated as just another of the players, just another guy,

a big one but just another guy, at the Turtle Bay Bar of the Nations—should one think, this is what I've always wanted, or should one be very, very afraid?

Leading nation-state guy acting in service to multilateral collective security is, after all, what the UN theorists always saw as the proper role for America: all that marvelous power, hard and soft, placed at the disposal of global institutions. The power of a mighty sovereign nation infused into, but also transformed by, the singular authority of a multilateral institution that governs with both power and legitimacy. It is a beautiful dream, from a certain standpoint: power and legitimacy that equal authority. But, just as with NATO, it does not work that way—and America's friends, allies, and even adversaries who rely on it for a certain amount of order know this. Be wary, O world, of an America that promises a smiling multilateralism. Perhaps it is sincere, perhaps not. Perhaps America has grown tired of its global responsibilities, an America *lasse de son métier*. Perhaps it just wants a good night kiss from its friends and then a good rest, though what this might mean in a competitive, multipolar, rising-new-power world is anyone's guess. Perhaps America has decided to *really* join the legitimate global system of the United Nations and embrace governance through multilateral institutions after all.

So let us for a moment indulge the fantasy that the United States has decided to do it as other countries do it: to engage in insincere promises and toss hard things to the Security Council, allowing America to focus on its fiscal problems and unemployment and education and health care and social security and unions and domestic protectionism. As for Iranian nukes and North Korean missiles, Russian expansionism and natural-gas blackmail, Chinese protection for Sudan in the Security Council, Turkey going its own way, the threatened collapse of smaller European economies and pressures on the eurozone, all the unanswered questions of the Arab Spring, civil strife in Thailand, and the ever-tense relations between India and Pakistan, well, we are all multilateralists now. The United States is a good global player, a team player in the big leagues of multilateralism. And if the United States acted like a bully, wouldn't everyone just hate us, and haven't we had enough of the hate? America just wants to be loved, so henceforth we will measure the success of our foreign policy according to the global polls that so fascinate our media and foreign policy experts. It's empirical, after all. We have a global vision—yes, of course we have a global vision. We want a world free of nuclear weapons and world peace.

But, by the way, if it is not too much to ask—America wants not to have too much to do with anyone else. We're really, really tired of having to deal with you, except on a strictly commercial basis, of course, and when we need to borrow your savings to finance our deficits. We will make some global charitable donations, too, when we can afford it—which is to say, just like you do. We've got our own problems and our own issues. Why can't we free ride for a while—everyone else does it. Pirates in the Indian Ocean? Let's form a UN piracy court and if the ocean needs policing, doesn't China have more at risk in commerce there than anyone? Let China do it, and where some might see decline, we see the brotherhood of man and burden sharing. And if you're complaining we don't do enough for human rights anymore, well, we supported taking down Gaddafi and even supplied the unmanned drones and most of the ammunition, too, so no one should say we aren't a team player on human rights, even if taking the lead is no longer our thing. Nowadays we like to join, we don't like to lead. And we can be a real joiner at the United Nations, too: member of the Human Rights Council and maybe even an American as president of the General Assembly someday, if we pay enough attention to *us* and stop paying so much attention to *you*. But if we do that, will you all just please piss off and leave us alone to figure out our new VAT tax?

And so the United States partakes of a multilateralism that is by turns too gregarious and yet is also a withdrawal. And even if the new multilateralism is not code for American withdrawal from the world, there is still the other ambiguity. Is it a multilateralism permanently about sovereigns and their agreements among themselves—or instead one that looks forward toward global governance and sets its behavior in the present as a function of that presumption about the future? It is always possible to shrug this ambiguity off and call it a strawman concerning global governance—no one serious holds that kind of wild utopianism, after all. But I do not think I would agree.

This form of multilateralism does not require any wild utopianism today. Far from it: all it requires is an embrace of multilateralism in a forward-looking way that sets expectations about how the United States should behave toward the United Nations today, as a function of what the institution is to become tomorrow. That is a modest thesis, because it requires only behavior today that paves the way for the presumed organization tomorrow. After all, it is how all of America's friends treat the institution—our role models in this exciting new exercise of multilateral engagement. Yet we know: this leads to endless excuses for present behavior and an unwillingness to demand accountability of the United Nations in the way that one might were one to acknowledge the possibility of letting it fail.

The behavior of leading Western sovereigns, and the thinking of senior intellectuals and officials—serious ones and not wild utopians—is consistent with this form of expectation-based multilateralism. Preserving the dream also seems the best explanation for the manner in which sovereigns with a strong attachment to the ideal of liberal internationalist global governance actually treat the United Nations: they do not insist that the United Nations keep its promises and they do not insist on accountability from the United Nations in the way one would of an organization whose performance one cared about in the present. This gives them the best, but also the worst, of both worlds: an organization that fails, but also fails much to task them seriously in the present, on the one hand—but one that will always succeed someday in the future, on the other. That otherwise unsustainable position is only possible, as this book has taken pains to emphasize, provided there is a deus ex machina that will provide at least some rough fundamentals of global order, the United States.

China views multilateralism differently. Seen from the outside, its fundamental stance appears to be simply an endorsement of naked sovereignty—sovereignty for its own sake and not because, as for the United States, sovereignty as the power by which liberal democracy is sustained. This is, however, too simple. True, China has no expectation of global governance in any liberal idealistic sense and seemingly no concept of the United Nations save as a vehicle for

its interests. It does not look forward toward global governance at least insofar as that means liberal internationalism,
and, to the extent it indulges that language, it sees liberal
internationalism as a trap and snare for the credulous which
it, surely, is not.

On the other hand, China poses risks to the liberal democratic hegemony of the United States precisely because it does
possess a distinct form of legitimacy—illiberal and undemocratic but broadly legitimate within its society, based around
the Party as the mechanism of coherence for harnessing global
markets to the end of economic growth and rising standards
of living. Whether the Party can carry this feat of illiberal
markets off in the long run is an open question; China faces
daunting internal incoherence. Whether a rising economic
tide will eventually produce political liberalization internally,
and likewise the prospects for a peaceful China in the world,
is, of course, the bet the United States has been making since
Nixon went to China. But with respect to hegemony and multilateralism, the issue the United States faces today is both the
Obama administration's preference for American geopolitical
decline coupled with its belief that managing decline is its
primary strategic task—including the jostling and shifting of
allies seeking new alliances and friends, starting with their
new largest trading partner, China—and the shift in the ideological basis of hegemony.

Since the end of the Cold War, at least, hegemony in
America's rather undemanding formulation has been based
around liberalism, democracy, and human rights as the apex
values. China offers the world a quite different ideal, one that
is far more congenial to many of the United States' fair-
weather allies, let alone its enemies. After all, an ideology of

economic growth—even if rich countries such as the United States sometimes disrespect it in better times than these—goes to a fundamental for the rest of the world. And if it is wrapped up with illiberal governance internally and a redefinition of human rights that shifts away from those matters that require looking inside a regime and its governance—well, all the better. China is a threat to hegemony precisely because it *does* have an internal legitimacy and offers it as a basis, along with investment, to the rest of the developing world. It is illiberal and undemocratic—those are its chief virtues in the eyes of those who would adopt it—and moreover it resists any examination of a regime's internal practices while yet being a claim of long-run economic growth.

Liberal internationalist global governance might well be losing its appeal among the mass of countries. Perhaps it already has. In that case, however, the fantasy of global governance as a future outcome of multilateralism becomes more dangerous, because the fantasy has no connection to a multipolar world that is not about either the banging billiard balls of the international-relations realists or the universal dreams of the international-law idealists. Global governance is instead defined by the mysterious attractions of shared internal ideologies, which is to say, the combination of power and legitimacy that constitutes hegemony—but those rising internal ideologies do not appear to be liberal. Talk of universal liberal internationalism continues apace, talk of global governance continues apace—but the world is actually one set by a rising new hegemony that owes little to universal institutions of international law and much to the mutual attractions of regimes that share a preference for illiberal authoritarianism, not liberal democracy.

With respect to democracy and human rights, as today conceived in liberal ideals, well, circumstances are not propitious if the United States declines or is gradually supplanted. This is quite apart from the increased likelihood of strife, war, and conflicts among the powers and great powers. What we are pleased to call "universalism" turns out to be an artifact—and a fragile one—of American hegemony. Beneath it, the values of liberal human rights and democracy shelter, even while proudly calling themselves universal, creatures of the "universal" system of multilateralism, liberal internationalism, proudly beyond geopolitics, creatures of pure universal law and institutions. If American hegemony is the deus ex machina of basic global security, that which rescues "collective security" from collective failure, it is also the deus ex machina of universal human rights, that which allows the NGOs to preen and prance about.

A few years ago, I had an illuminating conversation with a US official over the question of the United States' participating in the creation of the Human Rights Council. Why, asked this official, did I insist on "*never* giving the United Nations the benefit of the doubt"? My response, naturally, was to ask, "Why do you *always* insist on giving it the benefit of the doubt?" It was seemingly so simple a thing, a dispute so minor and about so little. Yet between the "never" and the "always" lies a profound chasm of the meaning of multilateralism in the present and future, the meaning of engagement, and the fundamental view that the United States takes toward the United Nations.

My fundamental undertaking in these pages has been to propose general rules of engagement with the United Nations in circumstances in which multilateralism is a common term concealing deep fault lines not merely of policy but of world-view. On the one hand, the United Nations is here for good, and it *is not going anywhere*. American conservatives need to understand this and take it on board. Get used to it.

On the other hand, the United Nations is here for good but it *is not going anywhere*. American liberals and liberal internationalists need to understand *this* and take it on board. Get used to it, too. The United Nations' long-running state of equilibrium is remarkably and powerfully stable, buttressed and hedged by factors as different and seemingly uncorrelated as undemanding hegemonic ordering and in-house UN rent-seeking behaviors. Overall, it is an equilibrium of internal contentment—happiness, even. Even the ability freely to complain and, on cue, bewail the inability to change seems remarkably just like one of the many benefits of the system.

Any force powerful enough to break this equilibrium will almost certainly come from outside of the United Nations itself. It is most unlikely to be congenial either to the United States or to the ideological flotsam of the international order—the Western NGOs that today exercise leveraged sway because of the stability provided by the United States as a loose and theologically undemanding hegemon. It is easier to see the forces that currently shore up the United Nations' powerful internal equilibrium than affirmatively to identify forces from that outside that might eventually shake it up. But any UN-on-the-march is not likely to be marching in the direction of US interests or ideals. An efficient United Nations is rather more likely to be a more efficiently anti-American United Nations.

Such an earthquake lies in a fuzzy future. In the present, we have a United Nations that, if it were about making real choices, choices that mattered, would have to make a fundamental one. Governance has never worked out well for it; sixty years into the institution's life, UN governance is still a dream of the future. Even matters that many writing about the United Nations take to be steps forward on the path to global governance—the indeed considerable progress of UN peacekeeping operations, for example—might find themselves challenged and moving backwards in a competitive multipolar world in which the new powers spar even over the global backwaters. But the anticipation of governance is utterly crippling to the United Nations of the present—crippling to its incentives, to all the things that it might do if it were to put away childish dreams of all the marvelous things it will be when it finally grows up. The United Nations *is* grown up—all grown up and dysfunctional. Its mature dysfunction is in large part because of the endless whispers of flattery and cajoling from people who insist that, with enough imagination, it will be something radically different from what it is.

This is not a counsel of despair, despite the fact that it bumps up against some of the fondest dreams of some very smart people with an even stronger sense of governing entitlement. The genuinely well-intentioned advice of this book is that the United Nations and its supporters get on with the business of the limited tasks the United Nations can do reasonably well in the present *and nothing more*.

Ban Ki-moon originally set something of an example at the beginning by being a secretary-general who appeared to understand that we need a UN-of-modesty, not a UN-of-rock-stars. This brought him in for criticism from those who persist in the fantasies. Those who focus at the United

Nations on their particular most-important-issue-the-world-faces are often remarkably blind to the long history of the United Nations' taking up one issue after another, engaging it to see how much it can serve a long-term agenda of global governance for the United Nations, and then dropping it when it does not work out. What happened at Copenhagen, and its tale of the hubris of global elites, the merging of the politics of global governance and the authority of science, is less than surprising if one studies the history of punctuated equilibrium and crisis at the United Nations.

But Secretary-General Ban's persona—of modest, behind-the-scenes demeanor—is far better suited to a United Nations that can gradually make itself a permanently useful organization. And it is better suited as well to persisting in its modest utility even as the international scene around it changes, possibly becoming much more dangerous. A United Nations that waits to discover that what matters is its modest effectiveness in limited tasks in the present until it is pushed by events to that realization will find that it is sidelined in the actual stream of events. A United Nations that casts a giant shadow based on flimsy and fake authority will discover, as US power wanes even modestly and other less-than-hegemonic powers struggle against each other, that the winds the world stirs up are stormy enough to whip the United Nations in every direction.

It is time to give up all the forward-looking expectations of glory for the United Nations. Even when dressed down in the deliberately modest terminology of multilateralism and realist claims that are themselves not quite believable, lurking just beneath the surface are extravagant dreams of a UN-of-tomorrow. This has been an essential part of the dynamic of UN stasis and UN crisis for decades. It was crucial to the dynamic of UN reform in 2005, to the Millennium Development Goals in 2000, and to Copenhagen in 2009. It will be so for whatever fresh cause the United Nations latches onto as fodder for its next foray into building global governance.

For that matter, it is time to give up the extravagant conceit that the UN is universal. Or that it somehow has a moral, political, or legal lock on universality and, with it, a monopoly on benign impartiality and the interests of all, as against those partial, parochial, benighted, and self-interested sovereign nations. Nor will the United Nations turn out, in the fullness of time, to be the glorious tree of global governance grown from today's modest sapling. There is no swan in this ugly duckling's future. It is what it is.

Give up the grand political eschatologies clothed in the too-cheap cloth of modern rationalities. There are things to do: children who lack vaccinations; places where blue helmets can bring a measure of order, even if they cannot and will not go everywhere and do not always behave with good discipline; food aid that can be usefully distributed; missions of diplomats and experts to Sudan and Southern Sudan to help those two states manage the breakup; good offices for states in need of neutral diplomacy to settle disputes before they get out of hand. There is no lack of discrete and useful tasks that can command agreement today as being worth doing. Why not stick with those? Forget the management committee of global security and just be a talking shop of the nations because, in today's increasingly jostling world, that's good, too. If the United Nations had vision and aspiration rather than permanently infantile dreams, and many fawning flatterers to stoke them, it would identify and perform discrete and narrow tasks, for which the measure of all things is competence in the present, with little thought of tomorrow except as a concrete list of tasks, a to-do list for tomorrow. Never dreams, however. Dreams of tomorrow at the United Nations only corrupt whatever competence might be achieved today.

So let the United Nations finally be a low yet sturdy run of hedgerows that perform precise, limited, and settled tasks, pruned to efficiency and competence. Unlike the ill-favored great tree, it might yet hedge up against winds of change that blow not necessarily for the good. Hedges against winds that blow across a wild and dangerous world: the anarchic, global state of nature that some, entirely too sanguine, still mistake for global community.

BIBLIOGRAPHY

A NOTE TO THE READER ON SOURCES:

This book is a policy essay rather than an academic monograph, and so it eschews much of the scholarly apparatus of extensive citation, original sources, and other features directed primarily at scholars. Citations are limited and sources listed here are secondary sources intended to be reasonably accessible and of interest to students or general readers. This bibliography lists sources mentioned in the notes and adds a selection of general sources and books on matters raised in the text, with particular attention to recent works on the United Nations.

Annan, Kofi. "Secretary-General, United Nations, Address at the Truman Presidential Museum and Library" (December 11, 2006). *Available at* http://www.un.org/News/ossg/sg/stories/statments_full.asp?statID=40.

Bodansky, Daniel. "The Copenhagen Climate Change Conference: A Post-Mortem." *American Journal of International Law* 104 (2010): 230–40.

Bolton, John R. *Surrender Is Not an Option: Defending America at the United Nations and Abroad*. New York: Simon & Schuster, 2007.

————. "Is There Really 'Law' in International Affairs?" *Transnational Law and Contemporary Problems* 10, no. 1 (Spring 2000): 31.

Bosco, David L. *Five to Rule Them All: The UN Security Council and the Making of the Modern World.* New York: Oxford University Press, 2009.

Clark, Ian. *Hegemony in International Society.* Oxford: Oxford University Press, 2011.

Collier, Paul. *The Bottom Billion: Why the Poorest Countries Are Failing and What Can Be Done About It.* New York: Oxford University Press, 2007.

Easterly, William. *The White Man's Burden: Why the West's Efforts to Aid the Rest Have Done Much Ill and So Little Good.* New York: Penguin, 2006.

Fukuyama, Francis. *America at the Crossroads: Democracy, Power, and the Neoconservative Legacy.* New Haven: Yale University Press, 2007.

Glendon, Mary Ann. *A World Made New: Eleanor Roosevelt and the Universal Declaration of Human Rights.* New York: Random House, 2001.

Glennon, Michael J. *The Fog of Law: Pragmatism, Security, and International Law.* Chicago: University of Chicago Press, 2010.

————. "Platonism, Adaptivism, and Illusion in UN Reform." *Chicago Journal of International Law* 6 (Winter 2006): 613.

Hanhimaki, Jussi M. *The United Nations: A Very Short Introduction.* New York: Oxford University Press 2008.

Hurd, Ian. *After Anarchy: Legitimacy and Power in the United Nations Security Council.* Princeton, NJ: Princeton University Press, 2007.

Inner City Press Service (project on United Nations investigative reporting, updated regularly). *Available at* http://www.innercitypress.com.

Kennedy, Paul. *The Parliament of Man: The Past, Present, and Future of the United Nations.* New York: Random House, 2006.

Korey, William. *NGOs and the Universal Declaration of Human Rights.* New York: Palgrave-Macmillan, 2001.

Krasner, Stephen D. *Sovereignty: Organized Hypocrisy.* Princeton, NJ: Princeton University Press 1999.

Krasno, Jean E., ed. *The United Nations: Confronting the Challenges of a Global Society.* Boulder, CO: Lynne Rienner Publishers, 2004.

Mandelbaum, Michael. *The Case for Goliath: How America Acts as the World's Government in the 21st Century.* New York: PublicAffairs, Perseus, 2005.

McGillivray, Mark, ed. *Achieving the Millennium Development Goals.* New York: United Nations University / Palgrave-Macmillan, 2008.

McKeon, Nora. *The United Nations and Civil Society: Legitimating Global Governance—Whose Voice?* London: Zed Books / United Nations Research Institute for Social Development, 2009.

Mead, Walter Russell. Via Meadia Blog (covering inter alia climate change and UN negotiations). *Available at* http://blogs.the-american-interest.com/wrm.

Mertus, Julie. *The United Nations and Human Rights: A Guide for a New Era.* New York: Routledge, 2005.

Meyer, Jeffrey A., and Mark G. Califano. *Good Intentions Corrupted: The Oil-for-Food Scandal and the Threat to the U.N.* New York: Public Affairs, Perseus, 2006. (Based on the reports of the Independent Inquiry Committee, Paul A. Volcker, Chair).

Mingst, Karen A., and Margaret P. Karns. *The United Nations in the 21st Century.* 3rd ed. Cambridge, MA: Westview Press, Perseus, 2007.

Mnookin, Robert. *Bargaining with the Devil: When to Negotiate, When to Fight.* New York: Simon & Schuster, 2010.

Moyo, Dambisa. *Dead Aid: Why Aid Is Not Working and How There Is a Better Way for Africa.* New York: Farrar, Straus & Giroux, 2009.

Muravchik, Joshua. *The Future of the United Nations: Understanding the Past to Chart a Way Forward.* Washington, DC: AEI Press, 2005.

New Zealand, Ministry of Foreign Affairs and Trade. *United Nations Handbook 2008/09.* New Zealand, 2009; updated regularly.

Power, Samantha. *Chasing the Flame: Sergio Vieira de Mello and the Fight to Save the World.* New York: Penguin, 2008.

Rabkin, Jeremy. *The Case for Sovereignty: Why the World Should Welcome American Independence.* Washington, DC: AEI Press, 2004.

Rieff, David. "Concerts and Silly Seasons." Posting to *OpenDemocracy,* February 23, 2007. *Available at* http://www.opendemocracy.net/democracy-americanpower/concerts_4380.jsp.

Roberts, Adam, and Dominick Zaum. *Selective Security: War and the United Nations Security Council since 1945.* London: Routledge, 2008.

Rosett, Claudia. The Rosett Report (ongoing investigative reporting on the United Nations). Pajamas Media. *Available at* http://pajamasmedia.com/claudiarosett.

Rubenfeld, Jed. "The Two World Orders." *Wilson Quarterly* (Autumn 2003). *Available at* http://www.wilsonquarterly.com/article.cfm?AID=386.

Sachs, Jeffrey D. *The End of Poverty: Economic Possibilities for Our Time.* New York: Penguin, 2005.

Schaefer, Brett D., ed. *Conundrum: The Limits of the United Nations and the Search for Alternatives.* New York: Rowman and Littlefield, 2009.

Sellars, Kirsten. *The Rise and Rise of Human Rights.* Phoenix Mill, UK: Sutton Publishing, 2002.

Slaughter, Anne-Marie. *A New World Order.* Princeton, NJ: Princeton University Press, 2004.

Smith, Courtney B. *Politics and Process at the United Nations: The Global Dance.* Boulder, CO: Lynne Rienner Publishers, 2006.

Soussan, Michael. *Backstabbing for Beginners: My Crash Course in International Diplomacy.* New York: Perseus-Nation Books, 2008.

Task Force on the United Nations. *American Interests and UN Reform: Report of the Task Force on the United Nations.* Washington, DC: United States Institute of Peace, 2005, update 2005.

Thakur, Ramesh. *The United Nations, Peace and Security.* Cambridge: Cambridge University Press, 2006.

Traub, James. *The Best Intentions: Kofi Annan and the UN in the Era of American World Power.* New York: Farrar, Straus & Giroux, 2006.

———. "Good Night, Ban Ki-Moon: The U.N. Secretary-General Must Go." *Foreign Policy,* July 22, 2010. *Available at* http://www.foreignpolicy.com/articles/2010/07/22/give_ban_the_boot.

United Nations, Department of Public Information. *The United Nations.* United Nations, 2008. (Updated regularly; previously known as *Basic Facts about the United Nations*).

United Nations Framework Convention on Climate Change. "Draft Decision -/CP.15, Proposal by President: Copenhagen Accord." FCCC/CP/2009/L.7, December 18, 2009. *Available at* http://unfccc.int/resource/docs/2009/cop15/eng/l07.pdf.

United Nations, Office of the Secretary-General. *A More Secure World: Our Shared Responsibility: Report of the Secretary-General's High-Level Panel on Threats, Challenges and Change.* United Nations, 2004.

United Nations, Office of the Secretary-General. "2005 World Summit Outcome" ("Final Outcome Document"). General Assembly Resolution A/Res/60/1. *Available at* http://daccess-dds-ny.un.org/doc/UNDOC/GEN/N05/487/60/PDF/N0548760.pdf?OpenElement.

United States. White House. "National Security Strategy." May 2010. *Available at* http://www.whitehouse.gov/sites/default/files/rss_viewer/national_security_strategy.pdf.

Walzer, Michael. *Spheres of Justice: A Defense of Pluralism and Equality.* New York: Basic Books, 1983.

Weiss, Thomas G. *What's Wrong with the United Nations and How to Fix It.* Malden, MA: Polity Press, 2009.

Weiss, Thomas G., David P. Forsythe, Roger A. Coate, and Kelly-Kate Pease. *The United Nations and Changing World Politics.* 6th ed. Cambridge, MA: Westview Press, Perseus, 2009.

Weiss, Thomas G., and Ramesh Thakur; Foreword by John Gerard Ruggie. *Global Governance and the UN: An Unfinished Journey.* Bloomington, IN: Indiana University Press / United Nations Intellectual History Project, 2010.

Zakaria, Fareed. *The Post-American World.* New York: WW Norton, 2008.

ABOUT THE AUTHOR

Kenneth Anderson is a professor of international law at Washington College of Law, American University, in Washington, DC, where he has taught since 1996. He is also a visiting fellow at the Hoover Institution and a member of its Task Force on National Security and Law, as well as a nonresident senior fellow at the Brookings Institution. During the 2005 debates over UN reform, he served as an expert on the US Institute of Peace Gingrich–Mitchell Task Force on United Nations Reform. A graduate of UCLA and Harvard Law School, he was general counsel to the Open Society Institute and director of the Human Rights Watch Arms Division before joining the American University faculty. Raised in California, he is married to Jean-Marie Simon; they reside with their daughter, Renee, in Washington, DC.

About the Hoover Institution's
**KORET-TAUBE TASK FORCE
ON NATIONAL SECURITY AND LAW**

The Koret-Taube Task Force on National Security and Law examines the rule of law, the laws of war, and American constitutional law with a view to making proposals that strike an optimal balance between individual freedom and the vigorous defense of the nation against terrorists both abroad and at home. The task force's focus is the rule of law and its role in Western civilization, as well as the roles of international law and organizations, the laws of war, and U.S. criminal law. Those goals will be accomplished by systematically studying the constellation of issues—social, economic, and political—on which striking a balance depends.

The core membership of this task force includes Kenneth Anderson, Peter Berkowitz (chair), Philip Bobbitt, Jack Goldsmith, Stephen D. Krasner, Jessica Stern, Matthew Waxman, Ruth Wedgwood, Benjamin Wittes, and Amy B. Zegart.

INDEX

France
imperialism and, 217
Libya and, 248
P5 status of, 135
free expression, 250–51
Fukuyama, Francis, 16

Gaddafi regime, 20, 51, 120, 141–43
Gaza war, 243
General Assembly
anti-Americanism in, 60, 170–71
bloc-voting in, 169–70
containment of, 21, 171, 234
engagement with, 58–59, 234
failed leadership in, 233–34
nonbinding resolutions of, 253
Obama and, 1
politicization in, 168
president, 171
suborgans within, 170
symbolism of, 234
UN budget and, 168–69
UN conferences and, 234–35
US and, 21
US rules of engagement with, 60
values in, 217
waste in, 233
genocide, 30, 95, 220, 248
Germany, 134–36
Gleneagles, 204
Glennon, Michael J., 36n3
global citizenship, 40–41
global civil society, 45, 47
global constitutionalism, 36, 39
global coordination, 30–32, 38
global governance
China and, 265–66
engagement and, 11
fantasy of, 13
global constitutionalism and, 36
without government, 28, 37
idealism of, 39
integration of, 40–41
liberal internationalism and,
38–39
loss of appeal of, 267

multilateralism as foundation for,
68–69
as necessity, 17
religious communalism and,
252–53
sovereignty and, 16–17
UN dues and, 150
UN platonism and, 31
US and, 150
US-UN relations and, 11
*Global Governance and the UN: An
Unfinished Journey* (Weiss &
Thakur), 36n3
global public order, 125
global security policy, US, 100
global vision, 263
globalization, 89
economic, 40
international development
and, 182
poverty and, 179
Goldstone, Richard, 243
good faith, 82
governance
becoming government, 37
international development and,
180–81, 195
UN, 71, 270
under universalism, 231–32
Group of 8 summit, 204
Group of 20 negotiations, 198
Group of 77, 170, 217
Guatemala, 106, 242
Gulf War I, 124

hegemony
China and, 266–67
legitimacy and, 122–23
See also US hegemony
Heritage Foundation, 200
heuristics, 19
High Level Panel, 108
HRC. *See* Human Rights Council
human rights, 25, 60–61, 210
abuses, in China, 125n5
changing context of, 223–24

**Books published by members and contributors to the
Koret-Taube Task Force on National Security and Law**

*Living with the UN: American Responsibilities
and International Order*
Kenneth Anderson

*Skating on Stilts: Why We Aren't Stopping
Tomorrow's Terrorism*
Stewart A. Baker

Israel and the Struggle over the International Laws of War
Peter Berkowitz

Terror and Consent: The Wars for the Twenty-First Century
Philip Bobbitt

*The Terror Presidency: Law and Judgment
Inside the Bush Administration*
Jack Goldsmith

Detention and Denial: The Case for Candor after Guantanamo
Benjamin Wittes

*Law and the Long War: The Future of Justice
in an Age of Terror*
Benjamin Wittes

Legislating the War on Terror: An Agenda for Reform
Edited by Benjamin Wittes

*Eyes on Spies: Congress and the
United States Intelligence Community*
Amy B. Zegart

Future Challenges in National Security and Law
Multiple Authors